CAMBRIDGE LIBRARY COLLECTION

Books of enduring scholarly value

Classics

From the Renaissance to the nineteenth century, Latin and Greek were compulsory subjects in almost all European universities, and most early modern scholars published their research and conducted international correspondence in Latin. Latin had continued in use in Western Europe long after the fall of the Roman empire as the lingua franca of the educated classes and of law, diplomacy, religion and university teaching. The flight of Greek scholars to the West after the fall of Constantinople in 1453 gave impetus to the study of ancient Greek literature and the Greek New Testament. Eventually, just as nineteenth-century reforms of university curricula were beginning to erode this ascendancy, developments in textual criticism and linguistic analysis, and new ways of studying ancient societies, especially archaeology, led to renewed enthusiasm for the Classics. This collection offers works of criticism, interpretation and synthesis by the outstanding scholars of the nineteenth century.

An Analytical Essay on the Greek Alphabet

Originally published in 1791, this work by classical scholar and connoisseur Richard Payne Knight (1751–1824) attempts to reconstruct the original pronunciation of ancient Greek. Emphasising the importance of knowing what the various ancient dialects sounded like in order to better appreciate surviving works of ancient literature, Knight engages in textual criticism of certain notable writings, including the poetry of Homer and Hesiod and the plays of Sophocles. Representing a learned contribution to classical philology, the essay also goes some way towards analysing the ways in which Greek sounds were distorted by their inclusion in other languages. Several plates at the end of the text reproduce a selection of ancient inscriptions on stone, coins and ceramics. Knight's *Analytical Inquiry into the Principles of Taste* (1805) and *Inquiry into the Symbolical Language of Ancient Art and Mythology* (1818) are also reissued in this series.

T0381737

An Analytical Essay on the Greek Alphabet

RICHARD PAYNE KNIGHT

CAMBRIDGE
UNIVERSITY PRESS

CAMBRIDGE
UNIVERSITY PRESS

University Printing House, Cambridge, CB2 8BS, United Kingdom

Cambridge University Press is part of the University of Cambridge.

It furthers the University's mission by disseminating knowledge in the pursuit of
education, learning and research at the highest international levels of excellence.

www.cambridge.org
Information on this title: www.cambridge.org/9781108066020

© in this compilation Cambridge University Press 2014

This edition first published 1791
This digitally printed version 2014

ISBN 978-1-108-06602-0 Paperback

AN
ANALYTICAL ESSAY
ON THE
GREEK ALPHABET.

By RICHARD PAYNE KNIGHT.

LEVIA QUIDEM HÆC, ET PARVI FORTE, SI PER SE SPECTENTUR, MO-
MENTI. SED EX ELEMENTIS CONSTANT, EX PRINCIPIIS ORIUNTUR,
OMNIA: ET EX JUDICII CONSUETUDINE IN REBUS MINUTIS ADHI-
BITA, PENDET SÆPISSIME, ETIAM IN MAXIMIS, VERA ATQUE ACCU-
RATA SCIENTIA.   CLARK. PRÆF. HOMER.

LONDON,
PRINTED BY J. NICHOLS FOR P. ELMSLY.
MDCCXCI.

I N D E X.

-εις,

AN
ANALYTICAL ESSAY
ON THE
GREEK ALPHABET.

THE Subject, which I here propofe to examine, will of courfe appear minute and frivolous to thofe, who are only acquainted with it from the keen ridicule, with which it has been treated by fome popular and elegant writers of the laft and prefent centuries (1). I would, however, entreat all perfons of this defcription, who honour the prefent attempt with their attention, to confider, that even the beft and keeneft ridicule is no teft, either of the truth or the dignity of the fubject, upon which it is employed, but has often been moft happily exercifed upon the beft-founded opinions and moft important and elevated objects (2). At all events, I hope that they will not condemn the defign before they know the confequences of its completion; and if they then find that, by facilitating the acquifition of Grecian Learning, it can bring the higheft efforts of human tafte and genius, into a ftronger or clearer light, they will confider it as adding to the intellectual pleafures of man, which are certainly the moft valuable belonging to his nature, becaufe they can be at all times enjoyed without injury to health, fame, or fortune.

(1) See Moliere's Bourgeois Gentilhomme; and Pope's Dunciad.
(2) See Gulliver's Travels; and Tale of a Tub.

I cannot

I cannot indeed but think, that the judgement of the Publick, upon the refpective merits of the different claffes of Criticks, is peculiarly partial and unjuft.

Thofe among them who affume the office of pointing out the beauties, and detecting the faults, of literary compofition, are placed with the orator and hiftorian in the higheft ranks; whilft thofe, who undertake the more laborious tafk of wafhing away the ruft and canker of time, and bringing back thofe forms and colours, which are the fubject of criticifm, to their original purity and brightnefs, are degraded, with the Index-maker and Antiquary, among the pioneers of literature, whofe bufinefs it is to clear the way for thofe who are capable of more fplendid and honourable enter-prizes.

But neverthelefs, if we examine the effects produced by thefe two claffes of Criticks, we fhall find that the firft have been of no ufe whatever, and that the laft have rendered the moft important fervices to mankind. All perfons of tafte and underftanding know, from their own feelings, when to approve and difapprove, and therefore ftand in no need of inftructions from the Critick; and as for thofe who are deftitute of fuch faculties, they can never be taught to ufe them; for no one can be taught to exert faculties which he does not poffefs. Every dunce may, indeed, be taught to repeat the jargon of criticifm, which of all jargons is the worft, as it joins the tedious formality of methodical reafoning to the trite frivolity of com-mon-place obfervation. But, whatever may be the tafte and difcernment of a reader, or the genius and ability of a writer, neither the one nor the other can appear while the text remains deformed by the corruptions of blunder-ing tranfcribers, and obfcured by the gloffes of ignorant grammarians. It is then that the aid of the verbal Critick is required; and though his mi-nute labour, in diffecting fyllables and analyfing letters, may appear con-temptible in its operation, it will be found important in its effect.

The office, indeed, of analyfing letters has been thought the loweft of all literary occupations; but neverthelefs as found, though only the ve-hicle of fenfe, is that which principally diftinguifhes the moft brilliant poetry from the flatteft profe; and as, in the dead languages, all found is to be known only from the powers originally given to the characters re-prefenting the elements of it; to analyfe thefe characters, and fhow what their

their Powers really were, is the only way to acquire a knowledge of thofe founds in which the antient poets conveyed their fenfe. A fuccefsful endeavour to obtain this end will not, I flatter myfelf, be deemed either trifling or abfurd in this age of tafte and learning.

S E C T I O N I.

AN articulate found is properly that which begins from, or ends in, a fuppreffion or obftruction of expiration, by the compreffion of fome of the organs of the mouth.

Thefe organs are the lips, the teeth, the tongue, and the palate; to which fome add the throat, but improperly, for guttural founds are not of themfelves articulate: the combinations of them known to the Greeks were only three; I. the lips with each other; II. the tongue with the palate; III. the tongue with the teeth: to which the Latins added a fourth, of the under lip with the teeth: but this the Greeks never employed, and therefore could not pronounce the Roman F (1), though we perpetually pronounce it in our corrupt manner of reading their language.

To reprefent thefe three modes of articulation, I am inclined to believe, the firft vifible figns for founds were invented; for, though articulation be only the *form*, and tone the *fubftance*, of fpeech, yet as the form is finite and fimple, and the fubftance infinitely variable, it is natural to fuppofe that the firft figns were invented to reprefent form rather than fubftance. It is alfo this form or articulation which diftinguifhes human fpeech from the cries of animals, which are all tones, or vowel founds, varioufly afpi-

(1) See Quintil. I. xii. c. 10.

B 2　　　　　　　　　　　rated,

rated, but neither begun, ended, or divided, by the compreffion of the organs of the mouth.

The firft figns or notes of articulation were, therefore, the G (as it was antiently pronounced, and as we ftill pronounce it when followed by an A, O, or U), the P and the T (1).

Each of thefe was pronounced two ways, with a greater or lefs degree of force in the compreffion of the organs; whence were formed three more letters, B, K, and D, which I rank next in fucceffion, though there is reafon to believe that neither of them (or, at moft, only the laft) was invented until feveral intermediate improvements had taken place in the art of expreffing founds by figns. The want of authentic monuments, however, prevents us from tracing the progrefs of thefe improvements, the earlieft infcriptions extant having been made when the Alphabet was even more perfect than it is at prefent. It fhould feem, indeed, both from the order of the Alphabet, and our manner of pronouncing thefe letters, that the B, G, and D, ought to rank together in the firft clafs; and the P, K, and T, in the fecond; which would certainly agree better with the analogy of found; but, neverthelefs, it is contradicted by the authentic teftimony of antient monuments, always to be preferred to any conclufions that can be drawn from mere analogy.

In a very antient Greek Infcription found in Magna Græcia, and now preferved in the mufeum of Monfignor Borgia, at Veletri, the G is expreffed by a fingle perpendicular line, thus I (2), which feems to be its moft antient form; for, upon fome of the earlieft coins extant, it is expreffed by the fame line a little curved, thus ((3); whence came the Roman C, which is ufed for the G in the Duillian infcription, engraved in the year of Rome 493. The G was not employed as a diftinct letter until introduced by Spurius Cervilius Ruga, twenty-feven years afterwards (4). Antiquaries have obferved that, in Manufcripts, the round forms moftly

(1) I employ the Latin letters becaufe much nearer to the primitive Greek than the Greek ones now in ufe.

(2) Plate I. Fig. 1, from a copy of it given me by Mr. Aftle.

(3) See thofe of Gela in Numm. Sic. vet. Pl. XXXI.

(4) Plutarch. Qu. Rom. Taylor's Civil Law, p. 557; alfo, in Marm. Sandvicenf.

predominate

predominate in the letters, and in infcriptions the fquare, becaufe the former are more eafily written, and the latter more eafily carved (1). Hence this curved Line, which reprefented the G, was made with an angular inftead of a circular curve, thus ⟨, or thus Γ.

The moft antient K is a combination of one of thefe forms with the antient upright line, thus)|, or thus Ӿ; fo that this letter is, in fact, a junction of two Gammas, in order to exprefs a ftronger and more emphatical enunciation by the fame organs. This will appear evident by examining the manner in which it is repeatedly written in the Etrufcan Infcription, called the Eugubian Table, publifhed by Gori; and alfo upon fome very antient medals of Lefbos and Syracufe, in both of which it is plainly reprefented by two diftinct characters (2). This Etrufcan Infcription Gori endeavours to prove, from a paffage of Dionyfius of Halicarnaffus, to have been written two generations before the Trojan war; but, though I do not think his argument quite fatisfactory as to this point, it is of very remote antiquity, for the Alphabet is the moft imperfect, and therefore, probably, the oldeft of any hitherto difcovered.

Upon fome very eminent coins of Croto, Corinth, and Syracufe, we find the Kappa expreffed by a circular fupported by a perpendicular line, thus Ҩ (3), from which comes the Roman Q. This is, however, equally a combination of the antient Gammas, the two curved lines being joined and divided by a perpendicular one, thus ʊ.

After the invention of the Kappa, the fimple Gamma feems to have fallen into difufe in fome dialects; for it is not to be found in any Etrufcan infcription; and the Etrufcan, as well as the Latin, is evidently a corrupt dialect of the Greek; a dialect by much the harfheft of any, and therefore probably employing only the harfheft and moft emphatical palatial confonant, which is the Kappa.

Both thefe letters retain their powers, with, I believe, little or no variation, in moft of the modern languages; except that the Englifh, French,

(1) See Aftle's Hiftory of Writing.

(2) See Plate I. Fig. 4 and 5, from coins in the cabinet of the Author.

(3) See Comb. Pl. XX. XXI.; and Torremozzi Sic. Pl. LXXVII. Similar medals are in the cabinet of the Author; who has quoted none that he has not feen, having too often proved the inaccuracy of books in thefe minute but important circumftances.

and

and Italians, have added a corrupt and barbarous dental found to the G, when followed by either of the flender vowels. The K is not employed by the Italians, Spaniards, or French, in their own tongues; and in reading the Greek they pronounce it in the fame manner as they do the Latin C, that is, like a barbarous femi-vowel, forced out between the tongue and the teeth with a harfh hiffing found.

The moft antient form of the P feems to be that of the Etrufcans, which confifts of a perpendicular line with another drawn obliquely from it, thus ꓕ. It exifts in the fame form, except that the oblique line is curved thus ꓶ, to diftinguifh it from the antient Lambda, upon the vafe reprefenting the hunt of the Caledonian boar, in the Britifh Mufeum, which is evidently Greek, and appears, both from the ftyle of the workmanfhip and form of the letters, to be one of the moft antient monuments extant of the art of that people. This curvature, being gradually increafed, formed the Latin P, which was previoufly employed by the Greeks in the fame form, as appears from the very antient Veletrian Infcription before cited. In the fame infcription, however, it appears in the form which they more commonly employed in early Times; which is indeed nearly the fame, only that the curved line is made fquare inftead of round (Γ), for the reafon beforementioned. The power of this letter feems not to have varied at all, for it is precifely the fame in all the languages of modern Europe, and, as far as we can judge from analogy and etymology, the fame as it was in Greece in the days of Homer.

The B feems to have been originally an afpirated P; for, in the Eugubian Infcription, it has that power; and the Macedonians employed it where the Greeks employed the Φ and Π, writing ΒΕΡΕΝΙΚΗ for ΦΕΡΕΝΙΚΗ, and ΒΥΡΓΟΣ for ΠΥΡΓΟΣ; whence it appears that our Northern words BURGH and BEAR come from the fame fource as the correfponding ones in the Greek. The Etrufcans reprefented it in two forms, thus ꓭ, and thus 8; the firft of which occurs only once, and that in the Eugubian Infcription; but the other is common. It is with the firft that both the Greek and Latin forms of this letter agree; but its power feems to have been that of the Phœnician Beth, at leaft if they pronounced it as we do now, which the Greeks feem evidently to have done in fome inftances; for the verbs ΒΟΜΒΕΩ, ΒΑΜΒΑΙΝΩ, &c. would not have anfwered

fwered the purpofe for which Homer employs them, in making the found correfpond to the fenfe, if the B were pronounced in any other manner. In other inftances, however, or, at leaft, in other times, they employed it as a palatial afpirate; for we find the Latin V (which we know had the power of our W) fometimes expreffed in the Greek by the B, and fome-times by the ΟΥ diphthong (1); whence it clearly appears that there was then an affinity between them, though they now differ fo widely. The Æolians and Dorians, in particular, employed it occafionally as a pure or fimple afpirate, like the Digamma, or Roman H, writing ΒΡΟΔΟΣ for ΡΟΔΟΣ, ΒΑΒΕΛΙΟΣ for ʽΑΕΛΙΟΣ, ΒΕΔΟΣ for ΕΔΟΣ, &c. (2). In the fame manner it was introduced into the words ΓΑΜΒΡΟΣ for ΓΑΜΕΡΟΣ, and ΜΕΣΗΜΒΡΙΑ for ΜΕΣΗΜΕΡΙΑ (3); but with what degree or form of afpiration it was pronounced it is impoffible for us now to tell; for though, like the ΟΥ diphthong, it had a refemblance to the Latin V, we cannot fay how near that refemblance was. In all modern languages it retains its antient power of a labial confonant, except in the Spanifh, and fome dia-lects of the modern Greek, in which it has acquired that corrupt and bar-barous found given by the other nations of Europe to the Latin V, a found which it feems to have derived from the Byzantine Greeks, as it is en-forced by the edict iffued by Stephen Gardener, Bifhop of Winchefter, for the fupport of their pronunciation in the univerfity of Cambridge, of which he was Chancellor. The Romans feem to have been very licentious and irregular in the ufe of this letter; for on the Duilian column, before al-luded to, the name, which in later times was written Duilius, is writ-ten Bilios; whence, as Gori obferves, bellum and bellona appear to be the fame words with duellum and duellona (4); and we find ac-cordingly, in the *Senatus confultum Marcianum*, infcribed about feventy-five years after, the name of the goddefs Bellona written Dvelona. In the infcription in honour of L. Scipio Barbatus, which is of the year after the Duilian, the B is alfo reprefented by the D and V in dvonoro, the

---

(1) As in the names Varro and Severvs, fometimes written by Greek authors ΒΑΡΡΩΝ and ΣΕΒΗΡΟΣ, and fometimes ΟΥΑΡΡΩΝ and ΣΕΟΥΗΡΟΣ.

(2) Prifcian, lib. I.

(3) Lennep, Analog. Græc. p. 286.

(4) Muf. Etrufc. Claff. V.

antient

antient form of the word BONORUM, the final M having been ufually omitted, and the U reprefented by the O in the old Latin.

The moft antient figure of the T, found in the Etrufcan infcriptions, differs little from that now in ufe. Its power has alfo probably continued the fame, except in the inftance of the hiffing found, which moft modern nations have given it, when followed by an I in the fame fyllable. This is undoubtedly a corruption, the Greeks having no letter to exprefs this kind of found but the Sigma.

The D, the other dental confonant, does not appear to have been known to the Etrufcans, having been probably borrowed from the Phœnicians after the Pelafgian alphabet had been carried into Italy. Its figure, indeed (which is always triangular, though often rounded at one angle), occurs frequently on the Etrufcan monuments; but it always ftands for the R. We find it, however, with the power of the D, or perhaps the ΔΣ or Z, upon the Zankléan medals, which contain fome of the moft antient fpecimens of Greek writing now extant (1).

Thefe fix letters are called mutes, becaufe, if employed according to their original intention, they exprefs no found of themfelves, but only mark the beginnings, endings, and divifions of found, by which it is articulated, or feparated into detached portions, called in writing fyllables.

Thefe portions are, however, often divided by other means, which I fhall now proceed to examine; but, in that cafe, it will appear that they are not, ftrictly fpeaking, articulate founds, or effentially different from the cries of brute animals.

The firft of thefe is a partial inftead of a total fuppreffion of the breath, by an approximation inftead of a conjunction of the organs of the mouth, reprefented by the letters called afpirates; which, like the mute confonants, are to be divided into three claffes, correfponding to the three different combinations of the organs of fpeech.

But, as each of thefe marks fignifies a particular mode of conftrained expiration, by the approximation of fome particular organs to each other, the moft natural and eafy way of expreffing them would be to invent fome

---

(1) See Torremuzzi Sic. Pl. XLV. Similar medals are in the Author's cabinet, and in moft others, they being common.

mark of general conſtrained expiration, which, being affixed to each of the ſigns before invented, might diſtinguiſh each different mode of conſtrained expiration according to the different combinations of the organs by which they are produced. Hence come the ſimple aſpirate, figured by the Phœnicians and Etruſcans thus ⊟, by the Latins thus H, and by the Greeks thus H, and thus Ͱ; which, being prefixed to a vowel, ſignifies that the tone, which it expreſſes, ſhould be uttered with a forced and condenſed expiration; and, when affixed to a conſonant, that the breath, which forms that tone, ſhould not be totally ſuppreſſed and interrupted by it, but only confined and conſtrained by the approximation only of thoſe organs, the entire junction of which is ſignified by the conſonant alone. The ſecond Greek character for this ſimple aſpirate does not ſeem to have been in uſe till the other was appropriated to expreſs another letter. An antient ſcholiaſt, cited by M. de Villoiſon (1), ſays, that, when the H became a vowel, it was divided into two letters, the firſt of which, Ͱ, was employed to ſignify the aſpirate, and the ſecond, ┤, the ſlender, or ſimple vowel ſound. Quintilian and other old grammarians ſeem to have held the ſame opinion (2); ſo that there can be no doubt but that theſe marks were ſo employed in the manuſcripts of their times. There is, however, no inſtance of the ┤ in any antient monument now extant, or in any manuſcript anterior to the ninth century, though the Ͱ occurs upon the medals of Tarentum, Heraclea, and Leſbos, and alſo on the Heraclean tables, and an earthen vaſe publiſhed with them by Mazochi; who has conjectured, with much ingenuity and probability, that theſe two notes were firſt employed in oppoſition to each other, to ſignify the thick and ſlender enunciation of tone, by Ariſtophanes of Byzantium, the inventor of the accentual marks (3). The preſent notes (c) and (ɔ) are corruptions of them, which were gradually introduced to facilitate writing (4). Dr. Taylor ſuppoſed that the H was the Ionian aſpirate, the Ͱ the Dorian,

(1) Proleg. in Homer. p. 5, where the marks, through an error of the copyiſt or printer, are tranſpoſed.

(2) Lib. I. c. 4. & Gramm. vet. Putch. Col. 1829, *& ſeq.*

(3) Comm. in Tab. Heracl. p. 127.

(4) Ibid.

and the F the Æolean (1); but we find the F in its Pelafgian Form, Γ, with the Ⱶ on the Heraclean tables; and the Lefbians, whofe coins have the latter afpirate, which he calls Dorian, were Æolians.

Diftinct marks or characters were invented for each of the afpirated confonants at a very early period; fo that, I believe, there is not more than one genuine example extant in which they are feparated in the primitive mode. This is a votive infcription preferved at Venice, in which we find KH for X, and ΠH for Φ, as in the Latin (2), which was derived from the Æolian or Arcadian alphabet, before the afpirated confonants had found a place in it. In the oldeft Etrufcan Infcriptions, however, as well as the Sigean, fuppofed to be the oldeft Greek extant except coins, we find them, both palatial, dental, and labial, expreffed by characters not only diftinct, but which have no apparent refemblance of form to the letters from which they are derived.

The palatial afpirate, which confifts of either the Gamma or the Kappa afpirated, was made by the Etrufcans, I believe, invariably, and by the Greeks fometimes, like a divided V, thus Ψ (3). Its ufual form, however, was compofed of two tranfverfe lines thus X; which, on the very antient medals of Naxus in Sicily (4), is employed, as in the Latin, to fignify the Ξ or abbreviated mark for the ΓΣ and ΚΣ, unlefs indeed, as I am inclined to think, the name of that city was really ΝΑΧΣΟΣ contracted to ΝΑΧΟΣ, as ΔΣΑΝΚΛΕ to ΔΑΝΚΛΕ, by an elifion of the Σ, much affected by the Greeks in the refinement of their language, when the found of that letter was deemed harfh and barbarous. The power of the Greek X feems to have been nearly the fame as that which the Spaniards now give to the Roman X, the Tufcans to the C, and the Scotch to the GH. We are apt to pronounce it as if it were a plain K without any afpiration; and the French have given it the barbarous found of their own CH, a found which to a Greek would have appeared fcarcely human. It was pro-

---

(1) Ad Marm. Sandvicenfe, p. 45.

(2) See Pl. I. Fig. 2. I have not feen the originals, nor any *fac-fimile* either of this or the Veletrian Infcription; but as both have been generally acknowledged to be authentic, and contain no internal evidence to the contrary, I have ventured to quote them.

(3) See Pierres gravees du Duc d'Orleans, Tab. II. Pl. II.

(4) See Torremuzzi, Pl. III. Fig. 2, from a medal now in the cabinet of the Author.

bably

bably pronounced more or lefs gutturally in different dialects, or according as it was compofed of the Γ or K, the latter of which letters was fome-times employed alone as a palatial, and the former as a guttural, afpirate. The Γ in particular was prefixed to words in fome dialects, and omitted in others, as the afpirates frequently were; whence Homer writes ΓΔΟΥΠΟΣ and ΔΟΥΠΟΣ, ΓΑΙΑ and ΑΙΑ, &c. as the metre requires. Hence too we may perceive that the Latin CUM and the Greek ΣΥΝ are the fame word, the original form of which was ΓΣΥΝ, now written ξυν, from which the one nation dropt the Σ, and the other the Γ. This is the rea-fon alfo that in the Latin the S is frequently prefixed to another confonant without rendering the preceeding vowel long.

From this ufe of the Gamma probably came the Digamma; which, from its form as well as name, feems to have been compofed of two Gammas placed one upon the other thus Ϝ, or thus Ⅎ; the former of which figures was employed by the Æolian and Ionian Greeks; and the latter by the Etrufcans, Campanians, and other Pelafgic clans of Italy. The Latins retained the Greek figure in their Alphabet, derived from the Arcadian, which was alfo the Æolian; but they corrupted the found of it in a manner that is difficult to be accounted for. The Digamma was cer-tainly pronounced rather as a fimple afpirate than as an afpirated confo-nant, and differed from the common note of afpiration in the impulfe, which caufed the forced expiration, being given from the throat rather than from the tongue and palate: but the Roman F was pronounced by a forced expiration from the under-lip through the intervals of the upper teeth, fo as not to refemble any voice, whether of man or animal, according to the obfervation of Quintilian (1). It is generally fuppofed among the Learned at prefent, that the Digamma was pronounced like our W, for it correfponded to the Latin V, the found of which was certainly the fame. The etymology of many Latin words proves this; VIS, VICUS, VINUM, &c. being evidently from ϜΙΣ, ϜΟΙΚΟΣ, ϜΟΙΝΟΝ, &c. the two laft of which were probably once written ϜΙΚΟΣ and ϜΙΝΟΝ, whence our words WICK and WINE; for, upon the very antient medals of Oaxus in Crete, we find the O omitted, and the name of the city written ϜΑΞΟΣ (2). In the Veletrian Infcription it is however inferted in the word ϜΟΙΚΟΣ. The

(1) Lib. XII. c. 10.   (2) See Dutens, p. 165.

W, as

W, as pronounced by us, is a palatial afpirate of the flendereft kind, having more of tone than articulation, and being rather a vowel than a confonant, for it is uttered with little or no conftraint of expiration. The Welfh commonly employ it to exprefs tone only, with confonants, as we do in fome inftances, though always accompanied by another vowel, as in TWINE, TWIST, DWELL, &c.; in all which the W is as much a vowel expreffing tone as the I or E. The difference, however, between a palatial and guttural afpirate is very fmall; for, if the tongue and the palate are a little more than ordinarily compreffed, while the breath is forced between them, the compreffure naturally extends to the throat, and the found becomes guttural. Local or temporary habit is always fufficient to caufe this; wherefore the fame letter, which in one age or province was employed as a palatial, might in another have been employed as a guttural, afpirate. The Æolic dialect, we know, had more guttural founds than any other, and more particularly employed the Digamma, which is thence called *Æolic* by the later grammarians. We may, therefore, fairly conclude that it reprefented this found, to which, perhaps, there is nothing nearer in modern language than our WH, as pronounced in the word WHIRL; or that of the Tufcan GU, as pronounced by the natives of Florence and Pifa in the word GUERRA. The Pelafgian VAU, from which is derived the Roman V, had certainly the fame power, and was often confounded with it; and we know that this letter was an afpirated Υ, from which the vowel Υ was diftinguifhed by the epithet ψιλον.

Both the F and the H or Ͱ feem to have been dropt from the Greek Alphabet nearly at the fame time, probably about the period of the Perfian war. The firft figure of the latter was, however, retained, to reprefent the double or long E, and the former feems to have continued in ufe in particular places, where a fondnefs for the antient dialects prevailed, even to the final fubverfion of the Greek republicks by the Roman arms. Strabo fays, that the people of Elis and Arcadia preferved the Æolic dialect pure when it was mixed or loft in every other part of the Peloponnefus (1), and of courfe in every other part of the world. In collections of antient coins we find a great many infcribed FA and FΑΛΕΙΩΝ (2); fome of them

(1) Lib. VIII.   (2) See Comb. Pl. XXVII. Fig. 21, 22, 23.

ftruck

ftruck at the earlieft period of the art ; and others apparently under the Achæan league, as they are of the lateft ftyle of workmanfhip, and have the ufual device of that federative republick imprinted upon them (1). ΓΑΛΕΙΟΙ we know muft be the Æolian manner of pronouncing ΗΛΕΙΟΙ, the people of Elis, to whom, I have no doubt, that thefe coins belong, and not to the Falifci, a people of Italy, to whom writers upon medals have ignorantly afcribed them, without confidering that neither the letters nor inflexion are fuch as could have been employed by the antient inhabitants of Latium or Etruria.

The labial afpirate Φ was ufually reprefented in the Etrufcan alphabet by two circles one above the other like the Arabic figure of eight (2). In the Sigean Infcription it is of the form now employed (3), which has fcarcely ever been varied, except in making the interfected circle fquare for the convenience of engraving. It was pronounced antiently by a conftrained expiration between the lips, which approached towards each other; but all the modern nations of Europe pronounce it like the Roman F, though that was a letter which the Greeks were abfolutely incapable of uttering, there being no found in their language which at all refembled it. Hence they were abfurdly and illiberally ridiculed by Cicero for bringing an accufation againft Fundanius when they could not pronounce his name (4). For the credit of modern manners, I believe there is no court of judicature now exifting that would liften to fuch a defence, if an advocate fhould be fo forgetful of decency as to attempt to employ it.

The Θ, or dental afpirate, was reprefented both in the Etrufcan and Ionian alphabets by a circle interfected by one or two tranfverfe lines, thus ⊘, or thus ⊗ ; or having a point in the middle, thus ⊙. The antient manner of pronouncing it was indifputably that which is ftill obferved by the modern Greeks, the Copts, and the Englifh; that is, by a conftrained expiration between the tongue and the upper teeth. All the other European nations pronounce it as a mute confonant, and throw the afpiration upon the next fucceeding vowel. This is a fort of hereditary defect; for

(1) See Gefner. Pl. XIV. Fig. 7.; alfo, Comb. p. 5.
(2) See Eugubian Table before cited.
(3) See Pl. II.
(4) Quintil. lib. XII. c. 10.

antiently

antiently the Northern nations could not pronounce any of the aſpirated conſonants; whence, among the barbariſms uttered by the Scythian, in the Theſmophoriazuſæ of Ariſtophanes, we invariably find the K. for the X, the Π for the Φ, and the T for the Θ (1).

The Σ, called San and Sigma, which is found under different forms in all alphabets, and which grammarians claſs ſeparately by itſelf, as being neither mute, aſpirate, or liquid, is in fact a dental aſpirate, differing from the Θ only in being pronounced with the tongue applied to the root inſtead of the point of the teeth, ſo as to produce a hiſſing, and what appeared to the refined ears of the Greeks, a barbarous ſound. This hiſſing pronunciation of the dental aſpirate ſeems to have been the only one known to the Lacedæmonians; for, when brought upon the ſtage by Ariſtophanes, they uniformly uſe the Σ for the Θ. It appears, however, to have been only a local and vicious habit of pronouncing; for, had it been an eſtabliſhed characteriſtick of their dialect, we ſhould have found the ſame ſpelling in the treaties of alliance entered into by them with other Dorian States, which are always in the Doric dialect, but without this peculiarity. In other inſtances both the Dorians and Æolians employed the T for the Σ, as in the pronoun ΣΥ, which they wrote ΤΥ. The poſſeſſive, however, derived from it, was written with either letter indifferently by the poets, as ſuited beſt with their rythm and metre; whence it is probable that this variation was, in all inſtances, rather habitual than provincial. Both the Engliſh and French now ſound the T as an S before the vowel I in many inſtances, particularly in the abſtract ſubſtantives derived from the Latin; unleſs, indeed, that the Engliſh have now almoſt univerſally corrupted it into the barbarous ſound of the SH. The caſe is, that the Σ being only a T aſpirated in a particular manner, would naturally be confounded with it in the different modes of pronunciation which habit or caprice give riſe to in languages not fixed by any eſtabliſhed rules of orthography, which the Greek was not till the Macedonian conqueſt, when the later Attic became the common dialect; nor any of the modern languages till within this century, when the French and Engliſh made etymology their ſtandard, whilſt the Italians and Spaniards more wiſely adhered to pronuncia-

(1) See Vſ. 1001, *& ſeq.* ed. Brunck.

tion;

tion; whence their words are fpoken as they are written, and a foreigner, who has learned the power of their letters, knows how to utter the founds which they reprefent.

The liquid confonants are thofe which partake of the nature both of mutes and afpirates, being pronounced by a fuppreffion of the breath in one part, and a conftrained expiration in another, except indeed the R, which is uttered by the breath being violently forced between the tip of the tongue and roof of the mouth, fo as to caufe a vibratory or jarring motion of the former, by which the natural current of expiration is broken and interrupted (1). In modern orthography, the note of afpiration is always affixed to it; but this is not fupported by the authority of any antient infcription, though it occurs in the common Roman form upon fome of the moft antient monuments of Grecian art now extant, fuch as the coins of Lefbos, Tarentum, Croto, and Syracufe.

The Lacedæmonians employed this letter inftead of the Σ in the terminations of their words, of which we have a curious example in the decree againft Timotheus, the Milefian mufician, preferved by Boethius in his Treatife upon Mufick (2), and more correctly re-publifhed, from a Manufcript at Oxford, in the year 1777 (3); fmall remains of it are alfo to be found in the Lyfiftrate of Ariftophanes (4); and Plutarch's Life of Pyrrhus (5); but the tranfcribers, not underftanding thefe curious provincial peculiarities, have expunged them from the orators and hiftorians, otherwife we fhould probably have had them in the other public acts of that people. This might poffibly have been the cafe with the Σ employed for the Θ, of which, however, there is no trace in any written monument of the Laconians, though it occurs in the converfations attributed to them;

(1) Διὰ τȣτȣ τȣ γραμματος (τȣ P) την φοραν μιμειται ειτα εν τῳ τραμῳ, ειτα εν τῳ τραχει· ετι δε εν τοις τοιοισδε ρημασιν, οιον ΚΡΟΥΕΙΝ, ΘΡΑΥΕΙΝ.————Την γλωτταν εν τȣτῳ, ἡκιστα μενȣσαν, μαλιϛα δε σειομενην. Plat. in Cratyl.

(2) Lib. I. c. 1.

(3) As this decree is a very important monument of antiquity, and particularly connected with the fubject of this Effay, I fhall confider it apart at the end.

(4) Παλαιορ for παλαιος. Vf. 987, ed. Brunk.

(5) Εἰς δε των ϖαρεοντων, ονομα Μανδρικιδης, ειπε, πη φοϩη λακωνιζων· αι μεν εαϛι τυ γε σιορ, ȣδε μη ϖαθωμεν· ȣ γαρ αδικευμαν· αι δ'ανθρωπορ, εσσεται και τευ καλλων αλλορ.

wherefore,

wherefore, I am rather inclined to think it a vicious habit of pronouncing, never authorized by orthography.

To pronounce the L, which has an affinity with the R, the vibratory motion abovementioned is ſtopped, and the tip of the tongue preſſed againſt the roof of the mouth, while the breath is forced out by the ſide of it.

The N is pronounced by the tongue being entirely compreſſed againſt the roof of the mouth ſo as to ſuppreſs expiration by that channel, which is, however, continued through the noſe.

The M has a near affinity with it, being equally uttered by a continuance of expiration through the noſe, whilſt it is in other reſpeᵭs ſuppreſſed by a compreſſure of the lips.

Neither the form nor power of the liquids have varied materially from what they were in the Latin alphabet, which is the oldeſt Greek except the Etruſcan. The Lambda has indeed been written ſometimes with the one and ſometimes with the other end upwards ; and the Latins retained one mode, and the Greeks the other, whence the two old forms were V and ʌ. The Sigma was alſo repreſented ſometimes by a ſimple waved line, thus S, and ſometimes by one more complicated and angular, thus Σ, which in the Venetian and Veletrian inſcriptions, and on the very antient coins of Sybaris and Paſidonia, is placed horizontally, thus M, while the Mu is diſtinguiſhed from it by the angular lines being of different lengths, thus *M*, or more complicated, thus *M*.

The laſt claſs of ſigns for ſounds are thoſe which repreſent the different tones of the voice, and which we, therefore, call vowels.

Tones being infinite in number, and varying in almoſt every individual, the arranging them under diſtinᵭ heads, and reducing them to any fixed and permanent rules, may be conſidered as the laſt refinement in language; a refinement which the ſimple and determinate harmony of the Greek tongue ſeems to have been alone ſuſceptible of; for none of the antient Oriental alphabets had any vowels (1) except the Phœnician, and that had

(1) The Shanſcrit has ; but whether that alphabet be original, like the language, I very much doubt, as both the forms and number of the letters ſeem to imply that it is made up from the ſpoils of others; and I believe there are no very antient inſcriptions to be found in it. The oldeſt that have been publiſhed are but little anterior to the Chriſtian æra.

properly only two, the Aleph and the Ain, fignifying (as I am inclined to think) merely the different degrees of aperture in the mouth, required to pronounce the words reprefented by the confonants (1).

The Greeks, even in the very earlieft ftage to which their Alphabet can be traced, had five; all which (except the Alpha, borrowed from the Phœnicians) appear to be of their own invention. The Latin, and other alphabets formed from the Greek, have confined themfelves to this number, though wholly inadequate to exprefs the licentious variety of tones employed in the corrupt dialects of the moderns; whence they are obliged to reprefent many different founds by one letter, to the utter confufion of all method and analogy in writing. The French, as I have heard from thofe who have minutely ftudied their language, pronounce the E only with more than ten different variations of tone; and in our own language the fame vague and licentious utterance prevails. In the Greek, on the contrary, each vowel fignified one tone, varied only in extenfion and accent; that is, in the length of time employed in the expiration of the breath, which formed it, and the degree of force and rapidity with which that breath was forced from the larynx. Vowels invariably long are not properly diftinct letters, but, like the double confonants, a fort of Sigla, by which the united founds of two letters were expreffed by one mark. They are faid to have been invented by Simonides, and began to be generally ufed about the time of the Perfian Invafion, although the Athenians did not adopt them till the Archonfhip of Euclides, which was in the fecond year of the xcivth Olympiad, 403 years before the Chriftian æra, and 77 after the retreat of Xerxes. The name of Gelo, King of Syracufe, who died in the third year of the lxxxvth Olympiad, 478 years before the Chriftian æra, is written, upon his Coins, with the Omega (2); and the Eta occurs upon the coins of the Rhegians, which, by the ftyle of workmanfhip, feem to have been ftruck nearly at the fame period, or a very little earlier. They have, however, the genitive plural written with the fingle O (PHΓINON), as thofe of the Coians have, though ftruck when the Omega was employed in the fame word, as KΩION, which we find upon

---

(1) Some, perhaps, will add the Jod; but, befides that this letter was not properly a vowel, I have never been able to difcover it upon any genuine monument of Phœnician writing.

(2) See Torremuzzi, Pl. XCVII.

D

many

many medals of the ifland of Cos (1). Thefe double vowels muft have relieved the Greek language from many ambiguities, efpecially after the difufe of the fimple afpirates, which, on many occafions, fupplied their place, as I fhall foon fhew. Their having, however, been licentioufly ufed, fometimes to fignify the coalefcence of two vowels into one, and fometimes the prolongation of a fingle vowel by a fucceeding paufe, has caufed confiderable confufion both in the analogy and profody of the Greek tongue, as I fhall prove when I come to examine the metrical powers of the letters, to afcertain which is the principal object of this Enquiry. It is generally fuppofed, that both the double vowels and diphthongs were unknown till many ages after Homer, as well as the double confonants Z, Ξ, and Ψ, which are in fact only abbreviated marks to exprefs two letters by one character, like thofe ufed in the manufcripts of the middle ages, and copied by the firft printers. This is, however, not quite fo clear; for the diphthongs are found in the moft antient infcriptions extant, though afterwards difufed. The firft Sigean, written about fix hundred years before the Chriftian æra, has EIMI; but the fecond, copied from it, probably about fifty years after, has EMI (2). The OI diphthong is alfo in the Veletrian infcription, which is at leaft as antient as the firft Sigèan (3). Upon a medal of Lefbos, more antient than either, we find the word ΝΩΙΧƷΗRΩ, written from right to left, with the double vowels (4); but upon another, of a lefs antient ftyle, the word NOIATƎ-1 has the fingle O in the genitive plural (5). The firft of thefe words feems to be a myftic title belonging to fome obfolete dialect, for it has no apparent affinity with the known roots of the Greek language; but the laft is probably the genitive plural of ⌐ETHΣ, employed equally as a myftic title. Words equally anomalous with the firft occur upon the very antient medals of Side, in Pamphylia, written alfo with the double vowels; but, as fome unknown

(1) See Dutens, Pl. IV. Fig. 4; Pellerin, Pl. CII. Fig. 1; and Magnan. Brut. Pl. XXIII. Fig. 2. Similar medals are in the cabinet of the Author.

(2) See Pl. II.

(3) See Pl. I. Fig. 2.

(4) See Pl. I. Fig. 4.

(5) The medal I faw in the cabinet of the King of France. There is one exactly fimilar in the Hunter collection, except the letters. See Comb. Pl. XXXIII. Fig. 3.

characters

characters are mixed with them, it is impoffible to decide whence they came, or to what language they belong (1). It is equally impoffible to afcertain the date of thefe antient medals; though we may fafely pronounce them to be as old as any written monuments extant, except the hieroglyphical infcriptions of Egypt; and, perhaps, fome Etrufcan or Pelafgian antiquities. Thofe of Lefbos, in particular, are of the moft antient fabrick known; and, from the numbers in the fame ftyle which have been found, muft have been ftruck when that ifland poffeffed great opulence and power.

This, according to the computation of Eufebius, was during the feventh century before the Chriftian æra, the Lefbians having poffeffed the empire of the Mediterranean from about the xxvith to the xliiid Olympiad; whereas Simonides did not flourifh till the end of the lxth Olympiad, full feventy years after (2). I am, therefore, perfuaded that the double vowels were ufed in Afia before the time of that poet, their fuppofed inventor; who might, neverthelefs, have brought them into Greece, and rendered the ufe of them more popular and general. The age of Homer is, however, fo much anterior to all monuments of art, or authentic records of hiftory, that we cannot even tell whether or not he had the knowledge of any letters; there being but one paffage in his Works where writing is mentioned, and that is fo equivocal, that it may mean either fymbolical or alphabetical writing (3).

The form of the double vowels feems not to have varied confiderably till the age of Hadrian, when the Omega, which was before written Ω or Ο, was, as Euftathius obferves, made out of two upfilons, and written (like our W) ω. I attribute the introduction of this form to that period, becaufe the Egyptian medal of Antinous is the oldeft monument of art, of which the date can be afcertained, that exhibits it; other medals of the fame perfonage having it in the antient form. As to what Abbé Winkelmann fays, of its being upon the medals of the Macedonian kings of

(1) See Pl. I. Fig. 6, from a medal in the cabinet of the Author.
(2) See Eufeb. Chron. lib. II. verf. J. Hieronym.
(3) —————— ————— πορὶν δ'ὄγι σημαῖα λυγρα
Γραψας ἰν πιναχι πτυχτῳ θυμοφθορα πολλα
Δειξαι δ'ηνωγιι ᾧ πι.θιρω, οφρ' απολοιτο.   Il. Z. 168.

Syria,

Syria (1), I can take upon me to affert that it is untrue, no fuch medal having yet been difcovered either of the Syrian or any other of the Macedonian Dynafties; though it is probable that the learned Antiquary was deceived by fome counterfeit, he having no knowledge of coins (2). It is, indeed, upon a brafs vafe, preferved at Rome, which appears, by the infcription, to have been prefented by King Mithridates to a Gýmnafium; but this Mithridates was probably the petty prince of Thrace, who reigned in the times of Trajan and Hadrian, and not the great King of Pontus, whofe tafte and magnificence would fcarcely have condefcended to make fo paltry a prefent, and much lefs to have put his name upon it. The fame kind of Omega is, indeed, in the names of the two artifts, which are infcribed upon the two celebrated ftatues of the Hercules Farnefe, and the Torfo of the Belvidere; but as thefe artifts are not mentioned by any antient writer, it is probable that they lived under Hadrian and the Antonines, and that the ftatues are copies from more antient works. The Coloffal head of Antinous, in the villa of Mondragone, at Frefcati, and the buft of Trajan, in the collection of Mr. Townley, prove that there were then artifts capable of the executive part of either of thefe figures, though the grand ftyle of compofition which peculiarly diftinguifhes the laft, had been long extinct. It is probably a copy of fome well-known groupe of Hercules ftrangling the lion, the attitude appearing to have been nearly the fame as that in which he is reprefented upon fome of the fmall filver coins of Heraclea, in Sicily (3).

The proper mode of pronouncing the Greek vowels has been a fubject of much controverfy ever fince the revival of learning in the Weft; it having been foon difcovered that the Byzantine Greeks, the only teachers of the language, had long loft the art of fpeaking it, though they continued to write it with purity, and even elegance. Erafmus firft compofed a whimfical dialogue upon the fubject; and foon after Cheke, Profeffor of Greek in the Univerfity of Cambridge, undertook to examine it; but his work was anticipated by an edict, publifhed in the year 1542 by Stephen

(1) Hift. des Arts, lib. IV. p. 122.

(2) See Hift des Arts, tom. III. p. 93; where he has publifhed one of the moft bungling modern counterfeits ever executed, as a true medal of Antigonus, King of Afia.

(3) See Torremuzzi, Pl. XXXV. Fig. 4 & 5.

Gardener,

Gardener, Bifhop of Winchefter, and Chancellor of the Univerfity, ftrictly commanding that the mode of pronunciation eftablifhed by the modern Greeks fhould be continued; by which the vowels H, I, and Υ, were confidered merely as different figns for one found, the diphthongs OI and EI for another, and AI and E for another. Cheke and his friends found no difficulty in confuting thefe abfurdities; but neither he, nor thofe who have followed him in the enquiry, have afforded us much real information, except that which was before given by Dionyfius of Halicarnaffus. " The " A," fays that Critick, " when extended, is the moft fonorous of the " long vowels. It is pronounced by the mouth being very much opened, " and the breath forced upwards. Next is the long E; to pronounce " which the mouth is moderately opened, and the found, following the " breath, preffed down about the root of the tongue. Then comes the " long O, which requires the mouth to be circular, and the lips contracted " round, againft the outward edges of which the breath muft be ftrongly " impelled. The Υ is lefs fonorous; for, the breath being conftrained by " a confiderable contraction of the lips, the found produced is flender. In- " ferior to all is the I; for, the mouth being but little opened, there is a " collifion of the breath with the teeth, and the lips are not employed in " elevating the found (1)." This paffage entirely fubverts the authority of the Byzantine Greeks, as well as that of our own fchools, none of which teach the true pronunciation of the vowels, except perhaps the Scotch. The Critick has confidered the long ones rather than the fhort ones, not becaufe there was any difference in the mode of pronouncing them, but becaufe tone can be better illuftrated and afcertained in a long found than a fhort one. It appears, from what he fays, that the A was pronounced as the Italians now pronounce it, or as we pronounce it in the words VAST, PAST, &c. The E was alfo as the Italians now pronounce it, or

---

(1) Αὐτῶν δὲ τῶν μακρῶν εὐφωνότατον τὸ α, ὅταν ἐκτείνηται· λέγεται γὰρ ἀνοιγομένου τοῦ ϛόματος ἐπὶ πλεῖϛον, καὶ τοῦ πνεύματος ἄνω φερομένου πρὸς τὸν ἐρανόν. δεύτερον δὲ τὸ η. ὅτι κάτω περὶ τὴν βάσιν τῆς γλώσσης ἐρείδει τὸν ἦχον ἀκόλουθον, ἀλλ' οὐκ ἄνω, καὶ μετρίως ἀνοιγομένου. τρίτον δὲ τὸ ω· ϛρογγύλλεταί τι γὰρ ἐν αὐτῷ τὸ ϛόμα, καὶ περιϛέλλει τὰ χείλη, τήν τε πληγὴν τὸ πνεῦμα περὶ τὸ ἀκροϛόμιον ποιεῖται. ἔτι δὲ ἦττον τούτου τὸ υ· περὶ γὰρ αὐτὰ τὰ χείλη συϛολῆς γινομένης ἀξιολόγου πνίγεται, καὶ ϛενὸς ἐκπίπτει ὁ ἦχος. ἔσχατον δὲ πάντων τὸ ι· περὶ τὰς ὀδόντας τε γὰρ ἡ κρότησις τοῦ πνεύματος γίνεται, μικρὸν ἀνοιγομένου τοῦ ϛόματος, καὶ οὐκ ἐπιλαμπρυνόντων τῶν χειλίων τὸν ἦχον. Dionyf. Halicarnaff. περὶ συνθεσ.

7   as

as we pronounce the A when followed by a confonant and mute vowel, as in the words MATE, PLATE, &c. The Italians have alfo the true pronunciation of the O, which we have miferably corrupted, except when followed by a confonant and mute vowel, as in the words MODE, BODE, &c. As for the Υ, I am in doubt whether any modern nation pronounces it exactly as the Greeks did: the Italians follow the Latins, whofe U correfponded to the ΟΥ diphthong of the Greeks, the true pronunciation.of which is retained by the French in their own ου. We pronounce it as the diphthong ΕΥ in fome inftances (as in 'ΥΔΩΡ), and in others, as the French pronounce the fame diphthong (as in ΣΥΣ), a barbarous found unknown to antiquity. Perhaps the neareft letter to it in modern alphabets is the French accented U; the found of which is, indeed, poor and flender; but fuch Dionyfius informs us that of the Greek Υ was.

The vowels have varied but little in their forms, except that the Upfilon was antiently written like the Latin V, and the Iota by an indented line, thus ς, to diftinguifh it from the Gamma, which was reprefented by the ftrait perpendicular line. The confufion between thefe two forms probably produced the *I* confonant; which feems, in the Roman alphabet, to have had that affinity with the G which it ftill retains in moft modern languages.

SECTION

SECTION II.

HAVING thus confidered the letters as notes of articulation, afpiration, and tone, it remains to be confidered in what modes and degrees particular acts of vocal utterance were lengthened or fhortened, in proportion to the number and clafs of the letters employed in reprefenting them; for, as the Greek Alphabet was adapted to the language, and not the language to the Alphabet, we fhall find the practice perfectly accord with the theory, unlefs where local or vicious habits corrupted it. Even there we have the peculiar advantage in this language of poffeffing the Works of a poet (the moft elegant, correct, and perfect, of all poets), who lived before many fuch habits had been formed, and whofe writings, therefore, though defaced by the varnifhes of criticks, grammarians, and tranfcribers, are compofed of materials fo pure and fimple, and executed with fuch precifion and regularity, that we can ftill trace the minuteft touches of the mafter's hand, and afcertain, with almoft mathematical certainty, the principles upon which he wrought (1). For this reafon I fhall admit

(1) This character of Homer's poems may, perhaps, ftartle thofe who are accuftomed to receive their opinions, ready-formed, from the futile, but pompous, affertions of certain felf-created judges of literature; whofe decifions, to the difgrace of the age, are not unpopular.

One of thefe has lately pronounced, with all the technical jargon of a profeffed bookmaker, that the Greeks had no ears for metrical harmony; but that all their poets, and more efpecially Homer, continually tranfgrefs the rules of their own profody; their verfification being, as he fays, always irregular, and generally rough and unmufical, and terminating in what he calls *cacophonies.* (Recherches fur les Grècs).

That there fhould be a mind fo perverfely organized as to form fuch opinions as thefe, when nurtured in the pride of pedantic ignorance, I am not at all furprized, for I have obferved as many *lufus naturæ* in morals as in phyficks; but that there fhould exift one, capable of forming or comprehending a fingle fyllogifm, and yet fo deftitute of common judgement and difcretion as to publifh fuch paradoxes to the world, and thus become the herald of its own imbecility and deformity, is fcarcely to be accounted for, even in the wide extent of human inconfiftencies.

no

no general rule or principle of metrical quantity that is not juftified by the practice of Homer; having found that his practice is always founded upon reafon and analogy, whereas that of later poets was often regulated by local and temporary habit.

Upon his practice, therefore, and the principles before ftated, I venture to draw the following general conclufions:

I. A fingle vowel, reprefenting a fingle act of vocal utterance or expiration, muft neceffarily be fhort, unlefs lengthened by a fucceeding paufe or obftruction of utterance; for the proper definition of a fhort fyllable is, one that occupies only the time ufually allowed to a fingle act of vocal utterance; whereas a long one is that which occupies the time ufually appropriated to two, either by being really a coalefcence of two, or elfe by being delayed or impeded by fome adfcititious paufe or obftruction.

If there be no fuch paufe or obftruction, and the fucceeding word begins with a vowel, this vowel, if ftanding alone, or terminating a word, will be fwallowed up, or, as the grammarians fay, elided; for tones, unlefs divided by a paufe or fufpenfion of the breath, naturally coalefce, or flow into each other.

The Greeks, however, in their Heroic or Hexameter verfe, admitted of an arbitrary or artificial paufe, and often fuftained one vowel entire before another in a different word; but in dramatic poetry this was not allowed; neither did the Latins, in their Heroic verfe, admit of it, otherwife than as a licence, juftifiable by the example of the Greeks, when Greek words were employed. I cannot indeed but think that it crept originally as a licence, introduced by the lofs of the afpirates, into the Greek language; and that it was never really juftified by the practice of the antient poets, whofe works, according to the prefent orthography, afford fo many inftances of it; for, if we reftore the afpirates according to etymology and antient practice, we fhall find fcarcely any inftances in Homer that may not be cured by a flight change in the order of the words, in which the Manufcripts and old editions continually differ; or the infertion of a particle, always admiffible, and often required by the fenfe. In the genuine poem of Hefiod too, I know of only four inftances, except thofe where the afpirates are wanting; and of thefe four the emendations appear fo obvious,

vious, that I fhall venture to propofe them, though without any better authority than my own conjectures.

For αζωςοι εκιον, I would read αζωςοι γ᾽ εκιον (1).

For αναβαλλεσθαι εϛ τ᾽ αυριον, αναβαλλεσθαι τ᾽ (i. e. τι) εις αυριον. Αλλοτε
αλλον fhould be αλλοθεν αλλον (2); or perhaps only have the paragagic N
added to the firft word; for the Bæotians frequently dropt the afpirates,
as appears from the very antient medals of Thebes, upon which the name
of that city is written with the T inftead of the Θ (3).

Μεσση επιδειελα may be μεσση᾽ επιδειελα (4); the adjective μεσσηος or
ΜΕΣΣΕϜΟΣ occurring in the feminine, μεσσηη, in Vf. 767, according to
a Manufcript collated by Grævius; and this reading was preferred both by
him and Robinfon (I think rightly), notwithftanding the decifive Manner
in which M. Brunk has rejected it.

Later poets, however, have continually inftances of vowels fuftained
before other vowels in different words; but thefe poets may be confidered
as writing in a dead language; for fuch the language employed in Heroic
verfe then was; both the words and flexions being taken upon the authority of the antient and popular bards, when no longer known as the ordinary means of focial intercourfe. Had they, indeed, poffeffed the works
of thofe antient bards in their genuine ftate, their imitations of them would
at leaft have been exact, as thofe of Vida are of Virgil; but between the
age of Homer and Hefiod, and that of Apollonius Rhodius and Theocritus, the alphabet, orthography, and pronunciation of the Greeks appear
to have been greatly altered; and with them, of courfe, the laws of profody, which regulated the old Hexameter verfe. Hence, in that verfe,
there is an appearance of arbitrary licence in the extenfion and abbreviation
of the fyllables, which none of the metres that employed only living dialects admitted, and which I cannot believe to have been admitted by this,

(1) Vf. 318, ed. Brunk.

(2) Vf. 685, ed. Brunk.

(3) Thefe medals are very fcarce. I do not recollect to have feen more than one, which
is a tridrachm, with the vafe on one fide, and quadrangulated incufe on the other, in the
cabinet of Mr. Vandamme, at Amfterdam.

(4) Vf 755.

E

when

when all the words and flexions which it employed were in familiar ufe, as they undoubtedly were in the time of Homer.

The *Iota fubfcriptum* of the dative cafe being, as will be more fully fhewn hereafter, a vowel of itfelf, regularly affixed to the preceeding one, as it is in other declenfions to the preceeding confonant, that preceeding vowel is guarded by it, and therefore not neceffarily elided. Hence the terminations in η and ω often remain long before another vowel. The η is alfo fometimes long before another vowel when affixed to an afpirate, as in the third perfon fingular of the Aorift and paffive, ἐ]υφθη, the reafon of which will appear when we confider the metrical power of the afpirates.

II. A fingle vowel before a fingle mute confonant muft neceffarily be fhort, unlefs there be a paufe between them; for, as the confonant terminates the found without adding to it, there will of courfe no paufe accompany it.

If, however, a fecond mute confonant follow, either in the fame or a different word, the fyllable, though not the vowel, will neceffarily be long; for, as its concluding confonant fignified a fuppreffion of the breath which produced it, and the opening confonant of the next fyllable the commencement of a new act of utterance from an equal fuppreffion of the breath, there muft neceffarily be an intermediate act of fufpenfion or expiration; which, how fhort foever it be, will require a paufe fufficient to lengthen the firft fyllable, to which it muft neceffrily be added, becaufe the fecond only began with its opening confonant.

I know that this intermediate act of fufpenfion or expiration, which conftitutes the paufe, is feldom perceptible in modern pronunciation, efpecially that of the Englifh, who never utter two confonants of the fame organs diftinctly when they come together in the fame word. The fecond D and T, in the words ADDED and PITTED, are never uttered, but only ferve to give the firft more than common force and emphafis. In the fame manner we pronounce the Latin words QUIDDAM, QUICQUAM, &c. and the few Greek which there are of this defcription.

The κ being, as was before obferved, formed out of two fingle confonants, is frequently employed by Homer with the power of a double one;

but,

but, when we find the fame power given to any other mute confonant, we may conclude that it was originally afpirated, or that fome letter has been omitted. ΤῩΔΕΥΣ is ufually derived from ΤΥΤΘΟΣ, *little*, which might account for the extenfion of the firft fyllable, if the etymology was admiffible, which, I think, it is not; for, though the Greek names were all defcriptive titles, they were never titles of diminution or degradation. The afpirate, we know, was dropt from the Τ in the dialeft of the antient Thebans(1); who, therefore, wrote the name of their city ΤΕΒΕ, inftead of ΘΗΒΗ. The fame pronunciation and orthography probably prevailed among the antient Ætolians, who muft confequently have pronounced and written the verb θυω or ΘΥϜΩ, ΤΥϜΩ; and if the name Τυδευς be derived from it, as it appears to be, it muft of courfe have been written upon the fame plan, ΤΥϜΔΕϜΣ.

The orthography, indeed, of moft of Homer's names may be confidered as merely traditional, for the oldeft infcriptions, in which any of them are recorded, are of an age long pofterior to his; and no reliance is to be placed in the copies of antient authors which have come down to us; for even a name fo well known, and of fo late a date, as that of the great King of Pontus, has not efcaped corruption: upon his coins, as well as upon every other antient monument that bears his name, it is uniformly written ΜΙΘΡΑΔΑΤΗΣ, according to its etymology from ΜΙΘΡΑΣ; but in all books, both Greek and Latin, it is as uniformly ΜΙΘΡΙΔΑΤΗΣ.

Whenever, therefore, this tradition is oppofed by radical etymology, or metrical analogy, we may, I think, venture to pronounce it wrong. ΑΒΤ̄ΔΟΣ was probably written with the Digamma, ΑΒΥϜΔΟΣ, it being derived from the verb ΒΥϜΩ. ΜΑΣΤΙΞ-ΙΓΟΣ was ΜΑΣΤΙΝΓΣ-ΙΝΓΟΣ, in the fame manner as ΦΟΡΜΙΝΓΣ-ΙΝΓΟΣ, ΣΑΛΠΙΝΓΣ-ΙΝΓΟΣ, and other words of the fame clafs; fome of which have dropped, and others retained the Ν(2). In fome editions of Homer we have, indeed, μαϛιγι, in Il. Ψ. 500; but the true word here, as the Venetian Scholiaft has ob-

(1) As in the medal before cited.

(2) In Hefychius we have βυϛ. μαϛιγξ. Heinfius, indeed, fuppofes the Γ in the laft word to be inferted erroneoufly; but it is in reality the antient form with the ufual variation ΜΑΣΤΙΓΞ for ΜΑΣΤΙΝΓΣ, the fame as πλαϛιγξ for ΠΛΑΣΤΙΝΓΣ, a word of fimilar meaning and formed upon the fame plan, from a different verb.

ferve

ferved, is μαςῖ, or rather ΜΑΣΤΙΙ, the Ionic dative of an obfolete word, ΜΑΣΤΙΣ; with the Δ elided in the fame manner as in θετῖ or ΘΕΤΙΙ for ΘΕΤΙΔΙ.

Such elifions are extremely common in the Greek language, as muft be obvious to every one who has even curforily examined it. The omiffion of the N before the palatial confonant is general in the prefent orthography, though its place is ufually filled by doubling the confonant, or adding another of the fame organ, as in εγχος, αγκων, &c.; which appear, from antient medals and infcriptions, to have been originally written, as they are ftill pronounced, ΕΝΧΟΣ, ΑΝΚΩΝ, &c. (1) The Σ was ftill more frequently elided, as being a letter the found of which was abhorred by the refined ears of the Greeks; whence great confufion has been introduced into the tenfes of the verbs, as I fhall more particularly obferve hereafter.

The firft fyllable of fome words compounded of the prepofition απο are occafionally pronounced long, though confifting only of a fingle vowel followed by a fingle mute confonant, as Ἄπολλωνος and απονεεσθαι, in which the Π was, by fome provincial habit, pronounced double; or (what is more probable) delayed in the utterance by the mufical paufe or cæfure; for this licence never takes place but in the firft fyllable of the foot; and, as all very antient verfe was fung to the lyre, there might have been fome particular ftrefs or paufe in the accompaniment on thefe occafions.

Παρθενοπῖπης fhould probably be ΠΑΡΘΕΝΟΠΙΠΤΗΣ, it being derived from ϖαρθενος or οπιπτευω, and the omiffion of a letter being marked by the circumflex. The letter might, however, have been elided in the time of Homer, and the cuftom of pronouncing the fyllable long continued after the change in the orthography.

A fingle vowel is often long before the adverbs δην and δηρον; but the firft of them is fometimes written Ͽην; and, as the fecond is derived from it, we may conclude that it was written in the fame manner, which is in-

(1) See Torremuzzi, Pl. XLV. Fig. 9 & 10; and Comb. Pl. V. Fig. 2. In the Heraclean infcriptions, however, which are in the Doric dialect, and about 300 years before the Chriftian æra, the N is more conftantly changed than at prefent, as appears from ΕΜΜΕΝ, ΕΜΜΕΣΣΩΙ, ΠΡΩΓΓΥΟΣ, &c. for εν μεν, εν μεσῳ, προεγγυος, &c.

deed

deed more conformable to etymology, the root being ΤΕΩ or ΤΕΙΝΩ. Written in this mode, the metrical analogy becomes perfectly regular; for,

III. A fingle vowel followed by an afpirate or liquid, either in the fame or a different fyllable, or even preceeded by one in the fame fyllable, may be either long or fhort, fince the conftrained expiration, employed in founding the afpirate or liquid, is a continuation of the vowel found differently modified by the approximation or compreffion of the organs of fpeech, and may therefore be fhortened or lengthened arbitrarily, according as the conftrained expiration is continued for a greater or lefs time. Hence both the afpirates and liquids are often written double when etymology requires that they fhould be fingle, as in αλλοφος, εμμεναι, εσσεται, &c. where there is no more reafon for writing the letters double than in δε λοφος, δε μεγα, απενιζοντο, βελος, &c. pronounced δελλοφος, δεμμεγα, απεννιζοντο, βελοσς, &c. Ariftarchus appears to have difapproved of this departure from etymology (1), which certainly ought to be entirely adhered to, or entirely neglected, for pronunciation; as the prefent orthography, being regulated upon no principle, gives the appearance of anomalies where there are none. In the flexions of the verbs the doubling the Σ is, however, fometimes regular; the old Æolian and Dorian terminations in -ΣΔΩ forming the future in -ΣΔΕΣΩ, contracted to -ΣΔΣΩ, and thence, by the Δ's being elided for the fake of fmoothnefs, to -ΣΣΩ. Neverthelefs, it appears from the Heraclean Tables, the moft complete and perfect monuments of the kind extant, that the antients adhered more to pronunciation than etymology, whence, in addition to other local peculiarities, we have uniformly ΗΟΣΣΟΣ, ΕΣΣΟΝΤΑΙ, ΕΣΣΗΤΑΙ, &c.

When two afpirates or liquids come together, or one of them be joined to a mute confonant, this conftrained expiration will naturally be lengthened or obftructed, either of which will prolong the fyllable. Neverthethelefs, the Attic writers, whofe dialect was fpoken more clofely and ra-

---

(1) See Schol. Ven. in Il. K. 258. See alfo Erneft. Not. ad Il. M. 281; and Callimach. Hymn. in Del. 110; and Clarke ad Il. N. Vf. 1; where, after having very ingenioufly and pertinacioufly defended an erroneous opinion throughout his firft volume, he very effectually, though not very openly, recants it; and thus at once fubverts the fine-drawn fyftem of metrical quantities, which he had laboured to eftablifh through all his preceeding notes.

pidly

pidly than that of the antient Æolians and Ionians, pronounced the vowel
fhort before ΣM, KN, ΠN, and TM; but, in all inftances of this kind,
the Σ, K, Π, and T, merely mark the commencement of utterance, or
preparatory fuppreffion of the breath, and were therefore very flightly, if
at all, pronounced in the rapid and concife fpeech of the Attics.   In the
works of Homer, however, the fyllable is, in fuch cafes, always long (1),
though he admits of the Λ or P to be joined to a mute confonant without
extending the preceeding vowel; for both thefe letters exprefs tone as
much as articulation, and therefore are properly called femivowels.   According to Dr. Clarke, indeed, he makes the fecond fyllable of Αιγυπτιος
fhort; but as it is always long in the fubftantive Αιγυπτος, I believe that
acute critick to have been miftaken, and that we ought to pronounce the
laft vowels, even in the oblique cafes, as one fyllable; the I having no
other power in this, as well as many other inftances, than the Y· in our
words YEAR, YAWN, &c. in which it is rather an afpirate than a vowel.

The firft fyllable of τεμνει is, neverthelefs, fhort in our prefent copies
in one inftance (2); but the Harleian Manufcript, collated by T. Bentley,
has τεμει, which is probably right, though the vowel might poffibly be
fhort, even according to the old Ionic pronunciation, before two liquids of
the fame organ; and if Homer had any other inftance of it, I fhould prefer
the common reading; but when a general conclufion is drawn from fuch

(1) Hence we may conclude that the Batrochomyomachia is not Homer's, but a burlefque imitation of his manner by fome antient Attic poet, who, though he adopted the
words and expreffions of the old bard, formed his metre according to the pronunciation of
his own country.

With equal confidence we may pronounce the Margites to have been a forgery, though
there are only four lines of it extant; and three of thofe are quoted as authentic by Plato and
Ariftotle: but in thefe we have a compound verb with the augment upon the prepofition
(κπιςατο); which Homer's grammar did not admit.

Similar objections may be made againft the hymns and epigrams, fome of which have
been ftated by Clarke, and others will be noticed in this Effay.

Thefe peculiarities are more certain proofs of the authenticity of the Iliad and Odyffey
than any hiftorical evidence would have been, for they fhew that the moft antient imitators
and moft learned readers of thofe poems never obferved the diftinctive fingularity of their
diction, and therefore could neither have forged or reverfified them, as fome have fufpected.

(2) Il. Ν. 707.

a numa number of examples as neceſſarily occur in the two long poems of the Iliad and Odyſſey, a ſingle exception is of courſe ſuſpicious.

We have alſo in our preſent copies one inſtance of εγναμψεν (1), two of ανδροτης (2), and ſeveral of ανδρειφοντης (3), with the firſt ſyllables ſhort. But the firſt word is, in the Venetian Manuſcript, written very properly εκαμψεν; and the ſecond, as Damm has obſerved, ſhould be αδροτης, as it is preſerved in a citation by Plutarch (4). Aldus's firſt edition of Plutarch has, indeed, ανδροτητα; whence Erneſti ſuſpects that αδροτητα is only a conjectural emendation of ſucceeding editors (5). Whether, however, it be ſo or not, it is certainly the true reading; for, beſides the analogy of metre, ſupported by the uniform concurrence of ſuch a number of inſtances in various dialects, the very principles of the language do not allow ſuch a word as ανδροτης to exiſt, any more than thoſe of our own tongue ſuch a one as *manneſs*; for the Greek abſtract ſubſtantives in -της, like ours in -*neſs*, are all neceſſarily derived from adjectives, and not immediately from other ſubſtantives: ανδρειος, therefore, being the adjective ſignifying *manly*, ανδρειοτης muſt have been the form of the abſtract ſubſtantive ſignifying *manlineſs*, if any ſuch in this claſs had ever been formed, which I do not find that there ever was. Even if there had, it could not have been known to Homer; for the adjective does not appear to have exiſted in his time, and prior to that the abſtract ſubſtantive could not have exiſted, any more than, in our own language, the ſubſtantive *manlineſs* could have preceeded the adjective *manly*.

Ανδρειφοντης occurs only in the dative caſe as an epithet to Mars (Ενυαλιω ανδρειφοντη), and, as it is now read, has the two firſt ſyllables ſhort, to the utter ſubverſion of all metrical analogy. The Leipſic Manuſcript has ανδριφοντη, which is little leſs objectionable, unleſs we elide the Δ, as in ανερι, and write ενυαλιω ανριφοντη, or, in antient letters, ENEΥΑΛΙΩΙ (6) ΑΝΡΙΦΟΝΤΗΙ.

(1) Il. Ω. 274.
(2) Il. X. 363; & Ω. 6.
(3) Il. B. 651; H. 166; Θ. 264; P. 259.
(4) De Poet. audiend.
(5) Ad Il. Π. 857.
(6) Thus is this title written on the Maſtrilli vaſe, found at Bari, in Italy, and publiſhed by Mazochi, which I believe to be right, for Suidas mentions the exclamation ENEΥ;

ΦΟΝΤΗΙ. We may, indeed, fuppofe the prefent reading to have been pronounced ΕΝΕΥΑΛΙ' ΑΝΔΡΕΙΦΟΝΤΗΙ, though the ΩΙ or ῳ of the dative cafe is not often elided. I wifh there was any authority to write ΑΡΙ- or ΕΡΙΦΟΝΤΗΙ, which, I think, would improve both the fenfe and metre, and which I cannot but fufpect to have been the original word, though it does not now occur any where. It is, however, equally confiftent with the idiom of the language as *εριβρεμιτης, εριχυδης, εριϰυνης,* &c. ; and its being little ufed was the natural caufe of its being corrupted.

When a confonant afpirate follows a mute, as in the Ζ, Ξ, and Ψ, the preceeding vowel, or rather the fyllable taken collectively, muft neceffarily be long; for though the Δ or ΤΣ, the Γ or ΚΣ, and the Β or ΠΣ, are each fignified by one character, they never completely coalefce in found, there being neceffarily a paufe, however fhort, between the fuppreffion of the breath, which produces the mute confonant, and the conftrained expiration, which produces the hiffing afpirate(1).

But when the conftrained expiration preceeds the entire fuppreffion, it feems only a preparatory or introductory part of it ; for the conftraint is itfelf a complete fuppreffion, which a continued approximation of the organs of the mouth to each other would render complete as foon as they came into contact. The Σ, therefore, fignifying the act of approximation, and the mute confonant, which follows it, that of contact, both are only different ftages or gradations of one exertion, and therefore form, when thus united, only one diftinct articulation ; which may, neverthelefs, be contracted or extended in the utterance, according as the idiom of the lan-

and the Latin verbs ENECO and NECO, and the Greek fubftantive NEKΥΣ, are apparently derived from the fame root, written according to different dialects ΕΝΕΚΩ, ΕΝΕϜΩ, ΕΝΕΥΩ, and ΕΝΥΩ.

(1) I am aware that there are fome very learned perfons who have been of opinion that the Σ preceeded the mute in forming the double confonants ; but I think, if this had been the cafe, the Doric verbs terminating in ΣΔΩ would have been written like the Attic and Ionic with the Ζ, otherwife the difference would have been to the eyes, and not to the ears, by which we know, neverthelefs, that all the variations of dialect in the Greek language were perceptible. The Κ alfo inftead of the Σ would have been elided before a confonant in the prepofition ΓΣ or ΕΚ, and the Latins would have written fuch Greek words as ΥΥΧΗ, ΥΑΛΤΡΙΑ, ΟΥΟΝ, &c. SPYCHE, SPALTRIA, OSPONIUM, &c. inftead of PSYCHE, PSALTRIA, OPSONIUM, &c.

guage,

guage, or cuſtom of the country, require. The extenſion, however, when it takes place, will not be in the ſyllable in which theſe letters are employed, but in the preceeding one; for the delay cauſed by the hiſſing ſound is not an extenſion, but a ſuſpenſion, of utterance, which utterance only commences with the conſonant that immediately preceeds the vowel. The Greeks, in almoſt all caſes, admitted this ſuſpenſion, ſo as to make a ſhort vowel, preceeding a Σ and mute conſonant, long; but the Latins, whoſe language was leſs flowing and melodious, and ſpoken with more abbreviation and rapidity (1), often paſſed it over, ſo that the vowel in many inſtances remains ſhort.

Homer, however, has ἱςιαια, which ſome would correct to ἰτεαια; but on the coins the name is always written with the Σ, which might neverthelefs have been elided in the earlier dialects, for I know of no coins of this city which do not appear evidently to have been ſtruck after the Peloponneſian war. He alſo makes the vowel ſhort before the names Ζακυνθος and Ζελεια, which ſome would therefore write Σακυνθος and Σελεια; but it is more probable that, in the old Ionic dialect, they were written ΔΑΚΥΝ-ΘΟΣ and ΔΕΛΕΙΑ, like the Zanclèan medals, which were ſtruck by one of the moſt antient Ionian colonies, and which have uniformly ΔΑΝΚΛΕ for ΖΑΝΚΛΗ (2). For the ſame reaſon the vowel is ſhort before the word Σκαμανδρος, which was antiently written Καμανδρος, as it ſtill is in ſome manuſcripts and old editions. In one inſtance we have alſo παρα ςαθμω; but in Euſtathius it is, more correctly, παρ ςαθμω (3).

It was either from not conſidering this, or, more probably, from being ſtartled at an apparent irregularity of grammar, that Ariſtarchus ſo injudiciouſly changed the antient verſe, which deſcribed the ſcene of action between the Greeks and Trojans, from μεσσεγυς ποταμοιο Καμανδρȣ, και ςομα λιμνης, to μεσσηγυς Σιμοεντος, ιδε Ξανθοιο ροαων (4); which, being preſerved in our preſent copies, has effectually puzzled the geographers who have attempted to fix the ſituation of Troy; for there is a chain of mountains between the ſea and the conflux of the rivers which the Greeks do not ap-

(1) Plutarch. in Demoſth. init.
(2) See Torremuzzi, Combe, &c. as before cited.
(3) Od. ς. 327.
(4) Il. z. 4.

F

pear

pear ever to have paffed; and in the XXIſt Iliad the ſcene is evidently be-
low the conflux, otherwiſe the Scamander could not properly call upon the
Simois to affift him in drowning Achilles.   According to the old reading
every thing is clear, the ſcite of the city being about the village of Borna-
baſchi, where are ſtill the ſprings deſcribed by Homer; which, flowing
down into the plain, formed a lake, ſtill viſible, between the outlet of
which and the river Scamander was the field of battle(1).   This outlet
was probably once into the Scamander, whence the fountains are called
πηγαι Σκαμανδϵυ.   They were two in Homer's time, one warm and the
other cold; but Mr. Wood ſpeaks of only one; and the ſubterraneous
channels may, perhaps, now be joined by the earthquakes that have frequently altered the face of that country.

By not duly conſidering the power of the aſpirates and liquids, ſome of
the moſt acute and learned Criticks have embarraffed themſelves with
imaginary difficulties; and then, by endeavouring to remove them, raiſed
real and almoſt unſurmountable ones.   This has been particularly the caſe
with thoſe who have attempted to reſtore the Digamma to the poems of
Homer; a taſk certainly of extreme nicety and difficulty, but which will,
I hope, be yet found practicable; for, until it is accompliſhed, the minuter beauties of his poetry, ſuch as elegance, purity, and correctneſs, in
which it excels as much as in ſublimity and expreſſion, muſt remain concealed from the generality of his readers.

When the ſagacity and erudition of Dr. Bentley had diſcovered the want
of this letter, Dawes, who, like many others, borrowed his ideas, and
repaid him with abuſe, aſſumed the taſk of pointing out the words to
which it ought to be added, and the figure by which it ought to be repreſented.   In the latter he has been proved to be miſtaken, as Bentley has
been proved to be right; but in the former his authority is ſtill held in
high eſteem, though but little deſerving it; for he has raſhly foiſted in
this aſpirate wherever the metre ſeemed to him to want propping, without
examining whether or not its power was ſuch as the place required, or the
etymology of the words admitted; whence he has brought this branch of
criticiſm into ſome diſgrace among the learned in other parts of Europe;

(1) See Mr. Wood's Plan and Deſcription

4   who,

who, with the natural prejudices of pedantry, have pronounced the enquiry to be vain, becaufe it has not been purfued with fuccefs (1).

The metrical power of the Æolic F is almoft, if not precifely, the fame as that of the H or ⊢ ; for it is equally a fimple or vowel afpirate, pronounced with nearly the fame degree of conftrained expiration, and, in the Æolian dialect, often occupied its place, or, at leaft, the place which it held in the Attic dialect; the tranfition being extremely eafy, in a language not fixed by any decided principles of orthography, from one letter to another, when both are of the fame clafs, and poffeffed nearly of the fame power (2). The Pelafgic clans of Italy feem to have employed it occafionally as a vowel, the antient medals of Capua being infcribed ꓱꓘ∀ꓘ (3). It is poffible, however, that the name of this city was then pronounced in two fyllables, ΚΑΡWΑ; but as the final A is never to be found upon the coins, it is more probable that the antient Ofc inhabitants did not employ it, but pronounced the name of their city ΚΑΡ'ΗΥ, which a Welfhman would now write ΚΑΡW. The Arabian Waw alfo, which has the fame name, and probably the fame power, as the Pelafgian Vau, or Æolian Digamma, is invariably ufed as a vowel in that language, though employed as a confonant by the Perfians, who have corrupted it precifely as we have the Roman V (4), which was originally the Pelafgian Vau or Waw. There is certainly no reafon why the Campanians might not, in their dialect, have ufed the correfpondent letter as a pure vowel, though the other natives of Greece and Italy employed it as a pure afpirate, fome with the metrical power of a fingle confonant only, and others with the general metrical powers of almoft every other letter, as I fhall now proceed to fhew.

(1) See D'Orvill. ad Charit. p. 202; and Erneft. ad Il. π. 172.

(2) See Salmaf. in Crenii Muf. Philolog. & Hiftor. p. 78. In the Heraclèan tables the fame word is written with the F (in the Pelafgian form Ⅎ) when alone, and with the ⊢ when compounded ; as ΙΕΤΟΣ and ΠѦΝΤΑⸯΕΤΗΡΙΣ, which occur invariably. The number six too, which in all other dialects is written ἰξ or ⊢-ΕΞ, is in thefe tables ⊏ΕΞ. ΙΣΟΣ is likewife written in one inftance ⊢-ΙΣΟΣ, and in two according to the ufual form. See l. 101, 122, and 127.

(3) See Comb. Pl. XIV.

(4) Afiatic Refearches, Vol. I. p. 30 & 31.

F 2

That

That Mr. Dawes fhould not have obferved this univerfal power of the
Æolian Digamma is rather wonderful; for, befides the analogy of found,
which might have led him to it, the very authority, which he quotes, afferts and exemplifies it. The word *confonant*, indeed, being improperly
applied to this letter, might naturally have mifled a lefs acute and learned
obferver, but could not, one fhould think, have mifled him, who employs
much argument to prove it an afpirate. "The Latins," fays the Grammarian Prifcian, in a paffage cited by Dawes, "employ the V for the Æo-
"lian F, both being ufually fimple confonants, as in

"ΟΙΟΜΕ**Ν**ΟΣ ϜΕΛΕΝΗΝ 'ΕΛΙΚΩΠΙΔΑ, and

"AT VENUS HAUD ANIMO NEQUICQUAM EXTERRITA MATEP.

"The Æolians, however, fometimes ufed the F for a double confonant,
"as in ΝΕΣΤΟΡΑ ΔΕ ϜΟΥ ΠΑΙΔΟΣ. In other inftances they ufed it
"as a fhort vowel, as in ΚΑΙ ΧΕΙΜΑ ΠΥΡΤΕ ΔΑϜΙΟΝ; and in others
"it has no metrical power whatever, as in ΑΜΜΕΣ Δ' ϜΕΙΠΑΝΑΝ ΤΟ
"ΔΕ ΤΑΡ ΘΕΤΟ ΜΩΣΑ ΛΙΓΑΙΑ." The reader, who is converfant with
the writings of Homer, will readily obferve that this is precifely the metrical power of the other fimple afpirate, fignified antiently by the figures
H and Ⱶ, and now by the mark ('). Dawes would, indeed, fubftitute
the Digamma to this afpirate in all inftances where the vowel is lengthened
or fuftained by it; but as he has no authority for fo bold an innovation
except his own fyftem, which is contradicted alike by etymology, analogy,
and antient monuments, his arguments, or rather conjectures, do not de-
ferve any very ferious confideration. He would even do away the authority of his own quotation from Prifcian, by reading the paffage of Alcman (1), AMMI or AMME ΔΕ ϜΕΙΠΑΝΑΝ, though the alteration, if otherwife admiffible, would render the verfe totally inapplicable to the purpofe
for which it is cited.

To attempt to point out the inftances in which the Digamma ought to be
inferted in Homer, after the failure of fo learned and ingenious a Critick,
muft of courfe appear rafh and prefumptuous in one whofe habits of life

---

(1) Alcman is faid to have been the firft poet who employed any verfe but the Hexameter of Homer. Both his age and country are unknown, for, though he is generally faid
to have been a Lacedæmonian, Velleius Paterculus pofitively afferts that their pretenfions to
him were ill-founded. See Meurf. Mifcell. Laconic. Lib. IV. c. xvii.

have

have not enabled him to apply his mind to the fubject with the unremitted diligence of a profeffed fcholar. As, however, I may throw out fome hints which may excite the curiofity, or guide the inveftigations, of more learned perfons, I fhall offer my conjectures in as few words as poffible. To do this with that method which is equally requifite to concifenefs and perfpicuity, it will be neceffary, in the firft place, to take an accurate view of the flexions of his words, and to confider them as written in the characters which he employed, or which were employed whilft his language was the familiar vehicle of focial intercourfe among his countrymen, and had not been confecrated by the ruft of time to the fole ufe of poets, who employed it only upon his authority, and when writing in his own metre. Not that I would infer, that the ftyle of Homer was what we fhould now call *obfolete* (that is, fo obfcured by time as to be intelligible only to the learned) at any period of Græcian literature; but that many of his words and flexions, having ceafed to be in familiar ufe before even the commencement of profe-writing, were ever after reftricted to the Heroic or Hexameter verfe, and not allowed even to the fublimeft dramatic poets who employed a different metre, though the loweft of the audience would have found no difficulty in underftanding them. The true meaning and etymology, indeed, of fome of his words, was loft; but cuftom had fupplied another which every one knew.

In the variety of the antient flexions confift the dialects of Homer, which muft not be underftood to have been, in his age and country, provincialifms, like the dialects of modern Italy, but merely variations upon one tongue, all equally authorifed by general ufe. Some of them, indeed, might have become provincialifms, even before his time, in particular parts of Greece; but, neverthelefs, the mixture of the Æolic and Ionic emigrants muft have again confounded them in Afia, and rendered them of general popular ufe before he wrote; for we may conclude that, as his poems were addreffed to the general mafs of mankind, and are remarkable, above any thing, for extreme perfpicuity, his words and flexions were all fuch as every hearer would readily underftand.

Thefe antient variations or dialects confifted chiefly of different modes and degrees of afpiration, and the broad and flender enunciation of tone fignified by the vowels A and E; which, though originally differences of

3

irregular

irregular licence, were, by degrees, as the language became fettled, transformed, by accidental habit or fafhion, into particular provincialifms, dif-
tinguifhing the Æolian and Ionian Greeks, whofe dialects were the pa-
rents of all the reft; for the Doric is principally a conftruction of the
Æolic, and the Attic of the Ionic (1). Homer, I am inclined to think,
was equally unacquainted with both thefe provincial contractions; for,
though Atticifms occur very frequently in his works, as we now have
them, they appear to have come from the Athenian and Alexandrine editors, through whofe hands they paffed in their way to us. Not but that
contractions and elifions were in ufe even in the earlieft times, but they
were entirely different from thofe which characterifed the Attic dialect.
From the fame corrupt channels flowed the anomalies and poetical licences
which commentators have pointed out and explained, but which were certainly unknown to the pure and regular diction of the poet, as will more
fully appear from a fhort analyfis of his flexions, which are all upon one
principle, though claffed and fubdivided by grammarians and fchoolmafters,
for no other apparent purpofe than to load the memories, and perplex the
underftandings, of their pupils.

It has been obferved by Dawes, that the nouns ending in -ΕΥΣ antiently
ended in -ΕΡΣ, from which their oblique cafes are regularly formed, as
ⱵΙΠΠΕΡΣ, -ΕΡΟΣ, -ΕΡΙ, -ΕΡΑ, -ΕΡΕ (by elifion ΕΡ), -ΕΡΕ, -ΕΡΟΙΝ,
-ΕΡΕΣ, -ΕΡΩΝ, -ΕΡΕΣΙ (contracted to -ΕΡΣΙ), -ΕΡΑΣ; each of which
fuffered various contractions in later times; but in Homer the lofs
of the Digamma is almoft conftantly fupplied by the Epfilon being
tranfpofed into an Eta; nor do I know of more than two inftances in his
works of an oblique cafe, or plural number, remaining without the aug-
mentation of an additional fyllable. Thefe two are the words ἱππεῖς (2)

---

(1) Though thefe four are the only dialects that were regularly cultivated and fixt, many
more exifted in the licentious variations of fpeech that took place through the wide difper-
fion of the Greek colonies. Herodotus mentions four different kinds of Ionic fpoken in
Afia only *, and it is probable that, before the Macedonian conqueft, almoft every ftate had
fome peculiarities of its own.

(2) Ἱππεὺς δ' ἱππηας· ὑπὸ δὲ σφισιν ωρτο κονιη.   Il. Λ. 151.

* Lib. I. S. 142.

and ὀδυσεὺς (1); to which we may add from Hefiod, whofe poem equally requires the Digamma, a third, βασιλεις. Thefe are all contractions of the antient forms; but in what manner they were antiently written is difficult to fay; for, though both the Υ and the I were employed to replace the F, we cannot reftore this letter without reducing the nominative and genitive fingular, and the nominative plural, to the fame form, only difcriminated by the circumflex. There is, however, no doubt but that, in the nicety of antient pronunciation, this circumflexed form was diftinguifhable by the ear as well as the eye; wherefore I am perfuaded, that the primitive contraction was from -ΕΦΟΣ and -ΕΦΕΣ to ΕΦΣ, changed in the genitive to -ευ̃ς, and in the nominative to -εις, and afterwards, by the Attics, to -ης; by which means any ambiguities which might have arifen were avoided.

Upon the fame plan the patronymics, and other words of the fame clafs, ending in -Α, -ΑΣ, -ΕΣ, or -ΗΣ, feem to have been declined, except that the afpirate was ufually dropt in the Ionic pronunciation; whence, when the penultimate fyllable is long in the oblique cafes, they are always in the Æolic, and, when fhort, always in the Ionic; for the Æolians retained the ufe of the Digamma after it had been neglected by the other Greeks, whence it was called *Æolic.* The genitives Ατρειδαο and Πηληιδαο abfolutely require the infertion of the afpirate, in order to give the penultimate vowel its due length,. and were, therefore, undoubtedly written ΑΤΡΕΦΙΔΑΦΟ and ΠΗΛΕΦΙΑΔΑΦΟ; but Ατρειδεω and Πηλειδεω require its omiffion, otherwife the two laft vowels could not coalefce into one fyllable as they ufually do; wherefore they muft have been written ΑΤΡΕΦΙΔΕΟ and ΠΗΛΕΦΙΔΕΟ, the two firft Digammas in the middle of the words ftill remaining, as they belong to the roots ΑΤΡΕΦΣ and ΠΗΛΕΦΣ. In words of the former clafs too the Digamma was retained even in the flexions through both

___

(1) Ὀδυσεὺς δε ·λαβων κυσι χειρ᾽ επι καρπῳ.   Od. Ω. 397.

We have, indeed, the accufative τυδη̃ in another inftance, which is generally fuppofed to be produced by an apocope of the laft letter, ευθ᾽ αυτ᾽ αγγελιην επι τυδη̃ ϛειλαν Αχαιοι (Il. Δ. 384); but the fingularity of this form renders it fufpicious, and a flight alteration in the order of the words makes it regular—ΕΝΘ᾽ ΑΥ ΤΥΦΔΕΦ᾽ ΕΠ᾽ ΑΝΓΕΛΙΗΝ ΕΣΤΕΛΛΑΝ ΑΧΑΙΟΙ.

dialects;

dialects; whence we have ΝΑϜΣ and ΝΕϜΣ, or, as they are now written, ναυς and νηυς, with their correspondent forms in the oblique cases always in two syllables, whereas the nominatives are always in one, which proves that the aspirate was retained in declension. The first syllable is, indeed, sometimes long and sometimes short, the short vowel before the aspirate being pronounced either way; whence we have νηα and νεα, both of which ought to be written ΝΕϜΑ or ΝΑϜΑ. The Ionians did, indeed, in some instances, drop the aspirates, and extend the vowels, contrary to etymology; but it is very uncertain whether this provincial innovation prevailed at all so early as the time of Homer, and very improbable that it ever prevailed in the declensions of the nouns.

Whether the Attic or Ionic terminations of the patronymics, &c. in -ΗΣ, and the formation of the genitives in -εω or -ΕΟ was at all known to Homer, I have some doubt, as the Æolic terminations in -ΑΣ and -ΑϜΟ favour more of antiquity, and the latter might have been reduced to one syllable, ΑϜ, by the elision of the last vowel, which we know was practised, even before the Digamma became obsolete, to form the Doric genitive in Α, which occurs on the very antient medals of Thebes and Macedon in the names ΕΥϜΑΡΑ, ΑΜΥΝΤΑ, ΠΕΡΔΙΚΚΑ, &c. (1) In the genitives plural of the same class, the Attics omitted one vowel, and the Dorians the other; whence we have ΣΙΚΕΛΙΩΤΩΝ, ΙΤΑΛΙΩΤΩΝ, &c. in the one dialect, and ΣΙΚΕΛΙΩΤΑΝ, ΙΤΑΛΙΩΤΑΝ, &c. in the other, both being contractions of the primitive Æolian forms, ΣΙΚΕΛΙΩΤΑϜΩΝ, ΙΤΑΛΙΩΤΑϜΩΝ, &c. originally, perhaps, written with the single vowels ΣΙΚΕΛΙΑΟΤΑϜΟΝ, ΙΤΑΛΙΑΟΤΑϜΟΝ, &c.

The aspirates, both vowel and consonant, were often elided even by the very antient Greeks; whence we find συς & υς, φη & η, &c. and the future tenses of the verbs, sometimes written with, and sometimes without, the characteristic Σ, the omission of which has caused the antient scholiasts to mistake them for present tenses, and to suppose a sort of licentious enallage, which, if admitted, must subvert all the principles of language. The Digamma was occasionally elided in the same manner; but whether αυταρ, δορυ, πελυς, βαλω, &c. were ever written ΑϜΤΑΡ, ΔΟϜΡΥ, ΠΟϜΥΣ,

(1) See Dutens, p. 158; and Frælich. c. VII.

ΒΟϜΛΩ,

BOFΛΩ, &c. as Dawes and his learned and ingenious editor have fuppofed, I much doubt; for though the ϒ was very generally inferted in the
later Attic for the F, it was alfo inferted where that afpirate never could
have been, and I believe, in fome inftances, reftored to words from which
it had been dropt; for the diphthongs were much lefs ufed in the fecond
than the firft ftage of Greek orthography, whence we have EIMI in the
firft Sigèan infcription, and EMI in the fecond. The negative Oϒ was at
one period very generally written O; but it does not follow that it was
ever written OF. In one inftance βϤλεσθε occurs with the firft fyllable
fhort, whence fome Manufcripts have βολεσθε and βολεσθαι.

Ει δ'υμιν οδε μυθος αφανδανει, αλλα βϤλεσθε

Αυτον τε ζωειν, και εχειν πατρϣϗα ϖαντα.   Οδ. Π. 387.

But though this elifion of the ϒ removes the metrical irregularity, the
greater difficulty ftill remains, for the word αλλα, as Clarke has obferved,
is totally incompatible with the fenfe, which requires a *conjunctive* inftead
of a *disjunctive*. I would therefore read,

Ει δ' υμιν οδε μυθος αφανδανει, ηδε και αυτου

ΒϤλεσθε ζωειν, και εχειν ϖατρωια ϖαντα.

Though the Digamma, as well as the other afpirates, could be thus
elided, no licence could ever add or infert either into words to which they
did not regularly belong. The antient fcholiafts and grammarians, indeed,
who wrote fo many ages after the two vowel afpirates had both been dropt
from the Alphabet, and the one wholly obliterated and difufed, finding
that, which was retained in pronunciation, fignified, when fignified at
all(1), only by the inverted comma ('), confounded it with the accentual
marks, and eftablifhed certain whimfical rules of their own for affixing or
omitting it.

The Alpha before a Delta, they decided, ought always to be afpirated,
unlefs it was a crafis, or fignificant of privation(2); but no vowel could
be afpirated in any cafe if followed by an afpirated confonant and a P,

(1) See Euftath. in Odyff. ᴢ. Vf. 151, where it appears that the manufcripts which he
ufed, though he wrote as late as the twelfth century, had no notes of afpiᴜᴛion. See alfo
Ernefti ad Loc.

(2) Schol. Ven. ad Il. Λ. 88.

G

whence

whence οφρα, αφρος, αχρις, &c. are without it (1).   The A alſo could never be aſpirated if followed by a Λ and a dental or palatial conſonant, whence αλτο is formed from άλλω (2) ; followed by a P and M it is, however, to be aſpirated, though there are ſome exceptions (3).

The αι diphthong, beginning words of more than one ſyllable, was never to be aſpirated (4) ; and the Σ, followed by an aſpirated conſonant, was ſuppoſed to prevent a vowel preceeding from being aſpirated, whence the Σ in εσθος is ſlender, though in the verb from which it is derived it is aſpirated (5).   In ελεοθρεπτος it was alſo to be ſlender, though aſpirated in ελος, becauſe followed by a Λ in a word the third ſyllable of which was a pure vowel (6).

Some Criticks were for aſpirating the augment in particular tenſes of particular verbs, and others of others (7).

Ptolemy of Aſcalon decided that the inſertion of the Υ ſunk the aſpirate; whence όλος became υλος, and άδω, when joined to the adverb ευ, ευαδω (8).

According to Dionyſius of Halicarnaſſus, the aſpirates coming in the middle of compound epithets ought to be preſerved, but elided in proper names, whilſt Herodian maintained the contrary (9).

Some, however, of the more antient grammarians underſtood the principles of their language better; and it appears from ſeveral paſſages of the Venetian Scholia, that Ariſtarchus and his followers were for aſpirating all words according to their etymology (10).   That this is the true opinion, we might venture to decide, even if it was not ſupported by ſuch reſpectable authority ; for, as the ſimple aſpirates were originally parts of the Alphabet as much as any other letters, it is natural to ſuppoſe that they were employed upon the ſame principles as the reſt.   They were, indeed, more

(1) Schol. Ven. ad Il. M. 391.
(2) Euſtath. p. 145, & 766; l. 41.
(3) Ibid. p. 140, 11.
(4) Ibid. p. 1626, l. 38.
(5) Ibid. p. 1431, 6.
(6) Ibid. p. 345, 1.
(7) Ven. Il. M. 55.
(8) Ibid ᵹ. 340.
(9) Ibid. Ο. 750.
(10) Ib. O. 365; and Ω. 235, and 247.

flexible

flexible than the confonants or liquids, and therefore more liable to local and habitual variation and corruption ; but, neverthelefs, lefs fo than the vowels, which were confequently more varied than either by change of dialect. The Heraclean tables, which apppear to have been written juft when they were falling into difufe, are more licentious and irregular in the omiffion and infertion of them than any other antient monuments extant. One inftance has been already given, and we find another in the verb εχω, which is fometimes, both when alone and when compounded, written ΗΕΧΩ (1), and fometimes ΕΧΩ (2). Many other words alfo, which are every where elfe unafpirated, are here uniformly afpirated, fucn as ΗΟΚΤΟ, ΗΕΝΝΕΑ, ΗΑΚΡΟΣ, ΗΟΙΣΩ, and ΗΑΡΝΗΣΙΣ. Others, on the contrary, which are every where elfe afpirated, are here unafpirated, fuch as ΟΡΟΣ, ΑΛΙΑ, ΑΜΑΞΙΤΟΣ, and ΔΕΚΟΜΑΙ. The cuftom of continuing the afpirate at the beginning of a word, when it has been added to the preceeding letter, appears from thefe tables to be modern, as we find Χ' ΥΠΟ, and not Χ' ΗΥΠΟ, though this prepofition is in every other inftance afpirated.

According to the antient principle of declination, the Digamma appears to have been the characteriftic letter of the oblique cafes in the mafculine and neuter words terminating in -ΟΣ and -ΥΣ, and the feminine in -Ω, -ΩΣ, or -ΥΣ, and -Α or -Η, though it is only wanting to fuftain the metrical quantity in the Æolic genitives plural of the laft, as ΜΟΓΣΑΓΩΝ, ΝΥΜΦΑΓΩΝ, &c. The general analogy of the language, however, makes it probable that it originally prevailed alike through all, and that -ΟΓΟ was the Æolic termination of the genitive fingular of mafculine words in -ΟΣ, as -ΟΙΟ was the Ionic ; which, being both gradually changed by the contractions and elifions common in the Greek language, became -ΟΟ, -Ο, and -ΟΥ, the laft of which was probably firft written ΟΓ, for no regular procefs of etymology could have placed the Υ here ; though, as this vowel was very generally fubftituted for the Γ, when it fell into difufe, we may reafonably fuppofe that it was fo in the prefent inftance. Even in the modern orthography of Homer, the genitive of the proper name Πηλεος

(1) Tab. Neap. I. l. 59, 72, 82.
(2) Ibid. l. 43, 68, 69, 73, 93, 109.

is Πετεωο, which, I think, can only be a corruption of ΠΕΤΕΟΓΟ; and not, as the Scholiaſt explains it, an Attic extenſion of the penultimate, and pleonaſm of the ultimate, vowel (1); ſuch arbitrary extenſions and pleonaſms being, I believe, wholly unknown to the Poet; whoſe words, though frequently contracted, were never amplified or prolonged but according to the ſtricteſt rules of etymology. This, I believe, may be, with equal truth, obſerved of the words-employed by all correct writers in all languages; for, though ſome degree of licence in contracting and abbreviating is allowed in all, there is none that I know of which admits of any licence whatever in extending or amplifying. Ιλιȣ and ανεψιȣ, each of which occur only once with the penultimate ſyllable long, though ſo often uſed with it ſhort, are probably remains of the ſame antient flexions; for the laſt ſyllable in both is long by poſition, ιλιȣ προπαροιθεν and ανεψιȣ κταμενοιο, which I would write ΓΙΛΙΟΓΟ ΠΡΟΠΑΡΟΙΘΕΝ and ΑΝΕΠΣΙΟΓΟ ΚΤΑΜΕΝΟΙΟ.

·The Cratylus of Plato ſeems to have furniſhed the antient ſcholiaſts with their notions of arbitrary extenſions, pleonaſms, adſcititious vowels, &c. &c. What the Philoſopher meant by that dialogue it is difficult to gueſs, for there is no appearance of humour or irony, and yet the etymologies which it contains are infinitely too abſurd for any man of common-ſenſe ſeriouſly to have believed. Every cobler at Athens muſt have known that ανδρια was not derived from αντι and ρεω, nor αμαθια from αμα and θεος. The reader who ſeeks for plain ſenſe, and not merely for fine periods, cannot but ſuſpect that Plato ſometimes wrote dreaming.

It is poſſible that the formation of the -ΟΥ diphthong in the genitive caſe might have been, by corruption, habitually introduced, as well as by the regular apocope or eliſion of the ending vowel; for we find the genitives in -ΕΟΣ or -ΕΓΟΣ contracted to -ΟΥΣ in the later Attic, or common Hellenic dialect, which can be accounted for by no rule or principle whatever, unleſs we admit the metatheſis, or abitrary tranſpoſition of letters, which will be conſidered in the proper place. The antient contraction was ΟΣ; whence in the Sigèan Inſcription, which is Ionic, we have ΗΕΡΜΟΚΡΑΤΟΣ for ΗΕΡΜΟΚΡΑΤΕΟΣ; and in the Sandwich, which is

---

(1) Schol. Ven. ad Il. Δ. 372.

Attic,

Attic, ΕΠΙΓΕΝΟΣ for ΕΠΙΓΕΝΕΟΣ. A fimilar contraction occurs in the verbs, the fecond perfon fingular of the imperfect paffive being changed from -ΕΣΟ to -ΕΟ and -ΟΥ. In the Venetian Manufcript we have θαρσεῦς, that is ΘΑΡΣΕΥΣ, inftead of θαρσυς, as in the common editions (1); which feems to be a fpecimen of the primitive contraction of the regular genitive ΘΑΡΣΕϜΟΣ, preferved by accident, as the contraction ΟΔΥΣΕϜΣ for ΟΔΥΣΕϜΟΣ, beforementioned, was by the metre. A corruption of the fame kind as that which appears in the common forms of thefe words has taken place in the nominatives plural of the comparatives in ΩΝ, as ΑΡΕΙΩΝ, the regular plural of which was ΑΡΕΙΟΝΕΣ, contracted by the Ionians to ΑΡΕΙΟΕΣ, pronounced in three fyllables, and thence corrupted by the Attics to ΑΡΕΙΟΥΣ. In Herodotus the contraction is more fimple, and the comparative formed with the Υ inftead of the Ι for the Ϝ; whence we find πλευνες for ΠΛΕϜΟΝΕΣ or ΠΛΕΙΟΝΕΣ, written by the Attics ΠΛΕΙΟΥΣ.

Thefe abbreviations have caufed the pofitive and comparative to be fometimes confounded in the flexions, as in ΧΕΙΡΕϜΣ, properly a *labourer*, or *handicraftsman*, but ufed figuratively to fignify any *private* or *common perfon*, the comparative of which, ΧΕΡΕϜΩΝ or ΧΕΡΕΙΩΝ, fignifying *commoner*, or *worfe in general*, and being contracted like other adjectives of the fame clafs, the regular flexions of the pofitive, fuch as ΧΕΡΕϜΙ, ΧΕΡΕϜΑ, ΧΕΡΕϜΕΣ, &c. now written χερηι, χερηα, χερηες, &c. became miftaken for abbreviations of it, and, I believe, ftill continue to be fo, though the fenfe of the context will eafily point out the difference. The word ΧΕΡΕϜΣ having grown obfolete at a very early period, whilft its comparative continued in general ufe, very naturally caufed the confufion.

Ἥρωος, the genitive fingular of ηρως, is a dactyle in Οδ. Ζ. 303, notwithftanding the double vowel in the penultimate; which proves that it was antiently written ϜΗΡΟϜΟΣ, the penultimate of which might be pronounced either long or fhort. It was probably from not underftanding this general principle of the antient flexions, that the rafh grammarian Zenodotus would have changed γοργω, γοργυς, to γοργων, γοργονος (2); for, had he un-

(1) Il. P. 573.
(2) See Schol. Ven. in Il. Θ. 349.

derftood

deritood this part of the analogy of his own language, he would have perceived that γοργυς was the regular contraction of the regular genitive ΓΟΡ-
ΓΟΦΟΣ, except that an obfolete letter was changed for a common one.
Modern interpreters feem to have erred in the fame manner when they con-
found αιδῶ, that is ΑΙΔΟΓΑ, the accufative fingular of ΑΙΔΩΣ, *reverence,*
or *virtuous fhame,* with a contraction of ΑΙΔΟΙΑ, *the private parts,* by
which means they render obfcene and ludicrous one of the moft pathetic
and folemn paffages of the Iliad (1).   This error feems to have originated
from the blunder of a tranfcriber, who, in another paffage, has put αιδῶ
for αιδεια, and has been followed by all the editors (2).

The accufative plural of the mafculine words in -ΟΣ, and feminine in
-ΥΣ, feems to have been formed by a change and contraction fimilar to
what has taken place in the genitives fingular and nominative plural abovementioned; for λογυς feems equally to ftand for ΛΟΓΟΦΣ; εριννῦς for
ΕΡΙΝΝΥΓΣ, the contraction of ΕΡΙΝΝΥΓΑΣ; and κλιτῦς for ΚΛΙΤΥΓΣ,
the contraction of ΚΛΙΤΥΓΑΣ; though I believe this laft word ought to
be written at length in every inftance where it occurs, and the firft fyllable
pronounced fhort, as it is in Euripides; and alfo in Homer in other words
derived from the fame root, fuch as ΚΛΙΣΙΗ, ΚΛΙΣΙΟΝ, &c. We have,
indeed, the accufative κλιτῦν in Οδ. Ε. 470; but this feems to be equally a
contraction of the antient accufative ΚΛΙΤΥΓΟΝ, which prevailed through
all words of this clafs; whence the vowel is now fuftained before ιτυν—
οφρα ιτυν καμψη, once probably written ϜΟΦΡ' ΙΤΥΓΟΝ ΚΑΜΠΣΗΙ. The
laft fyllable of the contracted form of the accufative is always long, becaufe, in antient orthography, it was -ΥΓΝ inftead of -υν. In Il. Φ. 318,
the penultimate in a genitive fingular of a word of this clafs is long—κεισεθ' ὑπ' ιλυος—which might have been antiently written and pronounced
ΚΕΙΣΕΘ' ΥΠ' ϜΙΛΥΓΟΣ, or ΚΕΙΣΕΘ ΥΠΟ ϜΙΛΥΓΟΣ; for though the firft
fyllable of ϜΙΛΥΣ is ufually long, there is no reafon from analogy why it
fhould be necefarily fo.

The earlieft inftances which I have met with of genitives in -ΟΥ are
upon the medals of Dionyfius, King of Syracufe, and Alexander II. and

(1) Il. X. Vf. 75.
(2) Il. B. 262.

Philip,

Philip, the fon of Amyntas, Kings of Macedon. I have, indeed, feen in books ΣΥΡΑΚΟΣΙΟΥ ΓΕΛΩΝΟΣ upon the medals of Gelo, King of Syracufe, who flourifhed near an hundred years before any of the abovementioned princes; but upon infpecting the original coins, of which I have feen vaft numbers in the different cabinets of England, France, Sicily, and Holland, I have uniformly found ΣΥΡΑΚΟΣΙΟΙ ΓΕΛΩΝΟΣ. This has given me fome fufpicion of the medals of Dionyfius, of which I have not feen any with the name at length; but neverthelefs, as both the kings of Syracufe, who were fo called, made the Attic dialect the language of their court as well as the kings of Macedon abovementioned, it is poffible that they equally employed the termination in -ΟΥ, which peculiarly belonged to it, but which does not appear to have been employed even at Athens till afterwards; for it is not to be found in the Sandwich infcription, which is public act of a later date. Probably the orthography of the Attic dialect was firft adapted ftrictly to its pronunciation in thefe courts, where, as we are informed, the moft powerful fovereigns of Europe thought it an object of ambition to be able to fpeak and write it correctly. This may account for its being formed with fo little attention to etymology.

This dialect was, at that period (about four hundred years before the Chriftian æra), becoming every where the fafhionable language of letters and philofophy, owing to the well-earned reputation of the Athenian writers, which having foon after recommended it to the patronage of the great conqueror of Perfia and his fucceffors, it became the general language of civilized men, and was thence confidered as the common Hellenic dialect, and the ftandard for purity, though it is in reality one of the moft corrupt dialects, as far as corruption confifts in deviation from primitive roots.

Whether the word ΣΥΡΥΚΟΣΙΟΙ upon the coins of Gelo be a nominative plural, or an abbreviation of the genitive fingular, is difficult to decide, though I think the latter moft probable. There is not indeed any inftance of fuch a genitive; but neverthelefs, by the fame rule of analogy that -ΟΓΟ is abbreviated by the apocopè to -ΟΓ, -ΟΙΟ may be abbreviated to ΟΙ. The moft fafhionable and polifhed dialect too, in the time of Gelo, was that of the Afiatic Ionians, which employed the I rather than the Υ inftead of the F; for the I was their ufual fubfidiary letter, as appears, not only in the genitive terminations, fuch as ΛΟΓΟΙΟ for ΛΟΓΟFΟ, and

ΣΕΙΟ

ΣΕΙΟ for ΣΕϜΟ, but alſo in variations of a more ſtable and permanent kind, ſuch as ΡΕΙΑ for ϼεα or ΡΕϜΑ, ΚΡΕΙΩΝ for χρεων or ΚΡΕϜΩΝ, &c. It was alſo employed for the F and Υ by the Dorians; and, on ſome oc-caſions, by the Æolians, if the preſent orthography of the fragments of Sappho, &c. is to be relied upon, which I cannot anſwer for. In the flexions it was inſerted or omitted arbitrarily, even long after the dialects had become eſtabliſhed provincialiſms; whence we find upon all the ſilver medals of Agathocles, of which great numbers are extant, the genitive caſe of his name written ΑΓΑΘΟΚΛΕΙΟΣ, whilſt the gold and braſs, the latter of which are equally common, have uniformly ΑΓΑΘΟΚΛΕΟΣ; ſo ſo that the accidental or habitual practice of different mints diverſified the orthography even in the ſame country, and under the ſame prince (1).

The antient Æolic termination of the genitive of nouns in -ΟΣ ſeems to be preſerved with but little variation in the relative pronoun, even in the preſent corrupt ſtate of Homer's poems; for I think ὃϜ cannot be de-rived from ὅς or ϜΟΣ any otherwiſe than by being a corruption of ϜΟϜΟ, whence the laſt ſyllable is never long but when rendered ſo by poſition (2).

The poſitive pronouns ΣΥ and ϜΟ were alſo declined upon the ſame plan, as appears from the genitives σεν and ἑν, evidently corrupt abbrevia-tions of ΣΕϜΟ and ϜΕϜΟ, often written at length, in the Ionic manner, σειο and ἑιο, The accuſative ἑε ſeems likewiſe to be the Ionic mode of writing and pronouncing the antient regular accuſative ϜΕϜΑ. The nomi-native plural and dative ſingular ἐς and ὁι belong to another declenſion, and are only diſtinguiſhed from the correſponding caſes of the relative pronoun by the accentual marks, which were not invented till the end of the third century before the Chriſtian æra, and not in general uſe till the middle ages (3). I ſuſpect, however, that this dative ſingular has been ſometimes introduced where the old regular form ϜΕϜΙ ſhould be; whence it ſome-times continues long before a word beginning with a vowel. The ſame may be ſaid of the dative εμοι, of which the laſt ſyllable is ſometimes long in the ſame predicament, and ſhould then probably be written ΕΜΕϜΙ or

(1) The I was very generally added to the E by the early Greek writers, as the Υ was to the O   Euſtath. p. 511, l. 1.

(2) Οϝ αλιϟς, Il. B. 335.   'Οϝ χϼατος, Odyſſ. A. 70.

(3) See Villoiſon. Prolegom. in Homer. p. 12.

4

EMEϜ',

EMEϜ', confiſtently with the antient genitives EMEϜΟ and EMEϜ, now written εμειο and εμεῦ.

In the dual and plural numbers the Φ has taken the place of the Ϝ, and the hiſſing dental aſpirate been prefixed to the third as well as to the ſecond perſon, which it probably was originally in the ſingular, at leaſt in ſome dialeƈts, for the aſpirates were changed even from the Σ to the Ͱ, that is, from the harſheſt to the ſofteſt, by the variations of dialeƈt (1). Hence we have σφωε or σφε, σφωιν or σφιν, σφεῖς, σφῶν, σφισι or σφι, and σφας, which ſeem to be only corrupted contraƈtions of ΣΕϜΟΣ, ΣΕϜΟΙΝ, ΣΕϜΕΣ, ΣΕϜΩΝ, ΣΕϜΙΣΙ, and ΣΕϜΑΣ, though it is probable that they had been adopted by general uſe even before the time of Homer.

Dawes would prefix the Ϝ both to the relative and poſitive pronouns, in contradiƈtion to many very antient inſcriptions, and without any ſupport from analogy, merely becauſe he thought the Ͱ inſufficient to ſuſtain the metre; but the very authority which he cites proves that the metrical power of both the ſimple aſpirates was the ſame, and that his conjeƈture was therefore founded upon a falſe ſuppoſition. In a verſe, indeed, of the Æolian poet Alcman, cited by Priſcian in the paſſage before quoted, the pronoun poſſeſſive begins with the Digamma (ϜΟΥ); but in Homer the ſame genitive is ἑυ, ἑοιο, and ἑηος, occaſionally contraƈted to ἑ; whence it ſeems that the word was ͰΕϜΟΣ, the regular adjeƈtive of Ͱ-Ο, which was declined ſometimes like the neutral, and ſometimes like the maſculine, nouns, in -ΟΣ, -ͰΕϜΕϜΟΣ, or ͰΕϜΟϜΟ and ͰΕϜΟΙΟ contraƈted to ͰΕϜΟϜ, written in modern orthography ἑυ, and, by an eliſion of the firſt ſyllable, common in the Æolic and Doric dialeƈts, ϜΟϜ, which, by a change of the aſpirates, became ἑ or ͱΟΥ. The declenſion after the manner of the neutral nouns in -ΟΣ is rejeƈted by the authors of the Venetian Scholia, who explain ἑηος to be the genitive ſingular of ἑυς, *good*, the genitive plural of which, pronounced after the Æolic manner, often occurs, ἑαων or ͱΕΑϜΩΝ. Others of the antient editors wrote ἑοιο inſtead of ἑηος; for which, however, it does not appear that they had any authority. Probably the opinion of the ſcholiaſts is right, and in that caſe ευς and ευ ought always to be aſpirated, ͱΕΥΣ and ͱΕΥ, which may account for the

(1) See Etymol. magn. in Voce υἱος; and Villoiſon. Prolegom. in Homer, p. 2.

H

firſt

firſt ſyllable in the diæreſis being ſometimes long and ſometimes ſhort, and alſo for the concluding vowel of the preceeding word being frequently ſuſtained.   It may alſo ſhow us the true meaning and etymology of the Latin appellative HEUS! which ſeems exactly to correſpond with the EH BIEN! of the French.   ΓΟΓΟΣ is formed from the relative pronoun as ΓΕΓΟΣ is from the poſitive, and declined and contracted in the ſame manner.

    I have often been inclined to ſuppoſe the paragagic particle φι a corruption of the antient dative caſe, and to think that βιηφι, ςρατοφι, οχεσφι, &c. were once written ΒΙΕΓΙ, ΣΤΡΑΤΟΓΙ, ΟΧΕΓΣΙ for ΟΧΕΓΕΣΙ, &c.; for, beſides the inſtance of the pronoun abovementioned, we find how eaſily the Γ became a Φ from the preſent practice of the modern Greeks, who terminate the words, antiently ending in -ΕΓΣ, and then in -ΕΥΣ, in εφς, as ΒΑΣΙΛΕΓΣ, afterwards ΒΑΣΙΛΕΥΣ, and now βασιλεφς. If, however, this was originally a corruption, it muſt have been authoriſed by general uſe even before the time of Homer; for in his works the terminations in φι are employed in a manner adverbially to ſignify both the genitive and dative caſes.

    The dative plural of neutral words in -ΟΣ has frequently the penultimate of the antient form ſhort, as ςηθεσι for ΣΤΗΘΕΓΣΙ, or, as it is now written, ςηθεσσι; in which caſe the aſpirate was elided, as even the leſs pliable conſonants frequently were in inflexion; whence we have the abbreviated comparatives beforementioned, and alſo the oblique caſes of other words, formed upon the ſame plan, ſuch as κυκειω, that is ΚΥΚΕΙΟΑ for the regular accuſative ΚΥΚΕΙΟΝΑ; ιχω or ΙΧΟΑ (for ſo it ought to be read according to the Venetian Manuſcript and Scholia) for ΙΧΟΡΑ, the accuſative of ΙΧΩΡ (1).   Where, however, the Γ is in the nominative, it is rarely, if ever, elided in the oblique caſes, wherefore, inſtead of πηλεος υιε, which occurs only once, I would venture to read ΠΗΛΕΓΟΣ ΓῨΙΕ; for, though the firſt ſyllable of ΓΥΙΟΣ is uſually long, it is not invariably ſo, and I think in this inſtance ought to be pronounced ſhort, as in Il. E. 612, in order that the I might be added to the E; which may, nevertheleſs, be rendered long by the ſucceeding liquid M.   The genitive πηλεος might alſo have been written ΠΗΛΕΓΣ, like ΟΔΥΣΕΓΣ, before conſidered.

(1) Il. E. 416.

Although

Although an aspirate may extend the succeeding as well as preceeding vowel, provided it be in the same syllable, it cannot, when placed between two single vowels, render both long; for, if it be not dwelt upon, both will be short; and, if it be dwelt upon, that alone to which it is added will be long. Hence we find, in the modern orthography νηος and νεως, κρονίονος and κρονιωνος, &c. but never νηως or κρονιωνος, because in the original flexions, ΝΕΓΟΣ and ΚΡΟΝΙΓΟΝΟΣ, the Γ might be added to the preceeding or succeeding vowel arbitrarily, but could not be added to both at once. We have, indeed, Περσηᾱ and Ωρίωνος, which must have been equally written ΠΕΡΣΕΓΑ and ΩΡΙΓΩΝΟΣ, but the aspirate and liquid, preceeding the second vowel in each, are sufficient to extend them, so that the Γ may be added to the third.

This effect of the Γ seems to have continued after it had ceased to be in use; for, in the oblique cases of this class, the preceeding vowel being long, according to the old Ionic pronunciation, always makes the succeeding one short, even in later writers, and the succeeding one being long, according to the Attic pronunciation, equally makes the preceeding one short. The converse, however, does not hold good, for either of them being short does not necessarily make the other long. Hence we find in the same passage of the Odyssey Νηλε̆ᾱ and Νηληᾰ, and in the Attic writers uniformly Νηλε̄ᾱ, Θησε̆ᾱ, Αχιλλε̆ᾱ, &c. which Homer never employs because incompatible with his metre. The word αμφηρεφε̆ᾱ, however, shews that they were not inconsistent with the customary pronunciation of his age and country, as most of the Attic peculiarities were.

The vowels being thus arbitrarily extended by the aspirates and liquids must be understood as a fundamental principle, but not as invariably adhered to in practice, for local or temporary habit had fixed the pronunciation of particular words to one mode even in Homer's time. Thus the adjective ΚΑΛΟΣ has the first syllable invariably long in the Iliad and Odyssey, and invariably short in the Attic writers; whilst Hesiod, Theocritus, and other later poets, who employed the dialects more arbitrarily, make it either long or short, as suited their purposes.

The final Α of feminine words, such as ΘΕΑ, &c. seems to have been rendered long merely by the emphasis or customary pause used in speaking, for there is no authority, either from etymology or antient monuments,

H 2   which

which can juſtify the inſerting the aſpirate or doubling the vowel. The ſame may be ſaid of the terminations in -H, which in all very antient inſcriptions is -E, though it was certainly pronounced uniformly long.

A very learned and ingenious perſon has attributed the extenſion of the vowel before liquids and aſpirates to a ſimilar cauſe, that is, to the muſical pauſe or cæſura (1), which muſt certainly have had greater influence upon the very antient verſe, that was always chanted to the ſound of an inſtrument, than upon that which was intended merely to be read. That this pauſe did regulate the actual quantities of thoſe ſyllables, which were common from their poſition, ſo far as to decide whether they ſhould be pronounced long or ſhort in each particular inſtance, I have no doubt; for, as the learned author has obſerved they are never extended but when beginning the foot where the pauſe naturally took place : but that this pauſe could ever make a ſyllable, ſhort by poſition, long, I can ſcarcely admit ; for the few inſtances which occur in Homer of the ſingle vowel A being pronounced long before the ſingle mute conſonant Π in the compounds of the prepoſition ΑΠΟ, are not ſufficient to eſtabliſh a general concluſion, as ſo trifling a licence might have been thought juſtifiable in works ſo long and ſo finiſhed ; or might even have been intentional irregularities, introduced to break the uniformity of the Hexameter verſe in the ſame manner as the ϛιχοι ακεφαλοι, or verſes beginning with a ſhort ſyllable.

As the nice ears of the Greeks abhorred the concurrence of conſonants, they altered many words, the original forms of which are, however, preſerved in the oblique caſes, and in the Latin. The participles in -ΑΣ and -ΕΙΣ ſeem to have once ended in -ΑΝΣ and -ΕΝΣ, like the Latin, whence the regular oblique caſes are in -ΑΝΤΟΣ, -ΕΝΤΟΣ, &c. ΠΑΣ ſeems alſo to have been originally ΠΑΝΣ, from which all the oblique caſes now in uſe in the maſculine and neuter genders are regularly formed, except the dative plural, which has become ϖᾶσι, though the primary form ΠΑΝ-ΤΕΣΙ or ΠΑΝΤΕΣΣΙ is preſerved in Homer, who, when he employed the contraction, probably employed the ſimpleſt and moſt direct, ΠΑΝΤΣΙ. Dıwes would, indeed, ſubſtitute the Digamma to the conſonants, and write ΠΑΓΣΙ from ΠΑΓΣ ; for which there is no authority but the ana-

---

(1) See Lib. ſing. de Rythm. Græc. Ox. 1789.

logy

logy of some words in which he suppofes that afpirate to have been inferted to fupply the place of elided confonants, fuch as οδυς or ΟΔΟΓΣ for ΟΔΟΝΣ, and the terminations of the third perfons plural of the prefent tenfe of the verbs, where the old Æolic termination -ONTI, preferved in the Doric, has been changed to -υσι or -ΟΓΣΙ. The words which originally ended in -ΟΓΣ were declined like ΒΟΓΣ, ΒΟΓΟΣ, or as now written βυς, βοος; and the oblique cafes in -ΟΓΣ or -ους are contractions of -ΟΓΟΣ, as ΑΙΔΩΣ, -ΟΓΟΣ, -ΟΓΑ contracted to -ΟΓΣ or -υς and -ῶ; ΛΗΤΩ, -ΟΓΟΣ, -ΟΓΣ, &c.

The participles of the prefent tenfe ending in -ΩΝ, -ΟΓΣ, or -ΟΓΣ, feem to have ended in -ΟΝΣ, whence the flexion is the fame ΔΙΔΟΝΤΟΣ and ΤΓΠΤΟΝΤΟΣ, from ΔΙΔΟΓΣ and ΤΓΠΤΩΝ. The appearance of the Τ in the oblique cafes induced Dawes to imagine that it had originally exifted between the Ν and the Σ in the nominative; but in this I believe he was miftaken, for it is not authorifed by the Latin of any period; and we find from the word ΑΝΑΞ or ΓΑΝΑΚΣ, which formed antiently both ΓΑΝΑΚΤΟΣ and ΓΑΝΑΚΟΣ (1), that the Τ was employed as a characterictic letter of thefe oblique cafes, as in thofe of ΣΩΜΑ ΣΩΜΑΤΟΣ, ΟΓΣ ΟΓΑΤΟΣ, &c. It may indeed be faid, that the laft word was originally written ΟΓΑΤΣ or ΟΓΤΣ; but, even if this be admitted, no fyftem-maker can transform ΣΩΜΑ into ΣΩΜΑΤΣ, for it belongs to a very numerous clafs, the laft fyllable of which is uniformly fhort in all the antient poets, unlefs rendered long by the initials of the fucceeding word.

The nouns in -ΙΣ feem to have been declined upon exactly the fame plan, and liable to the fame variations, except that the Δ, inftead of the Τ, was the characterictic letter of inflexion, as ΚΛΗΓΙΣ -ΙΔΟΣ, the dative plural of which was contracted from ΚΛΗΓΙΔΕΣΙ to ΚΛΗΓΙΔΣΙ and ΚΛΗΓΙΣΙ, or, as it is now written, κληῖσι, in the fame manner as ΠΑΝ-ΤΕΣΙ to ΠΑΝΤΣΙ and ΠΑΣΙ. Upon the fame principles, ΓΓΜΕΣΙ, or, with the paragagic Ν, ΓΓΜΕΣΙΝ, the regular dative plural of ΓΓΜΕΕΣ, or, as it was otherwife written, ΓΓΜΕΙΣ, was contracted to ΓΓΜΙΝ, or, as the Æolians pronounced it, without the afpirate, and with a ftronger

(1) Αναχοιν, Διοσχυροιν. Schol. Ven. in Il. ‌ω. 566; fee alfo Euftath. 1425, 56; and Hefych. The temple of Caftor and Pollux at Athens was called the ANAKEION.

emphafis

emphafis upon the M, ΥΜΜΙΝ or ΥΜΜΙ. The Ionian accufative fingular feems to have been formed by a fimilar contraction of an obfolete flexion, traces of which are preferved in the Latin, where we find the genitives, which the Greeks terminated in -ΔΟΣ, terminated in -DIS, as PARIS -IDIS; and the accufatives, which the Greeks terminated in -ΔΑ, terminated in -DEM; from which we may difcover the old form in -Δ N, contracted by the ufual elifion of the confonants, and fyncopè of the vowels, to what is called the Ionic accufative ΠΑΡΙΝ, ΟΦΙΝ, &c. In the latter word, indeed, and fome others, the contraction prevailed through all the cafes, whence fome grammarians have made a feparate declenfion of them; but improperly, for, as Theodore Gaza has obferved, all the names in -ΙΣ have their genitives regularly in -ΙΔΟΣ.

It was probably from a view of thefe facts that Lennep, in his excellent little Book upon the Analogy of the Greek Tongue, has not noticed the conjecture of Dawes, but concluded that the terminations of the participles in -ΟΥΣ and -ΩΝ were originally in -ΟΝΣ, and that the fubfidiary Υ and long -O were introduced merely to preferve the due length of the fyllable, when faftidious refinement had dropt the confonants. All the flexions of the feminine, and the dative plural of the mafculine and neuter, have been foftened u on the fame principle; whence we have ΤΥΠΤΟΥΣΑ inftead of ΤΥΠΤΟΝΤΕΣΑ, ΤΥΠΤΟΝΤΣΑ, or ΤΥΠΤΟΝΣΑ; and ΤΥΠΤΟΥΣΙ inftead of ΤΥΠΤΟΝΤΕΣΙ, ΤΥΠΤΟΝΤΣΙ, or ΤΥΠΤΟΝΣΙ. We have alfo ΤΥΦΘΕΙΣΑ or ΤΥΦΘΕΕΣΑ for ΤΥΦΘΕΝΤΕΣΑ, ΤΥΦΘΕΝΤΣΑ, or ΤΥΦΘΕΝΣΑ; and ΤΥΦΘΕΙΣΙ for ΤΥΦΘΕΝΤΕΣΙ, ΤΥΦΘΕΝΤΣΙ, or ΤΥΦΘΕΝΣΙ. In the Doric dialect, the antient forms of the dative plural were preferved, except that the E became an A, and the Σ was doubled, to exprefs the breadth and harfhnefs of this pronunciation. Hence, in the Heraclean tables we have ΠΟΙΟΝΤΑΣΣΙΝ, ΠΡΑΣΣΟΝΤΑΣΣΙ, Ϝ-ΥΠΑΡΧΟΝ-ΤΑΣΣΙ, &c. which in ordinary Greek would be ΠΟΙΟΥΣΙΝ, ΠΡΑΣΣΟΥ-ΣΙ, ΥΠΑΡΧΟΥΣΙ, &c. That the Ϝ was ever employed for the Υ in thefe forms is merely a fuppofition of Dawes, unfupported by authority or analogy, and probably untrue; for it is more natural to fuppofe that the Υ was inferted here, as in the inftances beforementioned, by the reformers of the Attic orthography, who, when the quantities appeared defective through the elifion of the confonants, fupplied them according to their

7   own

own pronunciation. In Homer the confonants were probably retained, though the contraction had certainly taken place in the participles. In the third perfon plural of the prefent tenfe of the verbs, the termination, being -ONTI in the old Æolic and Doric, was probably -ONΣI in the old Ionic, which being contracted to -OΣI or -ΩΣI, was again filled up, in the later Attic, with the OY diphthong, conformably to the pronunciation then moft in fafhion, and at length univerfally prevalent, though never juftified by etymology.

SECTION III.

THOUGH we cannot trace the antient orthography with the fame precifion by the mere rules of metrical harmony, as when aided by the regular analogy of the flexions, we have, neverthelefs, in the extreme accuracy of the moft antient poet, very plain directions to guide our en-quiries.

I. When we find a fingle vowel pronounced long, though followed by another vowel or fingle mute confonant, we may, unlefs in the inftances already excepted, conclude that an afpirate has been dropt, which we fhall generally difcover to be as requifite to etymology as to metre.

Moft of the following words have been remarked by grammarians for this defect, and, I believe, that the reft were written upon the fame plan, and in the manner here propofed :

Αμαιμαω——AMAIMAFΩ, whence αναμαιμᾱει, or ANAMAIMAFEI and αναμαιμακετος, probably written ANAMAIMAFETOΣ.

Αναξ——FANAKΣ, from FANAKΩ or FANAΣΣΩ, of which the imper-fect fhould be EFANAΣΣE, and not ηναссε ; which, as Dr. Bentley obferved, never begins a line, becaufe the two firft fyllables

lables in the time of the poet were fhort. The Italian Greeks, according to Hefychius, wrote it ΒΑΝΝΑΣ, in the Laconian idiom; and Homer has the vocative ανα or ΓΑΝΑ from ΓΑΝΑΣ.

Ανηρ——ΓΑΝΗΡ according to Dionyfius of Halicarnaffus (1); but it does not appear to have been fo in Homer, for I do not recollect its being preceeded by an open vowel unlefs where the paffage is corrupt, as κλεα ανδρων, which fhould be ΚΛΕΕΓ' or ΚΛΕΕ' ΑΝΔΡΩΝ, the antient accufative plural of ΚΛΕΟΣ being regularly ΚΛΕΕΓΑ, or ΚΛΕΕΑ.

Ανια, ανιω, ανιαζω——ΑΝΙΓΑ, ΑΝΙΓΩ, ΑΝΙΓΑΔΣΩ. The penultimate being uniformly long proves it to have been written with the afpirate, or diphthong; and the moft probable etymology, given by Damm, favours the former.

Αςυ——ΓΑΣΤΥ, being almoft always preceeded by an open vowel.

Ααtω, ατη——ΑΓΑΤΩ, ΑΓΑΤΗ. In Pindar, as now written, αυατα, but properly ΑΓΑΤΑ. In the genuine parts of Homer it appears to have been a trifyllable, as it muft be according to its etymology. The three lines alluding to the Judgement of Paris are evidently fpurious, being in every refpect unworthy of the poet (2); and the other inftance, where it is required to be read as a diffyllable, Mr. Dawes fays, is to be corrected from the various readings; which I have not, however, been able to difcover, the line being in all editions the fame:

'Οι τε μοι ειν αγορη φρεσιν εμβαλον αγριον ατην (3).

Perhaps for αγριον we fhould read ουλον, unlefs indeed ΑΓΑΤΗ might have been occafionally contracted to ΑΓΤΗ.   In the fame Iliad (4) we have ασσατο, or, as in other editions, ασατο, and ααsατο, the metre requiring that the word fhould form a dactyle—και γαρ δη νυ ποτε Ζην' ασσατο, τον περ αριsον. Clarke faw that this was corrupt, and therefore propofed to read—και γαρ δη ποτε Ζην' ααsατο τον περ αριsον; but, befides omitting the particle νυ, which gives peculiar force and elegance to the fentence, the ε in ποτε muft neceffarily be long before Ζην'. I would, therefore, read—και γαρ δη νυ ποτε Ζην' ηΓασαθ' ον περ αριsον; or, in antient orthography,

(1) P. 16, Ed. Hudf.
(2) Il. Ω. 28.
(3) Il. T. 88.
(4) Vf. 25.

KAI

ΚΑΙ ΓΑΡ ΔΗ ΝΥ ΠΟΤΕ ΔΣΗΝ' ΕΑΓΑΣΑΟ' ΟΝ ΠΕΡ ΑΡΙΣΤΟΝ, which gives both the fenfe and metre correct and entire. Ariftarchus is faid, by the Venetian Scholiaft, to have read Ζευς for Ζην'; but I can fcarcely credit it.

He would alfo have expunged the preceeding line, but without fufficient reafons. His judgement, indeed, however good in regulating the minuter delicacies of compofition, does not feem to have been adapted to decide upon the general fenfe of a poet of fo much fentiment as Homer, otherwife he would never have thought of rejecting the four lines from the IXth Iliad, in which Phœnix mentions the defign he had once entertained, in a fit of rage and defpair, of killing his own father; for, without thefe lines, we do not perceive the intent of Phœnix's narration, which was, to fhew the dreadful effects of anger; nor difcover the caufe why his father's houfe became hateful to him, which was, that it perpetually brought to his feeling mind the hideous ideas with which momentary paffion had filled it. The caufe of this ftrange rejection was probably their having been pufhed antiently from their place by a really fpurious line—Ζευς τε καταχθονιος, και επαινη Περσιφονεια; which feems, by a fpecies of advancement not uncommon, to have flipt from the margin into the text, and by that means to have removed the pronoun fo far from the fubftantive, that, to preferve its relationfhip, it was transferred over to the next repetition of it. The lines, as they now ftand in Berglerus's edition, the only one that has readmitted them, are,

———— Πατηρ δ' εμος αυτικ' οϊσθεις
Πολλα κατηρατο, ςυγερας δ' επεκεκλετ' ερινυῦς
Μη ποτε γυνασιν οισιν εφεσσεσθαι φιλον υιον
Εξ εμεθεν γεγαωτα· θεοι δ' ετελειον επαρας,
Ζευς τε καταχθονιος, και επαινη περσιφονεια.
Ενθ' εμοι υκετι παμπαν ερητυετ' εν φρεσι θυμος
Πατρος χωομενοιο κατα μεγαρα ςρωφασθαι.
Τον μεν εγω βυλευσα κατακταμεν οξεϊ χαλκω
Αλλα τις αθανατων παυσεν χολον, ες ρ' ενι θυμω
Δημυ θηκε φατιν, και ονειδεα πολλ' ανθρωπων
Ὡς μη πατροφονος μετ' Αχαιοισιν καλεοιμην.

I

Inftead

Inſtead of which they ſhould be,

——————— Πατηρ δ' εμος αυτικ' οϊσθεις

Πολλα κατηρατο, ςυγερας δ' επεκεκλετ' εριννῦς

Μη ποτε γυνασιν οισιν εφεσσεσθαι φιλον υἱον

Εξ εμεθεν γεγαωτα· θεοι δ' ετελειον επαρας.

Τον μεν εγω βυλευσα κατακταμεν οξεϊ χαλκῳ

Αλλα τις αθανατων παυσεν χολον, ὁς ρ' ενι θυμῳ

Δημυ θηκε φατιν και ονειδεα πολλ' ανθρωπων

Ὡς μη πατροφονος μετ' Αχαιοισιν καληοιμην.

Ενθ' εμοι υκετι παμπαν, &c.

The line Ζευς τε καταχθονιος, &c. is evidently a comment upon θεοι in the preceeding one, and probably an improper comment; for, though Pluto and Proſerpine were before invoked as the deities of deſtruction, they were not peculiarly the impeders of generation. Neither does Homer in any other place call Pluto by this title; which, being derived from the myſtic ſyſtem, was probably unknown to him.

ἄᾱᾱτος and ἄᾱᾱτος——ΑΝΑΓΑΤΟΣ and ΑΝΑΓΑΣΤΟΣ, the regular adjectives from the verb ΑΓΑΤΩ, according to Dawes.

The N, however, to ſuſtain the privative A, though conſtantly uſed by later writers, does not regularly belong to Homer's orthography(1); and as the Σ was frequently elided, and the conſonant doubled, in the old dialects, the antient words were probably ΑΑΓΑΤΟΣ and ΑΑΓΑΤΤΟΣ, from which the change to the preſent reading was very eaſy. Heſychius has ΑΑΣΤΟΝ, αναμαρτητον, αβλαβες, and ΑΑΤΟΝ, with nearly the ſame explication; but it is evident that an A has been loſt from both theſe words, and probably a T from the latter, as they are both the ſame, only formed according to different dialects. He adds, however, another explanation to the latter, ſignifying *inſatiable*, αναπληρωτον, the reaſon for which will be given.

The omiſſion or inſertion of the ſubſidiary and paragogic N, having been left in a great meaſure to the diſcretion of tranſcribers, has, I believe, produced conſiderable confuſion both in the meaning and etymology of ſeveral of Homer's words. Upon the medals of Alexandria Troas, the title of

(1) See Il. Σ. 536.

Apollo,

Apollo, which we now write Σμινθευς, is uniformly ΣΜΙΘΕΥΣ, that is, in antient orthography, ΣΜΙΘΕΥΣ, which has so near a resemblance to our word SMITE, and its various derivatives, that we cannot but suppose it to have come from the same root, and to have signified the SMITER or DE-STROYER, generally, according to a well-known attribute of Apollo, ex-pressed in the symbolical writing of antient art by the bow and arrows which he carried. The tale which deduces it from σμινθος, said to be the Cretan name for a *mouse*, is of later times, and gives a signification unwor-thy of the solemnity of the occasion on which Chryses invokes the God, in his character of Destroyer, to avenge his wrongs upon the Greeks. Like many others of the same kind, it was invented to give a fictitious meaning to one of those old mystic titles, the real signification of which was kept concealed from the vulgar. Aristarchus rejected it, and derived the title from a city of the Troade (1), which appears, however, to have been un-known to Homer, and which was probably named from the title.

From an improper insertion of the subsidiary N, as I am inclined to be-lieve, arose those unaccountable forms of verbs ανηνοθε and επενηνοθεν, which many have supposed to be præterites middle of ανθεω, *to bloom* or *blossom*, with the Attic reduplication, and poetic insertion of the O. But how there could have been a poetical licence of insertion, when poetry was the only species of literary composition; or how Homer's audience, who had no dictionaries and grammars to consult, could have understood forms so remote from common use, I cannot conceive. The sense also, as Dr. Clarke observed, requires an imperfect rather than a perfect tense; and the metaphor, according to this interpretation, is too forced and unnatural for Homer, who would scarcely have described *the blood blooming from a wound* (2), *the fur blooming from a skin* (3), or *the scattered hairs blooming upon a bald head* (4). I cannot, therefore, but think that these words are composed of οθω, *to push* or *move*, and are, therefore, regular imperfects ανα-εοθε and επι-ενι-εοθε, reduced by the ordinary crasis of the vowels to ανηοθε and επενηοθε, and then corrupted, by an improper insertion of the subsidiary N, to

(1) Apollon. Lex. ad Hefych. Albert. citat.
(2) Il. Λ. 266.
(3) Il. K. 144.
(4) Il. B. 219.

ανηνοθε

ανηνοθε and επενηνοθε. The verb οθω indeed, does not elfewhere occur in a neutral fenfe ; but moft of the Greek verbs had a neutral as well as active and paffive fenfe, which is oftener expreffed by the active than the middle voice(1). The pronoun might alfo, in thefe inftances, be underftood, as in ὁι μεν ανωσαντες πλεον ες πολιν (2). The Venetian Scholiaft would, how-ever, derive ανηνοθε and επενηνοθε from εθω, antiently FEΘΩ, whence the perfect FEFOΘA, now written ειωθα (3). According to his idea, therefore, the antient forms muft have been ΑΝFEFOΘE and ΕΠΕΝFEFOΘE, or with the afpirates elided, as in compounds, ANEFOΘE and ΕΠΕΝΕFOΘE ; but the perfect tenfe will not do in either inftance. In Οδ. Θ. 365, the fenfe feems indeed to favour this etymology ; but I think the line is fpurious.

Ενθα δε μιν Χαριτες λυσαν και χρισαν ελαιω

(Αμβροτω, ὁια θεvς επενηνοθεν αιεν εοντας)

Αμφι δε ἑιματα ἑσσαν επηρατα, θαυμα ιδεσθαι.

Aω, or αεω——AFΩ, or AFEΩ ; whence come the antient words AFOΣ -EFOΣ or -EOΣ, *morning*, and AFOFOΣ the adjective derived from it ; both of which are now written and declined, after the Ionic and Attic manner, ΗΩΣ -OYΣ, and ΗΟΙΟΣ (4). The Ionic va-riation might have taken place even before the time of Homer ; but the Attic termination of the genitive is, as before obferved, a corruption of no very early date, it being unauthenticated by any very antient monument. An immenfe number of words are derived from this root, all of which were antiently written upon the fame principle, as AFHP (in Ionic EFHP or HHP), AFHΔΩΝ, AFEIΔΩ, AFIΣΣΩ, &c. &c. The two laft were contracted by the Attics to ᾳδω and ᾳσσω ; but thefe abbreviations could not have taken place whilft the F was in ufe, wherefore they are unknown to Homer, who always makes the firft fyllable of αϊσσω long. In the old editions, indeed, of the Hymn to Apollo we have ᾳδον (5) ; but if this be

(1) Notum eft omnia fere verba Græca activa, fæpe & intranfitivè notare.   Damm.

(2) Od. O. 552.

(3) Hence ΓΗΘΙΑ (that is FHΘIA) ηθη in Hefychius.

(4) Other provincial forms are preferved by Hefychius, as ABΩ, πjωι, Λακωνις, and ΑΥΣιΣ. ἡμjρα.

(5) Vf. 22. Clarke has ἀδον, but cites no authority.

the

the true reading (as I believe it is), it is an additional proof that this elegant poem is not Homer's, though quoted as genuine by Thucydides.

Αυω——ΑΥϜΩ; whence are derived ΑΥϜΟΣ, ΑΥϜΤΜΗ, ΑΥϜΤΗ, &c.
It appears, however, from a paſſage of the Venetian Scholia, that Chryſippus the Stoick, and Dionyſius of Thrace, two antient Criticks of great eminence, wrote αυιαχος with the common aſpirate αὐιαχος, or ΑϜΤΙΑΧΟΣ (1); conſiſtently with which, they muſt have written theſe words in the ſame manner, ΑϜΤΩ, ΑϜΤΟΣ, &c. The authority of the beſt antient grammarians is, neverthelefs, but little in the uſe of the aſpirates, and general analogy favours the F in this inſtance; but, without the authority of monuments anterior to the ejection of theſe letters from the Alphabet, it is impoſſible to decide with certainty.

Αρς——ϜΑΡΣ.

Γῦπες——ΓΥϜΠΕΣ, the plural of ΓΥϜΠΣ, contracted from ΓΥϜΕΠΣ; whence, I believe, that αιγυπεες and αιγυπεοι are properly the ſame word, antiently written ΑΙΓΥϜΕΠΕΣ, the regular plural of ΑΙΓΥϜΕΠΣ, a particular ſort of ΓΥϜΕΠΣ, or vultur.

Διω, δεος, &c.——ΔϜΙΩ, ΔϜΕΟΣ, &c. according to Dawes. The vowels preceeding theſe words are uniformly long, whence the augments in the Aoriſt and perfect tenſes have been changed from Ε- and ΔΕ- to ΕΔ- and ΔΕΙ-, as in εδδεισα and δειδοικα.

Whether, however, the F or the Σ was the letter that has been dropt, I have ſome doubt, but am inclined to think the latter, for the word Ζευς or ΔΣΕϜΣ, and the Latin DEUS, are certainly from this root (2); and that the

(1) Ad Il. N. 41.

(2) ΔΕΥΣ, Ζευς, δεος, φοβος, η Θεος, Heſych. The account of this title, in the *new* Syſtem of *antient* Mythology, is ſo *new*, and, at the ſame time, ſo comic, that it may ſerve to enliven the dryneſs of the preſent Diſquiſition. Noah, according to the learned and ingenious Author, not only planted vines, and made wine, to intoxicate himſelf, but likewiſe ſowed barley, made malt, and brewed beer; which, being called in Greek Ζυθος, or (as he chuſes to write it) Ζιυθος, became, though a very contemptible liquor among that people, the name of their ſupreme god; who, it ſeems, was no other than Noah deified in the character of a great brewer.

Jupiter eſt quodcunque vides, quocunque moveris, ſays Cato, in Lucan; but, though Cato was fond of ſtrong drink, none but this ingenious gentleman, I believe, ever thought of giving ſo pleaſant a turn to his celebrated ſpeech, as the making him alleviate the real miſery, the Σ was occafionally dropt from the Δ, even in the early times, is proved by the high authority of the Zanclèan medals before cited, and alfo by the names Ζακυνθος and Ζελεια; which (as I have ventured to conclude from the facts above ftated, and the analogy of the metre, which requires a fingle confonant) were written, upon the fame principle, ΔΑΚΥΝΘΟΣ and ΔΕΛΕΙΑ.

The ufe of the Σ, like that of the other afpirates, depended much upon cuftom or dialect; for though no licence could infert it into a word to which it did not radically belong, it could, in almoft any cafe, be elided. Hence the apparent irregularities in the oblique cafes of the word Ζευς, which have, however, all been very naturally and regularly formed, from the different modes of writing and pronouncing it in different dialects, as

N. ΔΣΕΓΣ, ΔΣΗΝ, or ΔΣΙΓΣ, contracted, by eliding the afpirates to ΔΙΣ.

G. ΔΣΕΓΟΣ, ΔΣΗΝΟΣ, or ΔΣΙΓΟΣ, contracted to ΔΙΟΣ.

D. ΔΣΕΓΙ, ΔΣΗΝΙ, or ΔΣΙΓΙ, contracted to ΔΙΙ.

A. ΔΣΕΓΑ, ΔΣΗΝΑ, or ΔΣΙΓΑ, contracted to ΔΙΑ.

From the perfect tenfe of the verb ΔΣΙΩ or ΔΣΕΙΩ, the Greeks, as ufual, formed new verbs, fuch as δειδω, δειδισσω, &c. which fhould probably be written ΔΕΔΣΩ, ΔΕΔΣΙΣΣΩ, &c. in Homer, the I having been apparently inferted, as in many other inftances, to fupply the place of the afpirate.

In a very few inftances out of the great number in which thefe words occur, the vowel preceeding is fhort; but this, I believe, is always owing to corruption. Ειπερ αδειης τ' εςι(1) fhould be ΕΙΠΕΡ Τ' (or Κ') ΕΣΤ' ΑΔΣΕΙΗΣ. Βροντησας δ' αρα δεινον (2), fhould be ΒΡΟΝΤΗΣΑΣ ΔΕ ΑΔΣΕΙ-ΝΟΝ, the particle αρα being unneceffary. The fame alteration fhould take place in των δ'αρα δεισαντων (3), and it may be generally obferved throughout Homer, that the particles have been very licentioufly employed by the antient editors and tranfcribers to fill the vacancies which a change of Al-

---

fcry of thirft, which he felt upon the burning fands of Libya, with the ideal happinefs of being immerged in a barrel of beer.

(1) Il. H. 117.
(2) Il. Θ. 133.
(3) Odyff. ω. 533.

phabet has produced in his metre. Δεδίασι is, I believe, ufually pronounced in four fyllables, the two firſt ſhort; but it ought to be pronounced in three, the two firſt long, Δεῖδῖασι, or ΔΕΔΣΙΑΣΙ.

The vowel having been thus uniformly long, is, I think, a further proof that the Σ was the letter joined to the Δ, and not the F, as Mr. Dawes fuppoſed; for there is no reaſon from analogy why the vowel ſhould be always long before ΔF any more than before Δⱶ or Θ. I am ſtill more convinced of it, by finding the Σ omitted in the flexion of a verb of ſimilar form, in the theme of which it is ſtill retained. Ἐριδδησασ-θαι is evidently from ἐριζεω or ΕΡΙΔΣΕΩ, and ſhould therefore be regularly ΕΡΙΔΣΗΣΑΣΘΑΙ, though the claſhing of the rough and barbarous dentals induced either the Poet himſelf, or his antient editors, to prefer a trifling grammatical licence to a harſhneſs of ſound. This licence, indeed, like every other employed by the Poet himſelf, appears to have been previouſly authoriſed by familiar uſe; for, as the true antient forms were probably ΕΡΙΔΣΩ and ΕΡΙΔΣΕΣΑΣΘΑΙ, which are confiſtent with the other flexions of the ſame verb: the Æolians, who elided the afpirates, and doubled the conſonants, might have written and pronounced them ΕΡΙΔ-ΔΩ and ΕΡΙΔΔΕΣΑΣΘΑΙ, the third fyllable of the latter being rendered long by the emphaſis laid upon the Σ which terminates it. To prove that the Σ was occaſionally elided, and its place fupplied by doubling the conſonant, we have alſo the authority of Plato, in whoſe Dialogue upon the Immortality of the Soul we find the Bœotian interlocutor employing ΙΤΤΩ for ΙΣΤΩ, which in Homer's time would have been, in that dialect, FΙΤΤΩ; whence we may perceive the affinity between this verb and the Saxon pιτan, the root of our word WIT. We likewiſe find, in the Lacedæmonian Decree againſt Timotheus beforementioned, ΔΙΔΑΚΚΕ for ΕΔΙΔΑΚΣΕ, to which the Oxford Editor, with preſumptuous and inau-fpicious hand, has changed it; not confidering that Homer and Hefiod have employed repeatedly a ſimilar form in a word which is now written θηκε, according to the Ionian mode of extending the vowels and eliding the conſonants; but which, in the old language, was ΘΕΚΚΕ for ΕΘΕΚΣΕ, the third perfon ſingular of the Aoriſt of ΘΕΚΩ, the old Æolic form of ΘΕΩ or ΤΙΘΗΜΙ, it having been cuſtomary, in that dialect, to terminate verbs in -ΚΩ, which others terminated in -ΣΣΩ, -ΤΣΩ or -ΖΩ, -ΤΤΩ, and Ω pure;

pure; of which confiderable remains are obfervable in the Doric, and alfo in the future tenfes in -ΚΣΩ and -ΞΩ of other dialects. Whether it was ever allowable to change the dental afpirate for a dental mute in the beginning of a word, and to write ΔΔΕΙΝΟΣ for ΔΣΕΙΝΟΣ, ΔΔΕΙΩ for ΔΣΕΙΩ, &c. I cannot determine; but there is nothing in the analogy of the language againft it, and ΕΔΔΕΙΣΕ, the third perfon fingular of the Aorift, fo often repeated, and fupported by the invariable teftimony of fo many manufcripts and editions, is as great authority as there can be for any peculiarity of orthography not authenticated by antient infcriptions.

Διος——ΔΙϜΟΣ; whence came the Latin DIVUS. The firft fyllable of this adjective is always long, whereas it is always fhort in ΔΙΟΣ, the genitive of ΔΙΣ, from which it is derived. Hence we have uniformly διογενης, *nobly-born,* and διιπετης (properly διειπετης, as in Hefychius), *Jove-defcended*; the former having been antiently written ΔΙϜΟΓΕΝΗΣ, and the latter ΔΙΕΙΠΕΤΗΣ.

Δοω, contracted to δῶ——ΔΟϜΩ, contracted to ΔΩ, and varied by habitual or local corruptions to ΔΙΔΩΜΙ, ΔΟΣΚΩ, and ΔΟϜΚΩ; from which laft comes the Aorift εδωκα, properly ΕΔΟϜΚΚΑ for ΕΔΟϜΚΣΑ, often written without the augment δωκα for ΔΟϜΚΚΑ, in the fame manner as θηκε for ΘΕΚΚΕ, ἡκε for ϜΕΚΚΕ, &c. This cuftom, however, of eliding the confonants and afpirates, and extending the vowels, being Ionic, might have taken place in the time of Homer, who, upon the fame plan, has φῖλαι for ΦΙΛΣΑΙ, φῑλατο for ΕΦΙΛΣΑΤΟ, &c. whence the Criticks have been much perplexed; for φιλω, notwithftanding what Clarke fays (1), has the firft fyllable always fhort.

Εαρ——ϜΕΑΡ, written by Hefychius ΓΕΑΡ, according to his ufual practice of putting the Γ for the Ϝ.

Εαω——ΕϜΑΩ, written by the Laconians and Syracufians (who in this inftance employed the Laconian dialect) ΕΒΑΩ (2).

Ελπω——ϜΕΛΠΩ. The vowel being fuftained before this verb, proves that it began with an afpirate; and I have been induced to prefer the Ϝ to the Ϝ by an infcription publifhed by Abbé Winkelman,

----

(1) Ad. Il. τ. 304.   (2) Hefych.

in which we find, in Latin letters, the Greek names MINDIA HELPIS (1), the latter of which is evidently derived from this verb. Our word HELP feems alfo to be of the fame extraction; whence the verb TO HELP was formerly declined nearly in the fame manner as the Greek, HELP, HOLPEN —ϜΕΛΠΩ, ϜΕϜΟΛΠΑ.

Ειϰοσι and εειϰοσι——ϜΙΚΟΣΙ and ΕϜΙΚΟΣΙ. In the Heraclèan Infcription it is uniformly ϹΙΚΑΤΙ, except in one inftance, where we have ΕΙΚΟΣΙ, which is probably a miftake of the graver for ϹΙΚΟΣΙ, as ΕΕΤΟΣ, in another inftance, certainly is for ϹΕΤΟΣ.

Ειπω, επος, &c.——ϜΕΠΩ, ϜΕΠΟΣ, &c. In Hefychius we have ΓΙΠΟΝ (that is ϜΙΠΟΝ) ειπον; but the fubftantive fhews that it ought to be written with the E.

Ειδω——ϜΕΙΔΩ, and ϜΙΔΩ, with all the derivatives ϜΕΙΔΟΣ, ΑϜΙΣ, ΑϜΙ-ΔΗΣ, &c. It appears from Hefychius, that the Ϝ was once pre-fixed to the A privative in fuch words as the laft; whence he has ΓΑΜΜΟΡΟΣ (that is ϜΑΜΜΟΡΟΣ) αμμορος; but this does not feem to have been the orthography of Homer. Οφρ' ειδεω fhould probably be ϜΟ-ΦΡΑ ϜΙΔΩ, though the vowel may be elided before the Ϝ as well as be-fore the ϝ. ΓΟΙΔΗΜΑΙ (that is ϜΟΙΔΗΜΑΙ) επιϛαμαι of Hefychius is taken from the præterite of this verb, ϜΕϜΟΙΔΑ, ufually written without the augment ϜΟΙΔΑ.

Εερση——ΕϜΕΡΣΗ is probably the original term, and ϝΕΡΣΗ the abbrevi-ation; Lennep's doctrine of an adfcititious E, prefixed arbi-trarily to certain words, being contrary to the analogy of every language; but eliding the firft vowel was common in the Doric dialect, and probably in the old Æolic, from which it was derived. New forms alfo, both of verbs and nouns, arofe from the augmented tenfes, and re-tained the additional fyllable.

Εθος, ηθος, εθνος, &c.——ϜΕΘΟΣ, ϜΕΘΝΟΣ, &c. The fyllable ϜΕ may an-fwer to the long and fhort vowel, or the afpirate might have been dropt occafionally, and the vowel extended, fo that εθος and ηθος are probably the fame word, written differ-ently according to the cuftomary pronunciation of different countries. He-fychius has, however, ΓΗΘΙΑ (that is ϜΗΘΙΑ) ηθη; but his authority in

(1) Hift. des Arts, l: IV. c. vii.

K

the

the ufe of the double or fingle vowels is very little. Μαλις' ειωθε fhould probably be ΜΑΛΙΣΤΑ ϜΕϜΟΘΕ, the tranfmutation of the Ε into the Ο being common in the perfect tenfe; and the Ο, in the prefent inftance, being rendered long by the afpirates. Ειωθε may, however, poffibly be an Ionifm of the fame kind as thofe abovementioned.

Εικω, præt. εοικα——ϜΕΙΚΩ or ϜΙΚΩ, ϜΕϜΟΙΚΑ, as Dawes has juftly obferved; whence ϜΕΙΚΕΛΟΣ, ΑϜΕΙΚΩΣ or ΑϜΙ-ΚΩΣ, ϜΟΙΚΟΣ, &c. Ισος appears to be of the fame root, and accordingly we have ΓΙΣΓΟΝ (that is ϜΙΣϜΟΝ) ισον; and ΒΙΩΡ as Laconian for ισως in Hefychius. To this the analogy of our word WISE, in the compounds LIKEWISE, OTHERWISE, &c. exactly correfponds both in form and fignification. The firft fyllable's being uniformly long too favours the orthography of Hefychius, as does likewife the regular pro-grefs of etymology—ϜΙΚΟΣ, ϜΙΚΕΣΟΣ—ϜΙΚΕΣΕϜΟΣ contracted to ϜΙΣ-ϜΟΣ. In the Heraclèan tables, however (the only afpirated infcription in which this word occurs) it is ⱶΙΣΟΣ; but though authority is generally to be preferred to analogy in matters of this kind, I think, in this inftance, we may fafely attribute the peculiarity to local corruption.

Ἐως——ⱶΕϜΟΣ: wherefore the firft fyllable is frequently long and the fecond fhort. Barnes, indeed, fuppofed that ἑως εγω, at the be-ginning of a line, was an amphibrachys, equal to a dactyle; and Clarke, ftill more abfurdly, that it ought to be pronounced as a fpondee, by a fort of metathefis, ὡσε εγω (1). The learned author of the book upon Rhythm would, in one place, divide the intermediate long fyllable in a manner which I avow myfelf incapable of exactly comprehending (2); and, in another, elide the firft fyllable (3), as the Dorians frequently did; but, neverthelefs, without extending the third in confequence of it, as he muft do to fill the metre. All thefe refined conjectures are, however, fu-perfluous, if we read the word in its original form and antient letters. In fome paffages, indeed, we find it in one fyllable; as

Τω δ' ἑως μεν ῥ' επετουτο (4).——

Ειχε βιη ὁ δε τεως μεν ενι μεγαροις φυλακοιο (5);

Ἐως μιν (al. μεν) εν Οϝτυγιη——(6)

(1) Od. Δ. 12c. (2) Lib. fing. de Ryth. Græc. p. 37.
(3) Ibid. p. 142. (4) Od. B. 148.
(5) O. O. 131. (6) Od. B. 123.

Ἐως

Ἑως μεν γαρ τε θευσι — (1).

But in each of thefe there is fomething redundant. In the two firft the particle μεν encumbers the fenfe as well as the metre; and, in the third, the pronoun fhould be changed from μιν to the old regular form ἑ—ϜΕϜΟΣ Ϝ' ΕΝ ΟΡΤΥΓΙΗΙ. The fourth has been corrupted by two different readings, μεν and γαρ being (as has frequently happened) joined in the text, the firft of which is, in this inftance, the beft—ϜΕϜΟΣ ΜΕΝ ΤΕ ΘΕϜΟΥΣΙ—

In another paffage of the Odyffey, ὡς ὅτε is written for ϜΕϜΟΣ—Ησθιε δ' ὡς ὅτ αοιδος ενι μεγαροισιν αειδεν (2), inftead of ΗΣΘΙΕ Δ' ϜΕϜΟΣ ΑϜΟΙΔΟΣ ΕΝΙ ΜΕΓΑΡΟΙΣΙΝ ΑϜΕΙΔΕΝ; and though Bentley found ἑως in a manufcript, Clarke did not chufe to adopt it, becaufe Euftathius and the Scholiaft have ὡς ὅτε. With the fame timidity or negligence, and equally to the detriment of the fenfe, he has preferved ΚΑΙ for ΚΕΝ, in Odyff. P. 146, though the true reading is retained in Δ. 560, where the fame line occurs.

Ου γαρ οἱ παρα νῆες επηρετμοι και ἑταιροι

Οἱ κεν μιν πεμποιεν επ' ευρεα νωτα θαλασσης.

Ημαρ——ϜΗΜΑΡ probably, like ἡμερα or ϜΗΜΕΡΑ, whence the vowel is often open before it.

Θυω, &c.——ΘΥϜΩ, &c. the firft fyllable being always long.

Ιαχω——ϜΙϜΑΧΩ according to Dawes; but it fhould rather be ϜΙΑΧΩ, for the firft Ϝ is fufficient to prolong the fyllable and fuftain the preceeding vowel, and there is no authority or reafon for inferting the fecond. His emendation of αμφιαχυιαν to ϜΕϜΙϜΑΧΥΙϜΑΝ has certainly produced a much more monftrous word than any he could have found to remove; for fuch a flexion as -ΥΙϜΑ from -ΩΣ, or indeed from any other termination, could not have exifted at any period or in any dialect, it being inconfiftent with the analogy of the language. If he had thought -ΥΙΑ not fufficiently archaiic, he might have propofed -ΥϜΑ or -ΟϜΑ, which, though unfupported by authority, agree with the general principle of declination. The prefent reading ΑΜΦΙΑΧΥΙΑΝ is, however, probably right; the omiffion of the augment being common, and the elifion of the afpirates in compound words juftified, not only by the frail fyftems of the antient grammarians and fcholiafts, but by the indifputable

_____

(1) Il. P. 727.   (2) Ibid. 358.

authority

authority of the Veletrian Infcription, in which the word FOIKIA is written with the Digamma, whilft ΔΑΜΙΟΡΓΟΣ (which according to etymology fhould be ΔΑΜΙΓΟΡΓΟΣ) is without it (1). The prepofition ΑΜΦΙ has alfo a peculiar beauty in expreffing the tendernefs of the mother fluttering round her plundered neft while crying out. Ηχη and ηχεω are only variations from the fame root, and therefore were written FΗΧΗ and FΗΧΕΩ.

Ιδιος——ΣΙΔΙΟΣ uniformly in the Heraclèan infcriptions; but the metre does not require the afpirate in any of the inftances where Homer employs this word.

Ιψ——FΙΠΣ.

Ιρις, ιρος, &c.——FΙΡΙΣ, FΙΡΟΣ, &c.

Ις, ιφι, &c.——FΙΣ, FΙΦΙ, &c.; whence comes the Latin vis, and the ΓΙΣΚΥΝ and ΒΙΣΧΥΝ, both explained σχυν, of Hefychius. From the fame root are probably derived ιαομαι and ιητηρ, which fhould therefore begin equally with the F.

Ιτεα——FΙΤΕΑ; whence it is ΓΙΤΕΑ in Hefychius.

Κλυω, κλυμι——ΚΛΥFΩ, ΚΛΥFΜΙ.

Κταομαι——ΚΤΑFΟΜΑΙ. Hence κτησατο οιος in Odyff. Ξ. 450, fhould be ΚΤΑFΕΣΑΤ' ΟΙΟΣ; this being the old form of the Aorift, as I fhall fhow in confidering the flexions of the verbs. Κτησις fhould alfo be ΚΤΑFΣΙΣ or ΚΤΕFΣΙΣ, from the Ionic form ΚΤΕFΟΜΑΙ, whence ΚΤΕFΜΑ, now κτημα, ΚΤΕFΑΣ, ΚΤΕFΑΤΙΤΣΩ, now κτεατιζω, &c.

Κυκ εος, &c.——ΚΥFΑΝΕΟΣ, &c. whence the firft fyllable is long.

Κυδος, &c.——ΚΥFΔΟΣ, &c. probably from the fame root.

Κυμα——ΚΥFΜΑ.

Κωκυω, κωκυτος——ΚΩΚΥFΩ, ΚΩΚΥFΤΟΣ.

Λαω——ΛΑFΩ, written, through a difference of dialect, ΛΑΒΩ; which, acquiring a metaphorical meaning, became a different word, as it uniformly is in Homer. The derivatives fhould all be written after the fame manner, which will be found equally conformable to the rules of metre and etymology; as ΛΑFΟΣ, ΛΑFΑΣ or ΛΑFΣ, ΛΑFΙΝΓΣ,

---

(1) In the Heraclèan infcriptions the afpirate is ufually retained in the compounds.

ΛΑϜΡΗ, ΑΠΟΛΑϜΡΩ, &c.; alfo the proper names from thefe roots, fuch as ΛΑϜΕΡΤΗΣ, ΛΑϜΟΔΑΜΑΣ, ΛΕϜΚΟΘΕϜΗ, ΛΕϜΚΙΠΠΟΣ, &c. The original verb feems to have been antiently written with the Γ, employed as a guttural afpirate to exprefs the rough pronunciation of the old Æolian and Pelafgian clans; ΓΛΑϜΩ, whence γλαυσσω or ΓΛΑϜΣΣΩ, which is only a different mode of pronouncing ΛΕϜΣΣΩ. This gives us the true etymology and fignification of γλαυκωπις or ΓΛΑϜΚΩΠΙΣ, the epithet of Minerva, which means neither *blue-eyed* nor *owl-eyed*, but *keen-eyed* or *eager-eyed, having extremely quick and comprehenfive fight*, as Hefychius has rightly explained it. ΓΛΑϜΚΣ, *an owl*, was fo called from this quality; and ΓΛΑϜΚΟΣ, the adjective, fignifies the activity and violence of the fea rather than any particular colour; whence ΓΛΑϜΚΙΟϜΩΝ is employed as the epithet of a lion darting upon his enemy, to exprefs the eagernefs and ferocity of his look (1).

Λουω——ΛΟϜΩ. Hence λυσας and λοεσσας, which are the fame forms of the Aorift, except that the one is contracted and the other not; ΛΟϜΣΑΣ and ΛΟϜΕΣΑΣ, the penultimate Σ of which may be pronounced, as ufual, double or fingle.

Λυω——ΛϒϜΩ. The afpirate is elided in fome of the flexions, and alfo in the adjective and abftract fubftantive derived from it, ΛϒΤΟΣ and ΛϒΣΙΣ. This feeming irregularity perplexed M. L'Abbe very much; but Dr. Clarke treats his doubts with fome contempt; and, to prevent any one elfe from doubting, affures us, with great gravity, that it was an eftablifhed cuftom to pronounce the penultimate fhort in fome flexions and derivations of the fame words, and long in others (2). Of this L'Abbe had certainly no doubt, as the knowing it was the only ground upon which he could enquire into the caufe of its being fo. It did not, it feems, occur to him, that exactly the fame kind of elifion takes place in the flexions of fome Latin verbs, as AUDII, PERII, and FUI, for AUDIVI, PERIVI, and FUVI, where the correfpondent letter to the Digamma is funk. Both Clarke and Barnes fuppofe λυτο to be an abbreviation of ελελυτο, otherwife, they fay, the ϒ would be long (3). But this is a law of their own enacting; for the afpirate might be as eafily and properly

(1) See Il. ϒ. 172, and Π. 34; and Schol. Ven.
(2) In il. Λ. 314.   (3) Il. Φ. Vf. 114; and Ω. Vf. 1.

elided

elided in the imperfect (of which the second Aorist is a particular form) as in the perfect tense; and, in some instances where λυτο is used, the sense will not admit of a past-perfect without confounding and perplexing the narrative of the clearest and most accurate narrator that ever wrote. It is in these second Aorists too that the principal elisions take place through the flexions of all the verbs, as ετυπον from τυπτω, εβαλον from βαλλω, εφαιον from φαινω, &c.

Μαω———ΜΑΓΩ. Hence μεμαοτος and μεμαωτος for ΜΕΜΑΓΟΤΟΣ, the genitive of the participle ΜΕΜΑΓΩΣ, the F being, as usual, founded with either vowel. Μεμασαν seems to be an abbreviation of ΕΜΕΜΑΓΚΕΙΣΑΝ or ΕΜΕΜΑΓΕΙΣΑΝ, as δαμεν of ΕΔΑΜΗΣΑΝ, &c. (see Damm. Lex. Etym.). It may, however, be the Aorist of a new theme from the perfect.

Μυω, μεμυκα———ΜΥΓΩ, ΜΕΜΥΓΚΑ; whence ΜΥΓΩΝ, ΜΥΓΕΛΟΣ, &c.

Οϊς———ΟFΙΣ, whence the Latin ovis. In the oblique cases it is often pronounced in two long syllables, and often in a long and short one, as οιος αωτω, which, unless the F was elided, must have been pronounced ŌF-IŎΣ ĂFΩΤΩ, as it might have been without any violation of the laws of prosody; for, as OI and EI are sometimes short in ΟΙΟΣ and ΕΠΕΙΗ, ΙΟ might be equally so in the present case. The F might, however, have been occasionally elided as well as the Δ, the regular flexion being ΟFΙΣ ΟFΙΔΟΣ. The accusative plural is, in the present text of Homer, contracted to οϊς, with the first syllable short; but, as the second is always long, it might antiently have been written and pronounced regularly ŎFĪΑΣ.

Οινος———FΟΙΝΟΣ; whence, through the medium of the Latin, our word wine. Hesychius has, as usual, ΓΟΙΝΟΣ—ΟΙΝΟΣ.

Ομοω———FΟΜΟΩ, it being derived from FΟΜΟΣ.

Πιω, &c.———ΠΙFΩ; whence ΠΙFΑΡ, ΠΙFΔΑΚΣ, &c.

Πολις———{ ΠΟΛΙΣ -ΙΟΣ -ΙΙ -ΙΝ　　-ΙΕΣ -ΙΩΝ -ΙΕΣΙ -ΙΑΣ.
　　　　　{ ΠΟΛΕFΣ -ΕFΟΣ -ΕFΙ -ΕFΑ　　-ΕFΕΣ -ΕFΩΝ -ΕFΕΣΙ -ΕFΑΣ.
now written -ηχ -ηϊ -ηα -ηες -ηων -ευσι -ηας. Πολιτης or ΠΟΛΙF-ΤΗΣ seems formed out of both, unless it was antiently written ΠΟΛΙΣ-ΤΗΣ, which usually signifies the *founder of a city*; but in the Heraclèan Tablet we have the genitive plural ΠΟΛΙΣΤΩΝ, signifying the *ordinary inhabitants.*

4

inhabitants. The datives ϖοσέϊ, ἀιδρέϊ, &c. are probably from similar obsolete forms, ΠΟΣΕϜΣ, ΑϜΙΔΡΕϜΣ, &c. and not, as is generally supposed, Ionic flexions of the common terminations in -ΙΣ.

Πλεω or ϖλειω——ΠΛΕϜΩ or ΠΛΕΙΩ ; whence ΠΛΕϜΙΔΕΣ, now ϖληΐδες, and ΠΛΕΙΑΔΕΣ, the plurals of two different forms of the same word ΠΛΕϜΙΣ and ΠΛΕΙΑΣ.

Πνυω——ΠΝΥϜΩ.

Πτυω——ΠΤΥϜΩ ; whence the substantive ΠΤΥϜΟΝ.

Πυω or πυθω——ΠΥϜΩ or ΠΥΟΩ ; whence ΠΥϜΟΣ, ΠΥϜΕΛΟΣ, &c. the future of this verb, πυσω, seems to be formed from the first theme, ΠΥϜΣΩ, unless indeed it be formed by elision of the Θ, as οσω from οθω.

Σιγαλοεις——ΣΙϜΑΛΟϜΕΙΣ according to Dr. Taylor, who decides it to be the participle of the verb ΣΙΑΛΩΣΑΙ, ϖοικιλαι of Hesychius, the theme of which he of course supposes to have been ΣΙϜΑΛΟϜΩ (1). Hesychius, however, says also, that the material employed by curriers to prepare leather was called ΣΙΓΑΛΩΜΑ ; wherefore, as Hemsterhuise has observed, the present orthography must be right, unless (as has frequently happened in Hesychius, but never, that I know of, in Homer) the Ϝ was changed to a Γ.

Σπεος——ΣΠΕϜΟΣ or ΣΠΕΙΟΣ. Hence the datives plural σπηεσσι for ΣΠΕϜΕΕΣΙ or ΣΠΕϜΕΣΙ, and σπεσσι for the contracted form ΣΠΕϜΣΙ. The genitive, according to the usual change, has become σπειȣς, which may, however, be read ΣΠΕϜΕΟΣ or ΣΠΕΙΕΟΣ, in every instance, without injuring the metre.

Τιω, Τιεω, &c.——ΤΙϜΩ, ΤΙϜΕΩ, &c. Hence the first syllable in the future, &c. is always long, though short, as usual, by the elision of the aspirate, in the abstract substantive and adjective ΤΪΣΙΣ and ΑΝΤΙΤΟΣ.

Τρυγαω, τρυγοω——ΤΡΥΓΑϜΩ, ΤΡΥΓΟϜΩ ; whence ΤΡΥΓΟϜΩΣΙΝ, and ΤΡΥΓΟϜΟΙΕΝ ; by elision of the Ϝ, ΤΡΥΓΟΟΙΕΝ, now written τρυγωεν. This verb signifies the action of *stripping* or *depriving any thing of its fruit* ; whence ΑΤΡΥΓΕΤΟΣ has

(1) Let. Lys. C. IX.

been

been fuppofed to mean *flerile, that from which no fruit can be gathered,* or, which *is totally unproductive.* It is, however, applied to water and æther, the elements which are generally characterifed as the fource of all production (παντων γενεσις, and γενετωρ); wherefore, I am inclined to think that it means *that which is fo productive that it cannot be exhaufted or deprived of its produce.* The afpirate being dropt from the verbs of this form has given an appearance of licence in fome of the flexions where there is really none. Thus we find γελοωντες and γελωοντες, both of which are properly the fame, ΓΕΛΟϜΟΝΤΕΣ, the Ϝ being pronounced equally with either O. 'Ϝω——Ϝ·ϒϜΩ; whence Ϝ·ϒϜΑΔΕΣ, Ϝ·ϒϜΕΤΟΣ, &c.

'Ϝλη——Ϝ·ϒΛϜΗ. In the old Æolian ΣϒΛϜΑ, whence the Latin sʏʟᴠᴀ. Φυω, φυκος, φυλον, &c.——ΦϒϜΩ, ΦϒϜΚΟΣ, ΦϒϜΛΟΝ, &c. In the adjective, formed as ufual from the fecond Aorift, or contracted imperfect of the verb, the afpirate is elided φῠτος; whence a new verb, φυτευω or ΦϒΤΕϜΩ, was formed, which the Latins adopted in an obfcene fenfe. On an antient bafe of a ftatue, in the ifland of Delos, we have Ο ΑϜϒΤΟ ΛΙΘΟ ΕΜΙ ΑΝΔΡΙΑΣ ΚΑΙ ΤΟ ΣΦΕΛΑΣ; which Dawes would correct to ΤΟ ΑϜΤΟ ΛΙΘΟ ΕΜΙ Ο ΑΝΔΡΙΑΣ ΤΕ ΚΑΙ ΤΟ ΣΦΕΛΑΣ, the article having been, as he fuppofes, mutilated in the firft inftance, and omitted in the fecond, through a blunder of the tranfcriber, and the ϒ inferted in the pronoun by a later hand, as a comment upon the Ϝ. Both thefe conjectures are, however, very improbable; and I have been affured by thofe who have feen the ftone, that the letters are precifely as in the annexed plate (1). Is it not poffible that the article at the beginning may, by a local fingularity of fyntax, refer to ΑΝΔΡΙΑΣ, and ΑϜϒΤΟ ftand for Ϝ·ΑϒΤΟ, fignifying the fame as Ϝ·Ο ΑϒΤΟ, of which it is a contraction? for, though there cannot be any arbitrary tranfpofition of letters in any language, fuch corruptions might eafily arife amidft the licentious variations of local habits in a language which had no fixed rules of eftablifhed practice to confine it to etymology. In the fame manner, therefore, as ΑϜΙΔΗΣ became Ϝ·ΑΔΗΣ by a corrupt local change and tranfpofition of the afpirates, Ϝ·ΑϒΤΟΣ might have become ΑϜϒΤΟΣ, which might have been equally pronounced in

----

(1) Plate I. Fig. 3.

two

two fyllables; for Fϒ might have been pronounced merely as an empha-tical W, it being always to be remembered, that neither of the two vowel afpirates fignify, of themfelves, either tone or articulation, but merely certain modifications of them. Hence Homer has σευ αλλος (that is ΣΕϜ ΑΛΛΟΣ) in two fyllables (1); and Virgil DEHINC in one (2).

That there could be any literal error of fo much importance, or fuper-numerary character arbitrarily inferted, in a public infcription confifting of fo few words, and exhibited during fo many ages in one of the moft cele-brated and frequented fpots of the antient world I cannot admit, and muft therefore think it inexplicable if it cannot be explained without alteration.

II. When we find a long or double vowel, where etymology can account for only a fingle one, it will, I believe, invariably appear, upon analyfing the word, that fuch double vowel has been introduced merely to fill the vacuity in the metre caufed by the omiffion of the afpirate, which will be found as requifite to give the word its regular ftructure as its proper quantity. Some inftances of this have been already cited, and many others will pre-fent themfelves to the attentive readers of Homer, as

Βρισηις———ΒΡΙΣΕϜΙΣ. Alfo other patronymics and adjectives of the fame
    clafs, as ΧΡϒΣΕϜΙΣ, ΧΛΟΡΕϜΙΣ, &c.

Γρῆυς and γρῆϋς———ΓΡΕϜΣ and ΓΡΕϜϒΣ.

Hῦτε———ΕϜϒΤΕ. It occurs once as a diffyllable (3); but Ariftarchus dif-
    covered that this was corrupt, and therefore, in his firft edition,
    changed it to ΕϒΤΕ. Upon more mature confideration, how-ever, he found that αυτε was the true reading, which he judicioufly fubfti-tuted in his fecond (4), and which has been happily retrieved from oblivion by M. de Villoifon's important difcovery in the library of St. Mark's, at Venice, to the great improvement of one of the fineft paffages in Homer:

Πειρηθη δ'εο αυτʊ εν εντεσι διος Αχιλλευς

Ει οἱ εφαρμοσειε, και ετρεχοι αγλαα γυια.

Τῳ δ'αυτε πτερα γινετ' αειρε δε ποιμενα λαων.

Δ'εο αυτʊ, in the firft line, fhould be ΔΕ ϜΕϜ' ΑϒΤΟϜ, to make the eli-fion regular.

(1) Il. π. 31.   (2) Æn. IX. 480.
(3) Il. T. 386.   (4) Schol. Ven. in Loc.

L

Καοηα,

Καρηα, καρη——ΚΑΡΕFΑ, ΚΑΡΕF', or ΚΑΡΗ; generally confidered as an
anomalous and indeclinable word; but it appears really to
be an abbreviation by Apocopè of ΚΑΡΕFΑΣ, written by
the Æolians ΚΑΡΑFΑΣ, and thence contracted to ΚΡΑFΑΣ and ΚΡΑFΣ,
now written κρααϛ and κραϛ; whence comes the verb ΚΡΑFΩ, pronounced
by the Ionians ΚΡΕΙΩ, a verb fignifying *fupremacy* and *command*, of which
the participle ΚΡΕΙΩΝ only feems to have been in ufe in Homer's time.

Κωα, and κωος——ΚΟFΑΣ and ΚΟFΟΣ.

Ληις, ληιον, &c.——ΛΕFΙΣ, ΛΕFΙΟΝ, &c. probably from ΛΕFΩ, the fame
verb as ΛΑΒΩ, written in a different dialect; fuch
changes being, as before obferved, extremely common.
Hence we find both ληιϛος and λἔιϛος, which are the fame word, antiently
written ΛΕFΙΣΤΟΣ, and pronounced with the firft fyllable either long or
fhort, as fuited the purpofe of the writer.

Μαντηιος——ΜΑΝΤΕFΙΟΣ, from ΜΑΝΤΕFΩ, or μαντευω; other adjectives in -ηιος, and fubftantives in -ηις, were formed upon the
fame plan, and confequently written in the fame manner.

Μητρωος, μητρωιος——ΜΗΤΡΟFΟΣ, ΜΗΤΡΟFΙΟΣ. The firft fyllable of
thefe words was probably extended originally by the
afpirate, and not by the double vowel; for μητηρ is
derived from ΜΑFΩ, and therefore was written ΜΑFΤΗΡ, till adapted to
the Ionic pronunciation ΜΕFΤΗΡ or ΜΗΤΗΡ. For this reafon the firft
fyllable is always long, while that of ΠΑΤΗΡ is fhort, it being derived
from ΠΑΩ, and not from ΠΑFΩ, now written παυω, which has a different and incompatible meaning.

Πηος——ΠΕFΟΣ, or rather ΠΑFΟΣ, according to the more antient Æolian pronunciation.

Πωυ——ΠΟFΥ; or, perhaps, ΠΑΟFΥ or ΠΑΟΥ, from ΠΑΩ; the junction of the Α and Ο in an Ω being common.

Ρηιδιος, ρηιϛος, &c.——ΡΕFΙΔΙΟΣ, ΡΕFΙΣΤΟΣ, &c. from ΡΕFΑ, written
ΡΕΙΑ, in the Ionic manner, as often as the firft fyllable is pronounced long. In one inftance only it
occurs as a fingle fyllable at the end of a line—ϭ με μαλᾱ ῥε̄α(1); where

(1) I.Υ. 101.

the

the afpirate muſt have been elided, unleſs, as I fuſpect, the paſſage be corrupt. The Venetian Manuſcript has ȣ κε μαλᾱ ρ̄ε̄α; from which, com-
pared with the other, I think the true reading may be diſcovered—ΟΥ ΚΕ
ΜΕ ΡΕFΑ or ΡΕΙΑ. Ρεια is, indeed, pronounced in one ſyllable in another
paſſage (1), according to the preſent reading; whence Barnes, upon the
authority of a manuſcript, altered it to ρ̄εα. Ρεια, however, is twice pronounced as one ſyllable in the Proœm to Heſiod's εργα και ημεραι—as ρεια
μεν γαρ βριαει, ρεια δε βριαοντα χαλεπτει; and though this Proœm, confiſt-
ing of the firſt ten lines, be the contemptible performance of ſome rhapſo-
diſt, it is, neverthelefs, of ſufficient antiquity to prove that the antient
copies of Homer exhibited the paſſage in queſtion in the ſame form as we
now have it. I cannot, however, but think that it is erroneous, and that
inſtead of ρ̄εια μ̄εν γᾱρ, we ſhould read ΡΕΙΑ ΜΕΝ ᾹΡ; the latter particle
being much better adapted to the ſenfe as well as the metre, than the former; for the reference is not to the ſimile of the vultur, contained in the
preceeding line, but to the general action of Automedon expreſſed in that
before:

Τοισι δ' επ' Αυτομεδων μαχετ', αχνυμενος περ εταιρȣ
Ἱπποις αἰσσων, ὡς' αιγυπιος μετα χηνας.
ΡΕΙΑ ΜΕΝ ΑΡ φευγεσκεν ὑπ' εκ τρωων ορυμαγδȣ,
Ρεια δ' επαιξασκε, ϖολυν καθ' ὁμιλον οπαζων.

Τηΰγετος——ΤΕΓΥΓΕΤΟΣ or ΤΑΓΥΓΕΤΟΣ, probably derived from ΤΕ-
ΓΟΣ or ΤΑΓΟΣ, though its being the proper name of a
mountain renders the etymology leſs certain, there being no
information to be had from the ſenfe.

III. The ſubſidiary Ι and Υ, which, Euſtathius ſays, the early Greek
writers very generally affixed to the Ε and Ο (2), have very often ſupplied
the vacuity cauſed by the loſs of the Digamma as well as the double vowels. Hence we have, in different dialects, ΜΟΥΣΑ, ΜΟΙΣΑ, and ΜΩΣΑ,
whilſt the antient form was ΜΟΕΣΑ, from the obſolete verb ΜΟΕΩ, from
which came the Latin MOVEO. The Laconians elided the Σ, and wrote
ΜΟΑ, or perhaps, in earlier times, ΜΟFΑ (3) or ΜΟΒΑ. Κρȣνος is alſo
from ΚΡΟFΩ, and therefore ſhould be written ΚΡΟFΝΟΣ; but, neverthe-

(1) Il. P. 461.   (2) P. 511.
(3) See Decree againſt Timotheus.

L 2   leſ

lefs, it is impoffible to decide whether the practice of Homer's age and country was, in thefe refpects, ftrictly conformable to etymology, or whether local habits had not even then changed the afpirate to a vowel in many inftances. Dawes would write ΑΧΕΛΩΦΟΣ for ΑΧΕΛΩΙΟΣ; and there is no doubt but that, in the Dorian and Æolian countries, the name of the river was fo pronounced; but Homer might have pronounced it differently, as an Ionian, as he appears to have done in the name of the city Elis, which, though beginning with the F on the medals, feems to have begun with the vowel in all the numerous inftances where he mentions it. ΑΧΕΛΩΙΟΣ might alfo have been pronounced in three fyllables as well as ΛΟΓΩΙ in two, though it might likewife have been pronounced in four. In the ordinary manner of writing it Αχελωος, the Iota is equally retained though placed under the preceeding vowel, according to the mode adopted in the manufcripts of the middle ages, inftead of after it, according to that of all antient infcriptions. It is probable that the termination of the adjectives in -ΥΣ and -ΗΣ was once in -ΕΡΣ or -ΙΡΣ, contracted from -ΕΡΟΣ or -ΙΡΟΣ, the -ivus of the Latins; and that thence came the formation of the feminine in -ΕΡΑ or -ΙΡΑ, now written -ΕΙΑ. The tranfition from E to I is extremely eafy, fo that -ΕΡΑ or -ΙΡΑ might have been only variations of dialects. The termination in -ΙΟΣ belongs to a different clafs, and anfwers to the Latin in -ius, the penultimate of which is always fhort in both languages, whereas it is always long in -ivus.

SECTION

SECTION IV.

WHETHER Homer's pronunciation and orthography, which muſt have been thoſe of his age and country, were moſt Ionic or Æolic, it is impoſſible for us now to aſcertain, though general tradition, and the preſent ſtate of his text, join in favour of Ioniſm. At all events, it is ſafeſt to ſuppoſe our preſent copies right, unleſs where anomalies, or ambiguities of metre or grammar, certain analogy, or antient authority, prove them to be wrong. As the removal of the anomalies and ambiguities can, in al-moſt all inſtances, be accompliſhed merely by reſtoring the antient Alpha-bet and orthography, without ever changing the ſenſe, and ſcarcely ever the order of the words, we may conclude that our text is, upon the whole, accurate. The tones and flexions have, indeed, been changed, as local or temporary faſhion required ; but in other reſpeǎs, I believe, the poet paſſed through the hands of his Athenian and Alexandrine editors with leſs muti-lation and injury than Shakeſpeare ſuffered from their ſucceſſors at Oxford.

The very learned Dr. Heyne, indeed, thinks that, as far as relates to the integrity of the ſenſe, he has ſuffered leſs than Virgil and Horace, and many other writers, both Greek and Latin, who have flouriſhed ſince the Chriſ-tian æra ; and I cannot but think this opinion right, though Wolfius and Villoiſon have employed many learned and ingenious arguments to prove the contrary (1). The latter in particular has given a curious and elaborate account of the various editions through which his works paſt, and the vo-luminous diſputes of the criticks concerning the right readings, the ambi-guity and obſcurity of which was a very antient ſubjeǎ of complaint. It appears, however, from the ſpecimens of them publiſhed in his Venetian Scholia, that their diſputes were in general minute and frivolous, and the amendments they propoſed ſeldom well-judged ; ſo that all perſons of real

---

(1) Wolf. Præf. in Heſiod. Theog. Villoiſon. Prolegom. in Homer.

I   taſte tafte and difcernment among the antients fought for the old editions which had never paffed through their hands. Interpolations there certainly were, and ftill are, in the text; but even thofe confift chiefly of verfes which are really of the Poet's own compofing, but which the Homerifts chofe to repeat in places where he did not intend them to be introduced. The lines that are really fpurious are principally marginal explanations which have flipped into the text, where they are generally fo eafily difcernible, that we cannot but wonder how the Alexandrine Criticks could have overlooked them, more efpecially when we confider that their extreme faftidioufnefs induced them to condemn verfes undoubtedly genuine. Shall we fay with an ingenious gentleman fond of paradoxes, that the Greeks did not underftand their own language (1)? Without going fo far, we may venture to affirm, that the writers who fucceeded the Macedonian Conqueft, and confidered the later Attic as the univerfal dialect, and ftandard for purity, were not likely to form very accurate notions of the ftyle of Homer; for, inftead of confidering their own grammatical flexions as corruptions of his, they confidered his as licentious or poetical deviations from their own; wherefore they began their refearches at the wrong end, and confequently, the farther they purfued them the farther they were from the truth.

Happily, however, Homer appears to have had a Steevens among his editors, as well as many Hanmers and Warburtons; for our prefent copies are certainly lefs adulterated than thofe which were read by the moft learned of the Attic, and later Hellenic, writers. Many, indeed, of the citations which we find fcattered through the works of the orators, hiftorians, and philofophers, might have been incorrectly quoted from memory, or corrupted by tranfcribers; but others are fo remote from the prefent reading, that they muft have been taken from different copies. We find, for inftance, both in Plato and Plutarch (2), the 528th verfe of the laft Iliad cited:

$$Κηρων εμπλειοι· ὁ μεν εσθλων, αυταρ ὁ δειλων,$$

Inftead of

$$Δωρων, ὁια διδωσι, κακων, ετερος δε εαων;$$

which is fo different, that the quotation muft have been from fome reverfi-

(1) See new Syftem of antient Mythology.
(2) Plat. de Repub. lib. II.; Plutarch. de aud. Poet.

fication into more modern dialect; for the ufe of the word κηρ, as employed in it, is not of Homer's age. It may, indeed, appear prefumptuous in a modern Critick to diffent from Plato and Plutarch concerning the right ufe of a Greek word, or the right reading of a verfe in a Greek poet; but in this inftance we have ftill greater authority to oppofe to them in fupport of critical analogy. Pindar, who lived a century before Plato, and who probably read Homer in his own dialect before he had been newly dreffed by the Athenian editors, alludes to the paffage in words which clearly prove that he read it as we now have it, though he underftood it in a fenfe fomewhat different from the common interpretation, which appears neverthelefs to be right:

'Εν ϖαρ' εσθλον, ϖηματα συν
Δυο δαιονται βροτοις
Αθανατοι (1).

But though the general fenfe of Homer has been refcued from depravation, it does not follow that the minuter accuracies of his language have not been extremely corrupted. Befides the changes in the flexions and orthography, the articles, particles, and prepofitions (in the ufe of which the antient Æolic and Ionic Greek differed extremely from the Attic), have been frequently omitted, transferred, and inferted, much to the detriment of the metre, and critical nicety of the expreffion, though I do not recollect more than one inftance in which the general fenfe is injured, fo as to make the corruption difcernable to any but a very experienced eye. This is in the XXIId Iliad, where Hector, certain of his death, on finding himfelf oppofed, unaffifted and alone, to Achilles, fays,

Νυν δε δη εγγυθι μοι θανατος κακος, κ δε τ' ανευθεν,
Ουδ' αλεη· η γαρ ρα ϖαλαι το γε φιλτερον ηεν
Ζηνι τε και Διος υιει εκηβολω, οι με ϖαρος γε
Προφρονες ειρυαται· νυν αυτε με μοιρα κιχανει.

Which, in its prefent form, literally fignifies—*Evil death is near me—not even feparate—nor refuge—for it was indeed formerly agreeable to Jupiter and Apollo, who before cordially defended me; but now Fate overtakes me.*

(1) Pyth. III. 145.

Inftead

Inſtead of which, by only dropping the conjunction from the negative, and tranſpoſing a particle, we have

Νυν δε δη εγγυθι μοι θανατος κακος ε δε τ' ανευθεν·
Ουκ αλεη γαρ'——η ρα παλαι τογε φιλτερον ηεν, &c.

Evil death is near me—not even ſeparate ; for no refuge.——It was, indeed, formerly agreeable to Jupiter and Apollo, &c. &c. The break in the ſentence after γαρ, where ετ' εςι is underſtood, has peculiar beauty in expreſſing the troubled ſtate of Hector's mind ; but, as the antient copies had no points or marks to diſtinguiſh it, the paſſage was miſunderſtood, and then corrupted to give it another meaning, or rather no meaning   The languid uniformity of modern language, which requires a continual repetition of the verbs and pronouns to make it intelligible, is ſcarcely ſuſceptible of this beauty.

In many other paſſages of the Iliad and Odyſſey theſe minuter parts of ſpeech have been equally deranged, of which there needs no other proof, than that all the manuſcripts and old editions, which have hitherto been inſpected, differ in a variety of inſtances ; nor is there one from which ſome emendation has not been drawn.   Much, however, yet remains to be done—more perhaps than can be done with ſuch aids as we are likely to have ; for though the ſtrict adherence to analogy, which characteriſes Homer's language, may guide us to the true form of his words in general, the almoſt imperceptible nicety with which theſe indeclinable particles were uſed in the ſtructure and connexion of the ſentences, renders it frequently impoſſible to decide where they might or might not have been introduced.   The tranſcribers, however, oftener tranſgreſſed in the omiſſion than the inſertion of them, as appears from the various readings collected from manuſcripts and old editions ; and I am perſuaded that, could we recall them all, with the aſpirates, into their proper places, it would be found that all the arbitrary extenſions or ſuſtentations of the vowels, by the cæſure, or otherwiſe, as well as all other anomalies, ambiguities, and obſcurities, would diſappear.

When I ſpeak of ambiguities and obſcurities in Homer, I do not mean ambiguities and obſcurities of ſenſe ſo much as of form ; for the luminous ſimplicity of his ſtyle is ſuch, that his meaning is almoſt always clear and

obvious ;

obvious; though, by the omiſſion of the aſpirates ⱶ and F, and other changes in the dialeᴅ and orthography, many of his words have loſt their difference of form, whilſt they have retained their difference of meaning.

This will appear diſtinᴅly by comparing and examining the following words in their antient and modern forms:

I. 1. Αγω   duco   ΑΓΩ.
   2. Αγω   frango   FΑΓΩ.

The firſt was probably once written ⱶΑΓΩ, whence the Ionic form ⱶΕΓΕΩ; but Homer ſeems to have uſed it without the aſpirate, though he often employs the Æolic form ΑΓΑΓΩ, derived from the paſt tenſes.

The ſecond was written by the Laconians ΒΑΓΩ, as appears from the explanation of ΒΑΞΟΝ and ΒΑΓΟΣ in Heſychius (1); whence we may conclude that it was generally written as here propoſed. It may be ob-ſerved too, that the augment, which always coaleſces with the initial of the firſt, ſo as to make ηγον, is always detached from the ſecond in Homer, ſo as to make εαγον; the place which the aſpirate occupied in the antient form EFΑΓΟΝ, being kept void by the metre. We have indeed, in one inſtance, an exception—ιππειον δε οι ηξε θεα ζυγον; but, by only changing the eliſion, we may make it regular—ⱶΙΠΠΕΙΟΝ Δ' ⱶΟΙ ΕFΑΓΣΕ ΘΕΑ ΔΣΥΓΟΝ.

In two paſſages of Heſiod, and no where elſe that I know of, we have the ſingular word καυαξαις employed in the ſame ſenſe; which, I there-fore conclude, was compoſed of this verb and the prepoſition κατα, con-traᴅed, as it often was in compoſition:

—— —— —— ᵾτε κε νηα
καυαξαις —— —— ——
—— —— —— ΟΥΤΕ ΚΕ ΝΕFΑ
ΚΑFΑΓΣΑΙΣ —— —— ——
αξονα καυαξαις—————ΑΓΣΟΝΑ ΚΑFΑΓΣΑΙΣ (2).

The derivatives, which are numerous from both theſe verbs, of courſe follow the roots, though now written, in many inſtances, without any variation, and only diſcriminated by the ſenſe.

ΑΓΗ or ΑΓΑ, *admiratio* (from which are formed the verb ΑΓΑΟΜΑΙ, ſhortened by eliſion to ΑΓΑΜΑΙ, and the adjeᴅive ΑΓΑFΟΣ or αγαυος,) be-longs to a different root from either.

---

(1) Ed. Alberti.   (2) Εργ. ⱶ ἡμ. Vſ. 611 & 638, ed. Brunk.

II.   1. ἅδω   *placco*   ҒΑΔΩ.

2. αδω or ἀδέω   *fatio*   ҒΑΔΩ or ҒΑΔΕΩ.

From the firſt comes εαδοτα, properly ҒΕҒΑΔΟΤΑ; or, without the Ionic eliſion of the characteriſtic letter of the perfect tenſe, ҒΕҒΑΔΚΟΤΑ, the accuſative ſingular of the participle perfect of ҒΑΔΩ; which Dawes would write ΓΕΓΑΝΔΟΤΑ, but without any good authority. The editors and commentators of Heſychius would, indeed, perſuade us that ΓΑΔΕΙΝ, ΓΑΔΕΣΘΑΙ, ΓΑΝΔΑΝΕΙΝ, &c. which appear evidently, from the explanations annexed to them, to be forms of this verb, are literal errors, common in that author, for ҒΑΔΕΙΝ, ҒΑΔΕΣΘΑΙ, ҒΑΝΔΑΝΕΙΝ, &c.; but the analogy of ΓΑΝΥΜΑΙ, ΓΗΘΕΩ, and the Latin GAUDEO, prove that this was the antient and primitive form, anterior to Homer. The Γ was, as before obſerved, occaſionally employed as a guttural aſpirate, which, in the progreſs of refinement, was ſoftened down to the Ғ, not only in this, but in other inſtances, as in ΓΕΡΕΣ or CERES, originally the ſame name as that which in more poliſhed dialect was written ҒΗΡΗ, and applied to another perſonification of the ſame deity. I have, therefore, no doubt but that the preſent mode of aſpirating this verb is right according to the Ionian dialect of Homer; and that, conſequently, ἥνδανε ſhould be ΕҒΑΝΔΑΝΕ, or without the augment, ҒΑΝΔΑΝΕ; the ſpecies of metatheſis employed in the preſent orthography being, I believe, like every other, a corruption of later times, unknown to the pure and regular diction of Homer. At preſent, indeed, the ſimple aſpirate is uſually transferred from the theme of the verb to the augment; whence we have uniformly ἑαδε for ΕҒΑΔΕ, which an antient ſcholiaſt very gravely tells us was a diæreſis of the corrupt contraction ᾅδε (1). This is perfectly conſiſtent with the abſurd prejudices of the old grammarians concerning the purity of the Attic dialect, but as inconſiſtent with ſenſe and analogy as it would be to write ΤΕΥΠΤΕ for ΕΤΥΠΤΕ, the Ғ being, in the old Alphabet, a letter as much as the Τ, and no otherwiſe liable to licentious and arbitrary tranſpoſition.

From the ſecond of theſe two verbs comes αδδηκοτες, properly ҒΕҒΑΔΗΚΟΤΕΣ, the plural of the participle perfect of ҒΑΔΕΩ, of which the

_____

(1) Το μεν τει ἑαει ειαιρεσις εςι τε ἥδε. Schol. Ven. ad Il. Ξ. 340. See alſo ad Il. N. 543.

conſonant

confonant has been doubled to fupply the defect of the afpirates, as in the adverb αδδην, which was originally written FAΔHN, and the fubftantive FAΔOΣ; for the initial afpirate is fufficient to extend the firft fyllable. Ariftarchus feems to have feen the irregularity of doubling the confonant, and the propriety of adding the afpirate; but, not being acquainted with the F, he propofed to read αδην, which would fignify *at pleafure* inftead of *to fatiety*; and therefore might do in fome inftances, as ειωθοτες εδμεναι αδδην (1), &c. but not in fuch as αδην ελεαν κακοτητος, &c. It was, however, as before obferved, a peculiarity of the Æolian dialect to drop the afpirates on fome occafions, and pronounce the confonants double, as in ΥΜΜΕΣ and ΑΜΜΕΣ for ϝΥΜΕΙΣ and ϝΗΜΕΙΣ; and, as this variation muft have extended to the F as well as the ϝ, Homer might have employed both forms in the verb and adverb as well as in the pronoun. How far he did fo or not, the analogy of his metre is our only criterion; for no light is to be obtained from the antient grammarians.

According to Hefychius (2), fome antient interpreters did not allow ασαι, in αιματος ασαι αρηα, to belong to this verb, but deduced it from the fame root as ασις, αση, ασαμινθος, &c. I doubt, however, whether a verb fo derived, and of fuch a meaning, could, confiftently with the Greek idiom, be ufed with a genitive cafe. Aσειν or FAΣEIN, the future infinitive of FAΔΩ, is in other inftances employed with a dative (3).

The adjective ατος, properly AFATOΣ, *infatiable*, is derived from FA-ΔΩ. It is employed as the characteriftic epithet of Mars, the god of difcord and deftruction, whence AFATH, the feminine before treated of, became the title of the goddefs of mifchief, and was employed figuratively to fignify *mifchief* or *misfortune* in general.

III.	1.	αιω	*audio*	AIΩ.
	2.	αιω	*exhalo*	AFIΩ.
IV.	1.	αλω or αλεω	*coacervo*	FAΛΩ or FAΛEΩ.
	2.	αλεω	*molo*	AΛEΩ.
	3.	αλεω or αλευω	*evito*	AΛEFΩ.
	4.	αλυκω or αλυσκω	*evito*	AΛΥΚΩ or AΛΥΣΚΩ.

(1) Schol Ven. ad Il. E. 203; and K. 88.　　(2) In αιματος.

(3) See Il. I. 817.

5. αλυσσω

5. αλυσσω, *rabie actus sum*, ΑΛΥΣΣΩ, in the Attic ⊢ΑΛΥΣΣΩ (1).

6. αλυω, *mente turbatus sum*, ΑΑΥϜΩ, according to others ⊢ΑΛΥΩ (2), and ⊢ΑΛΥΙΩ (3).

7. αλαω, αλοω, αλαλημαι, *cæcutire vel errare facio*, ΑΛΑϜΩ, ΑΛΟϜΩ, and ΑΛΑϜΕΩ.

8. ἁλόω   *capior*   ⊢ΑΛΟϜΩ.

9. αλοαω or αλοιαω   *tundo*   ΑΛΟϜΑΩ.

10. ἁλλω   *salio*   ⊢ΑΛΛΩ.

From the firſt probably came our word WALL, through the medium of the Latin VALLUM. According to the preſent orthography, it is aſpirated in ſome tenſes, and thus confounded in the flexions with the tenth, ⊢ΑΛΛΩ; and, to complete the inconſiſtency, the note of aſpiration is placed upon the augment, ſo that we have ἑαλη for ΕϜΑΛΗ, notwithſtanding that the metre requires the aſpirate at the beginning of the ſimple forms, and not of the augmented; as in

Αχιληα αλεις μενεν (4), properly ΑΧΙΛΕϜΑ ϜΑΛΕΙΣ ΜΕΝΕΝ;

and Αινειας δ' ἑαλη (5),   properly ΑΙΝΕΙΑΣ Δ' ΕϜΑΛΗ (6).

The ſecond occurs only in the derivatives ΑΛΕΤΡΙΣ and ΑΛΕΤΡΕϜΩ, which ſufficiently point out the form of it.

From the third are derived αλευρη or ΑΛΕϜΟΡΗ, and αλεη or ΑΛΕϜΗ, *refuge* or *evaſion*; but whence αλεη, *warmth*, is derived, or how it was written, is difficult to gueſs, as it occurs but once in Homer, and there ſeems to want the aſpirate—ἐπει κε ταυρος θερεω, αλεη τε γενηται (7). In other writers, however, it is frequently employed; and Heſiod has επαλια λεσχην; all which confirm the preſent form. Perhaps, inſtead of θερεω, we ſhould read ΘΕΡΕΩΜ' (that is ΘΕΡΕΩΜΑΙ), for the ſenſe ſeems to require the middle or paſſive voice in this verb as well as that which follows. We have, however, the correſpondent forms of other verbs with the firſt vowel equally ſuſtained before another vowel; as in

ὁν κεν εγω δησας αγαγω η αλλος Αχαιων (8),

(1) Euſtath. p. 1636. B. 28.   (2) Ibid.   (3) Ibid. ad Od. I. 398.

(4) Il Φ. 571.   (5) Il. Υ. 278.

(6) In the Heraclèan Table, the aſpirate is dropped from ἁλια, *a congregation*; which, according to this hypotheſis, ought to be ϜΑΛΙΑ.

(7) Od. P. 23.   (8) Il. B. 231.

                             and

and κυρην δ'υ γαμεω Αγαμεμνονος (1);

no do I recollect an instance in which the first person active occurs in this form, and with this *potential* or *conditional sense*, followed by a consonant. Hence I cannot but suspect some corrupt apocopè or abbreviation, though I have no more probable emendation to offer than substituting the common form of the potential mood, which I should not deem admissible without authority ; for though the change of obsolete to common forms has been general and uniform, it is very improbable that a corrupt change of one common form to another should have taken place uniformly through so many passages, and been supported by the concurrent testimony of so many copies and editions.

The fourth is only a different theme of the third, such as were perpetually arising in the infinite flexibility of the Greek tongue.

The fifth is derived from ΛΥΣΣΑ, the *canine madness*, and seems to have a near affinity with the sixth, ΑΛΥΓΩ, though differently applied. Both, probably, are ultimately derived from ΛΥΓΩ.

The sixth seems to be derived from the adjective ΑΛΑΓΟΣ, composed of the Α privative and the verb ΛΑΓΩ.

The reduplication of the first syllable in the third theme of it I have ventured to consider as a corruption, introduced, like many others of the same kind, to fill the metre when rendered defective by the loss of the aspirate. In its present form, it seems to have an affinity with αλαλητυς, the *military shout* (so called from the exclamation ΑΛΑΛΑ, whence came the verb ΑΛΑΛΚΩ), which is, however, a word of a totally different class, being one of the very few employed by Homer not of Greek extraction, and perhaps the only one that can be supposed, with any degree of probability, to have come from the East.

The eighth is regular and unvaried through all its flexions ; but the ninth might be ΑΛΟΙΑΩ as well as ΑΛΟΓΑΩ, did not the substantive, which is uniformly αλωη or ΑΛΟΓΗ, and never αλῳη or ΑΛΟΙΗ, point out its true form.

The tenth is written, in different tenses, with and without the aspirate, but never occurs in Homer with the two Lambdas. The occasional omis-

(1) Il. I. 387.

fion of the afpirate is probably a licence of later times, though it may have been dropt, as the confonauts were elided, in particular tenfes, or according to particular dialects.

V. 1. αιρω or αιρεω   *tollo*   { ΑΗΕΙΡΩ, ΑΗΕΙΡΕΩ, &c.
    2. ἁίρω or αἱρεω, fut. αρῶ, *capio, fumo* { ΑΗΕΙΡΕΩ, ΑΗΑΙΡΩ, &c.
    3. αρω   *convenio*   ΗΑΡΩ.

The two firft being equally abbreviations of αειρω, antiently written ΑΗΕΙΡΩ or ΑΗΑΙΡΩ, were probably originally of the fame form; but the afpirate having been dropt in fome dialects, and the initial vowel in others, two verbs were formed, differing a little, but very little, in meaning, for our verb TAKE comprehends every fignification of both. I fufpect, however, that they were not difcriminated in Homer's time, but that both were written ΑΗΕΙΡΩ, &c.; for the vowel is never fuftained before the fecond or afpirated form; and the contraction in the flexions is perfectly regular.

Upon a very antient medal of Thebes, in the cabinet of the Author, is the word ΕΥΗΑΡΑ (1), the contracted Æolic or Doric genitive of ΕΥΗΑ-ΡΑΣ; which, whether it be the name of a magiftrate, or title of a deity, muft, I think, be derived from the third verb, the perfect tenfe of which is now αρηρα, and the correfponding participle both αρηρως and ἄραρως. It appears, however, from the medal, that the original form of the verb was, as I have fuppofed, ΗΑΡΩ, and confequently its regular flexions ΗΕΗΑΡΑ and ΗΕΗΑΡΩΣ, the penultimate of which, beginning with an afpirate and ending in a liquid, may, on either account, be either long or fhort, and thus fupply both the metre and fenfe without any anomaly. We have, however, ἄραρω, with its paft imperfects ἄραρον and ἄραρισκον, and alfo the participle ἄραρων; but, in all inftances where they occur, ΗΑΡΩ, ΕΗΑΡΟΝ, ΗΑΡΙΣΚΟΝ, and ΗΑΡΩΝ, will equally fill the places.

The derivatives of the fecond and third verbs were of courfe afpirated confiftently with the roots; but it is not always eafy to diftinguifh them from each other; for, as the one was ufed metaphorically to fignify *choice*, its meaning approached that of the other, which fignified *fitnefs*. The one afpirate having alfo been totally loft from the Alphabet, and the other

---

(1) See Dutens, p. 158, where the fame medal is publifhed.

funk

funk into a fort of accentual mark, applied according to certain whimfical rules, independent of etymology, fuch corruptions have taken place, that it is impoffible in every inftance to afcertain the original orthography, more efpecially where fo little information can be had from the metre. The original form of the fecond, indeed, being ΑϜΕΙΡΩ or ΑϜΑΙΡΩ, naturally produced the derivatives ΑϜΟΡ, ΑϜΟΡΤΗΡ, ΜΕΤΕϜΟΡΟΣ, &c. now written αορ, αορτηρ, μετηορος, &c. the A in the two firft being either long or fhort, and the E in the third long on account of the afpirate. Αρμα is alfo from the fame root; but ἁρμοζω fhould be from the third verb, though uniformly written with the common afpirate. Αρτια, αρτυνω, &c. āre alfo from the third, and therefore fhould be ϜΑΡΤΙΑ, ϜΑΡΤΥΝΩ, &c. unlefs the afpirate was habitually dropt in thefe derivations, which was probably the cafe even in the time of Homer, for I do not recollect an inftance where it is required to fuftain the metre. Αριςον, *prandium*, was, however probably ϜΑΡΙΣΤΟΝ, and thus diftinguifhed from ΑΡΙΣΤΟΝ, *optimum*, and not by the firft fyllable being long, as Clarke has fuppofed. The inftance of αναριςος with the fecond fyllable long, cited by him from Ariftophanes and Theocritus, is wholly irrelevant; new habits and different dialects having in their times totally changed the pronunciation of the language; fo that he might as well have cited a word from Pope to prove the right accent of a word in Chaucer. All the manufcripts and printed editions have uniformly εντυνοντο ἀριςον, and not εντυνοντ' ἀριςον, as he has given it; wherefore I conclude that the true reading is ϜΝΤΥΝΟΝΤΟ ϜΑΡΙΣΤΟΝ.

VI. 1. αρη   *precatio*   ΑΡΗ.
  2. αρη   *noxa*   ϜΑΡΗ or ϜΑΡΗ.

The fecond word is always preceeded by a vowel or the paragagic N, except in one inftance, and there we fhould probably read ΑΜΥΝΕ ϜΑΡΗΝ or ϜΑΡΗΝ for αμυνον αρην, the verb being an imperative. Hence we may fafely conclude that it was afpirated; but whether with the F or Ϝ is very much to be doubted. The Venetian Scholiaft certainly favours the former when he fays that αραιος, *flender* or *ductile*, ought to be written ἁραιος, otherwife it would fignify *noxious* (1). Our word WAR alfo, apparently derived from the fame root, feems to fupport this orthography; though

(1) In Il. Σ. 411.

there

there is no reafon to believe that Αρης was fo written in Homer. It muft, however, be of the fame extraction, and was probably terminated originally in -ΕΦΣ, whence the oblique cafes are αρτος -ητι -ηα, properly ΑΡΕΦΟΣ -ΕΦΙ -ΕΦΑ. The accufative αρην, which occurs only before a vowel, is a corruption of ΑΡΕΦ' (1).

VII. Αργης -ητο , and αργης -ετος, are generally fuppofed to be the fame word; but, neverthelefs, I believe they are totally different; for I know of no licence that can double or extend the penultimate vowel in the oblique cafes, without the aid of a liquid or afpirate, but what would fubvert the analogy of all language. They are applied too to objects fo different in their natures, that it is fcarcely poffible that they fhould fignify the fame properties; for when the penultimate vowel in the oblique cafes is long, the epithet is always joined to fomething fplendid or agreeable, as αργητα κεραυνον, εανω αργητι φαεινω, &c.; but, when it is fhort, it is never employed except to defcribe the fat of a dead carcafe, as ασειν εν τροιη ταχεας κυνας αργετι δημω. It is poffible that the firft might have been written ΑΡΓΕΦΣ -ΕΦΟΣ, and fignified *emitting whitenefs or fplendor*; for moft, if not all, words ending in -ΕΦΣ, were fignificant of *action*. The other might have been written ΑΡΓΕΣ -ΕΤΟΣ, and have fignified *the dead inactive quality of whitenefs*. This diftinction may perhaps appear refined; but fuch refinement belonged to the Greek language: thus ⱶΠΠΕΙΟΣ or ⱶΠΠΙΚΟΣ fignified any *perfon or thing which paffively belonged to horfes*; but ⱶΠΠΕΦΣ *the perfon actively belonging to them*, that is, *he who rides or drives them*.

VIII.
1. δαιω	*accendo*	ΔΑΦΩ.
2. δαιω	*divido*	ΔΑΙΩ.
3. δαεω	*difco*	ΔΑΕΩ.

From the firft come ΔΑΦΙΣ, ΔΑΦΟΣ, ΔΑΦΙΟΣ or ΔΕΦΙΟΣ (employed metaphorically to fignify *deftructive* in general); and thence ΔΕΦΩ, ΔΕ-ΦΙΟΩ, &c. which are all written in the antient manner, except that the afpirate has been dropt, and the Η introduced inftead of the Ε, to fupply its office in giving the fyllable its due length. The Ι has alfo, in the flexions of the verbs, been joined, in the form of an *Iota fubfcriptum*, to the preceeding inftead of the fucceeding vowel; whence we have δηωσας,

---

(1) See Il. Σ. 100.

&c.

&c inſtead of ΔΕΓΙΟΣΑΣ, &c. Δηουν I believe to be a corruption of ΔΕ-ΓΙΟΝ, formed according to the common mode of the Attic contractions; but neverthelefs, ΔΕΓΙΟΟΝ, the regular flexion of the more uſual theme, may equally be a word of two ſyllables, and therefore the true antient form. The firſt ſyllable of the adjective δηιος is frequently ſhort, which proves in-diſputably that it was antiently written ΔΕΓΙΟΣ, the firſt ſyllable of which might naturally be either long or ſhort, whereas no licence could ſhorten a double vowel in this place. Δαλος and δῆλος are from the ſame root, and were originally written ΔΑΓΕΛΟΣ, both being the ſame word, employed literally and metaphorically, and contracted, according to different local idioms, to ΔΑΓΛΟΣ, ΔΑΕΛΟΣ, ΔΕΕΛΟΣ, and ΔΗΛΟΣ. Hence we find in Heſychius ΔΑΒΕΛΟΣ, δαλος, Λακωνες, ΔΑΕΛΟΝ, διαδηλον, and ΔΕΕΛΟΝ, δηλον. Δαï is ſuppoſed by Damm and others to be a contraction of δαïδι or ΔΑΓΙ-ΔΙ, the dative ſingular of δαïς or ΔΑΓΙΣ, *a torch*; but as it is always uſed, when thus abbreviated, in a ſenſe which it never ſignifies when at length, I ſuſpect it to be a different word from the ſame root, the regular flexions of which would be ΔΑΓΣ -ΑΓΟΣ, -ΑΓΙ, &c.; though, as it only occurs in one caſe, the analyſis of it cannot be very certain. It is evidently em-ployed metaphorically to ſignify a *fight*, in the ſame manner as ΔΕΓΙΟΣ or ΔΑΓΙΟΣ (which ſeems to be the adjective regularly formed from it), is to ſignify *deſtructive*.

From the ſecond verb came ΔΑΙΣ -ΙΤΟΣ, a *feaſt* or *entertainment*, ſo called becauſe the proviſions were always divided regularly among the gueſts. Hence come various other words, ſuch as ΔΑΙΝΥΜΙ, ΔΑΙΤΕΟ-ΜΑΙ, ΔΑΙΤΡΟΣ, &c. which will be all found conformable to their roots through all their flexions and variations.

The third is regular through all its flexions in the preſent orthography.

IX.

1.	δεω	*ligo*	ΔΕΩ.
2.	δηω	*invenio*	ΔΗΩ.
3.	δεω	*egeo*	ΔΕΓΩ.
4.	δευω	*rigo*	ΔΕΥΩ.
5.	δυω	*ſubeo*	ΔΥΓΩ.

The forms and flexions of theſe verbs are obviouſly pointed out by the ſenſe and metre. From the firſt came ΔΗΜΟΣ or ΔΕΕΜΟΣ, *a people*; and from the fourth, probably, δημος or ΔΕΥΜΟΣ, *fat*, which ſome an-

tient

tient grammarians, however, derived from δαιω or ΔΑΓΩ, *to burn* (F);
in which cafe it muft have been written ΔΕΓΜΟΣ; and this may poffibly
be right.

X. 1. διω   *fugio*   ΔΣΙΩ or ΔΔΙΩ.

     2. διω or διεω   *fugo*   ΔΙΩ or ΔΙΕΩ.

The forms of thefe two verbs are diftinguifhed by the fingle vowels
preceeding the former being always long, and thofe preceeding the latter
always fhort; otherwife they might be really the fame word, ufed fometimes in a neutral and fometimes in an active fenfe.

The firft has been already very fully examined, and the fecond has nothing particular in any of its flexions. It feems to have been doubted
among the antient Cricks to which the word employed by Hector in Il.
X. 251 belonged; whence fome editions gave it in the firft perfon, διον,
and others in the fecond, διες, the latter of which was moft generally ap-
proved, though the former prevails in our modern copies.

XI. 1. ἑλω   *capio*   ΗΕΛΩ.

     2. ελω or ειλω   *volvo, congrego*   ΓΕΛΩ or ΓΕΙΛΩ.

The flexions and derivations of thefe two verbs have been much con
founded by the modern reftorers of the Digamma, who, becaufe both began with a letter capable of fuftaining the preceeding vowel, concluded
that both began with that afpirate (2). The one, however, being already
afpirated, there is no reafon for altering it, efpecially as the afpirate ferves
to diftinguifh it from the other, which is fo different in meaning. The
fame may be faid of its derivatives ΗΕΛΩΡ, ΗΕΛΔΟΜΑΙ, &c.; from the
latter of which, indeed, the afpirate has been dropt in compliance to the
abfurd rules of the fchool-reformers of the orthography, though both are
equally derived from ΗΕΛΩ (3), and fhould confequently be written according to etymology.

ΓΕΛΩ or ΓΕΙΛΩ, having begun with a letter long obliterated and forgotten, has of courfe been more difguifed, though not fo much fo as to be
very difficult to be traced in any of its flexions and derivations. Dawes has
remarked that ελσαι fhould be ΓΕΛΣΑΙ, and εελμενος, ΓΕΓΕΛΜΕΝΟΣ; and
confequently the fame analogy muft regulate the orthography of every

(1) Schol. Ven. in Il. Θ. 240.   (2) See Dawes de Conf. vel Afpirat. Vau.
(3) See Euftath. p. 35. l. 42.

           word

word derived from it. Ελιξ should be FEΛIKΣ; ελισσω, FEΛIΣΣΩ; and the reduplications ελελιξε, ελελιχθησαν, &c. only the regularly augmented tenses, EFEΛIKΣE, EFEΛIXΘHΣAN, &c. Hence the last syllable of κυανεος is extended before ελελικτο, not by any stress or emphasis upon the Σ, but by the natural effect of the F.—KYFANEOΣ FEFEΛIKTO ΔPAKΩN(1). The imperfect might indeed seem more proper in this place; but the past perfect, OPΩPEXATO, having been employed a few lines before to express the same time (2), proves that this must be equally a past perfect. EΛEΛIΔΣΩ, *to shake* or *vibrate*, is a word of a different extraction, though confounded in the flexions with FEΛIΣΣΩ, *to turn*, by the defects of the present orthography.

From FEΛΩ and FEΛΩ are derived ολοὸς or ᵾλος, properly FOΛOΦOΣ or FOΛFOΣ, *baneful* or *destructive*, and ᵾλυς, afterwards ὁλος, properly FOΛOΦOΣ or FOΛFOΣ, *collected* or *whole*, and metaphorically *curled* or *woolly*, whence the Latin verb voʟvo was formed without any change but that of the F to its correspondent letter in that alphabet. When the first adjective is in three syllables the penultimate is in a very few instances long, whence the Venetian Manuscript has it with the diphthong, as μειναι ολοιη μοιρ᾽ επεδησεν (3); and η γαρ ἐγ᾽ ολοιησι φρεσι θυει (4); which may possibly be right, though OΛOΦH is the more regular form, the penultimate of which may be either long or short. It should, I believe, be pronounced in the same manner in some instances where the contracted form is now employed, as in δειδια γαρ μη ᵾλος ανηρ— (5); Aγαμεμνονι ᵾλον ονειρον— (6); and βασκ᾽ ιθι ᵾλε ονειρε (7); which should probably be ΔEΔΔIA ΓAP MH-FOΛOΦOΣ ANHP—; AΓAMEMN᾽ FOΛFON ONEIPON—; and BAΣK᾽ IΘ FOΛOΦOΣ, ONEIPE. In this last instance I would substitute the nominative on account of the metre, as in φιλος ω Μενελαε—; αλλα φιλος, θανε και συ—, &c.; in which φιλος is not an Attic vocative, as some have supposed, nor a nominative put for a vocative, but a nominative regularly joined to a vocative by means of a verb or participle understood, the expression being elliptic for ὁς ει φιλος or φιλος περ εων: In the same manner BAΣK᾽ IΘ᾽ FOΛOΦOΣ, ONEIPE, means literally *go baneful, O dream!* or

(1) Il. Λ. 39. (2) Ibid. 26. (3) Il. X. 5.
(4) Il. A. 342. (5) Il. Φ. 536.
(6) Il. B. 6. (7) Il. B. 8.

go dream! that art baneful (1). It is poſſible that the initial aſpirate might have been dropt from this adjective even in the time of Homer, and that it might have been written ΟΛΟϜΟΣ and ΟΛϜΟΣ; from which the verbs ΟΛϜΩ, ΟΛϜΥΜΙ, and ΟΛϜΕΚΩ, are derived, as voLvo is from ϜΟΛϜΟΣ, and of courſe ſhould follow the orthography of the root, except that the Ϝ is elided in the flexions as the ſecond Τ is in the flexions of ΤΥΠΤΩ. Ελεος, a table *to turn or dreſs meat upon*, and ελεος, *mercy*, were antiently diſtinguiſhed in the ſame manner, the firſt being from ϜΕΛΩ, and written ϜΕΛΕΟΣ, and the ſecond, a word of leſs certain etymology, ΕΛΕΟΣ. Ἑλος, *a bog*, ιλυς, *mud* or *clay*, ιλιδον (or, as in the Venetian Manuſcript, ειλαδον), *collectively on bodies or troops*, ʊλαμος, *a mob or crowd*, ωλξ, *a furrow*, the name of the city Ιλιος, &c. are likewiſe from ϜΕΛΩ or ϜΕΙΛΩ, and ſhould conſequently be written ϜΕΛΟΣ, ϜΙΛΥΣ, ϜΙΛΛΔΟΝ or ϜΕΙΛΛ-ΔΟΝ, ϜΟΛΛΜΟΣ or ϜΟΛϜΛΜΟΣ, ϜΟΛΚΣ, ϜΙΛΙΟΣ, &c. by which means the metre will be rendered correct as well as the etymology diſtinct.

Αολλος and αολλιζω ſhould alſo be ϜΑϜΟΛϜΟΣ and ϜΑϜΟΛϜΙΔΣΩ, for the Α prefixed, being what is called the αθροιϛικον, or *collective*, ſhould be aſpirated (2); whence Ariſtarchus aſpirated αθροος (3), as the Attics did αθρεω (4), and others αδελφος, αμαξα, αθυρμα, and all the words of this kind (5) from which the initial letter had been dropped through local and habitual corruption, and the defects of a new Alphabet. It was dropt from ϜΑΘΡΟϜΟΣ for no better reaſon than becauſe an aſpirated conſonant followed, which was contrary to the rules of the later grammarians (6). For reaſons equally frivolous it was probably dropt from αδινος, which Damm would derive from the ſame root as αδην; but the ſenſe in which it is always employed ſhews that the initial is the Α αθ‌ιοιϛικον, and therefore, that it ought to be preceeded by the aſpirate. Similar corruptions ſeem in ſome inſtances to have taken place in affixing it; whence probably the Α privative is aſpirated in ἁμαρτω, contrary to general analogy, and, apparently,

(1) Damm ſuppoſes that ʊλος in both theſe inſtances means *whole* or *entire*; but I think Clarke's interpretation, which is alſo that of the Scholiaſt, better.

(2) Euſtath. p. 16, l. 32.　　(3) Ibid. p. 996, l. 10.　　(4) Ibid. 1387, l. 7.

(5) In the firſt Sigean Inſcription we find ΗΑΔΕΛΦΟΙ.

(6) Euſtath. p. 1387, l. 1.

to the practice of Homer (1); for in the numerous passages where this verb is employed the aspirate is never required by the metre. It appears also from an obsolete word, which occurs only in some copies (2), and which has been explained by the antient Critics, that there must have been two verbs of this form, very different in meaning, and only discriminated by the aspirate, ͱΑΜΑΡΤΩ from ͱΑΜΑ and ΑΡΤΩ or ͱΑΡΤΩ; and ΑΜΑΡ-ΤΩ from Α and ΜΑΡΠΤΩ.

XII.   1. ερω, ερεω or ειρεω   *dico*   ͱΕΡΩ, ͱΕΡΕΩ or ͱΕΙΡΕΩ.
       2. ερω, ερεω or ειρεω   *rogo*   ΕΡΩ, ΕΡΕΩ or ΕΙΡΕΩ.

The metre points out the different forms of these two verbs, the first requiring the aspirate to sustain the preceeding vowel in almost every instance, which the second never does. The derivatives, however, from the first are ρητος, ρητηρ, ρητωρ, &c. but as the Laconians wrote them with the Β, ΒΡΗΤΟΣ, ΒΡΗ ΓΗΡ, ΒΡΗΤΩΡ, &c. we may conclude that the old Homeric form was with the F, ͱΡΗΤΟΣ, ͱΡΗΤΗΡ, ͱΡΗΤΩΡ, &c. the regular contractions of ͱΕΡΗΤΟΣ, ͱΕΡΗΤΗΡ, ͱΕΡΗΤΩΡ, &c. which were the regular nouns, formed according to the common rules of analogy from the verb. In their present forms they appear to be from ρεω, *fluo*, which was antiently written ΡΕͰΩ, whence came ΡΟͰΟΣ, contracted to ΡΟͰΣ, and now written ρυς. The antient grammarians and scholiasts found a difficulty in the flexion of the word χειμαρρυς; for not all the licence of contraction and extension, in which they so freely indulged themselves, could deduce from it the plural χειμαρροι (3). The case is, that this word has suffered a double corruption; first, by omitting the second Ο and substituting the Υ for the F, and then by doubling the Ρ to make the second syllable long. The true word, formed according to the regular analogy of the language from ΧΕΙΜΑ and ΡΕͰΩ, is ΧΕΙΜΑΡΟͰΟΣ, the regular plural of which is ΧΕΙΜΑΡΟͰΟΙ; and I believe that, if these forms be adopted instead of the present, in every instance where Homer uses it, the descriptive beauty and rapidity of his metre will be as much improved as

(1) Hesychius has neverthelefs, as before obferved, an Α privative with the F; but this was probably another local corruption.

(2) See MS. and Schol. Ven. Il. E. 656; Σ. 571; Φ. 162; and Ψ. 414.

(3) See Schol. Ven. in Il. Δ. 452.

the

the regularity and precifion of his grammar. If it was contraincluded, it muſt have been to XEIMAPΓOΣ.

Eῤῥω, *eo in perniciem*, is of an extrainduction different from any of theſe, though it appears from Hefychius to have been written FEPPΩ (1).

XIII.   1. εω or ω   *ſum*   EΩ or Ω.

      2. εω, βεω or βxω, *vado*   FEΩ, BEΩ, or BAΩ, the Laco-
                                     nian idiom having in this inſtance become general.

      3. ἑω   *mitto*   ΗEΗΩ.

      4. ἑω   { *ſedeo*, vel } ΗEΩ.
                         { *ſedere facio* }

      5. ἑυω   *uſtulo*   ΗEFΩ.

      6. ὡ   *veſtio*   FΩ.

To theſe ſome add ἑω, *expleo*, and thence derive ἑῶμεν or ἑσμεν (2) (which occurs only once), and ἑντο (3), but the laſt is from ΗΗΜΙ, the form in -MI of ΗEΗΩ, and the former is probably a corruption. The Scholiaſt ſays, that ſome antient editors gave χεομεν (4), ſignifying ὑποχωρησομεν; and this is probably right, χεομεν or XEFOMEN being the Ionic mode of writing XAFOMEN, from XAFΩ, the primitive form of χαζω, whence comes χαα or XEFA, the *retreat* or *hole* of a ſerpent. Xεω or XEFΩ is uſually employed metaphorically to ſignify *pouring out*, whilſt XAFΩ and XAΔΣΩ retain their primitive' ſignification of *yielding place* or *vacuity*, whence came XAFOΣ, XAΣMA, &c. In Od. Σ. Vſ. 17, we have how-ever, ουδος δ' αμφοτερυς ὁδε χεισεται, *this threſhold will afford room for us both*.

The verbs which I have colleinducted under this head being compoſed en-tirely of vowels and aſpirates, the moſt flexible and variable parts of the moſt flexible and variable language ever ſpoken by man, they have naturally varied their forms more than any others, ſo that it is extremely difficult to trace every flexion to its proper theme, and ſtill more ſo to diſcriminate the corruptions of later times from the cuſtomary dialeincts of the Poet's own age and country. Each of them has its termination in -MI, as indeed

---

(1) In BAPPEI and ΓEPPΩ, that is, FEPPΩ.

(2) Eπει χ' ἰωμεν πολεμοις. Il. T. 402, al. ἰσμεν.

(3) Eξ ἱει ιντο, *expelled the deſire.*

(4) Eπα χιομεν πολεμοια.

every other verb had; but in thefe it was fo prevalent that the original form grew obfolete, except in the flexions, at a very early period.

The forms of the tenfes in the firft are ftill quite regular, except that the future εσομαι is from the paffive, though the Aorift ησα, εσα, or ηα, is from the active. The imperfect εον is ufually replaced by εην, from the termination in -μι, which was alfo pronounced ηεν, the middle vowel being made to coalefce indifferently with the fucceeding one, or with the preceeding augment. When the augment was omitted it was ην, as the Aorift was εσα, which being the Attic forms, became general for the imperfect, the Aorift having grown obfolete, except in the third perfon plural, εσαν, and that was adopted for the imperfect. Ηην, which occurs only once in the Iliad (1), and twice in the genuine parts of the Odyffey (2), is the paft perfect, regularly ηειν. Other variations, fuch as the Σ in the future and Aorift being pronounced double, fingle, or not at all; the fecond perfon fingular being contracted or at length, &c. will point out themfelves to all who are converfant in the language, and will confider it according to its analogy, without placing too much confidence in our common fchoolgrammars, where he may find the antient regular forms of the tenfes given as licentious deviations of dialect.

The fecond varied its form to ΕΕΙΩ, ΙΩ, &c. from which various flexions and derivatives were formed. The Latin vado, however, which is the fame word in a different dialect, proves that the original was written with the F. Our old verb wend too, of which we ftill ufe the paft tenfe went, feems to have come from FENTI, the antient form of the third perfon plural of FHMI. Hence likewife came FETOΣ (now written ετος, but in the Heraclèan table ϹΕΤΟΣ, and in Hefychius ΓΕΤΟΣ), *a year*, or *period of the going round of the fun* (3); and FEΔΝΟΝ or ΕFΕΔΝΟΝ, *a marriage portion*, probably formed from the antient theme FEΔΩ, correfponding with the Latin vado, whence comes our word wed. The adfcititious E, which often occurs both in verbs and fubftantives, is not, as Lennep fup-

(1) A. 807.

(2) T. 283, and Ω 342; the recapitulation in Ψ. 310, &c. feems to be fpurious.

(3) Hence, as Mazzochi has obferved, came the Latin word vetustus, of which vetus is a contraction; the old Greek being ϹΕΤΟΣΤΟΣ, literally *annofus*.

pofes, an arbitrary prefix (for no fuch licence can exift in any language), but marks a new theme, formed from an augmented tenfe, fuch as the Greeks were continually in the habit of making. Ετης, *a fellow-citizen*, feems, in its prefent form, to be of the fame extraction as ετος or ϜΕΤΟΣ, though it is in reality very different. Some antient grammarians fuppofed it to be an abbreviation of ἑταιρος, and that therefore it ought to be written ἑτης, unlefs the afpirate was dropt by local or temporary habit (1). It appears, however, to be rather the root than the derivation of ἑταιρος; and that it ought to be written with the afpirate, we have the undoubted authority of the very antient Lefbian medal, on which we find the genitive plural ϜΕΤΑΙΟΝ, either as the title of the local deities reprefented upon the coin, or as an appellation of the citizens, in the fame manner as ΠΟΛ-ΚΟΣ (a word of the fame origin as the Latin voLGUS, and our FOLK) is employed for ΔΗΜΟΣ upon a medal of Cnoffus, in Crete, belonging to the collection of Mr. Cratcherode. From ἑτης, or at leaft from the fame root, comes ετεος, *true* or *certain*, which therefore ought to be ϜΕΤΕΟΣ; but ετωσιος, *vain* or *tranfitory*, muft be from ϜΕΩ, and therefore written with the other afpirate, ϜΕΤΩΣΙΟΣ. From the form ΙΩ probably came the adjective ὁμοιος, regularly ϜΟΜΟΙΙϜΟΣ, *that which comes equally upon all*, which is therefore pronounced in four fyllables with the penultimate long; but ηιων and ηια are from ΕϜΙΩ, and were therefore ΗϜΙΩΝ and ΗϜΙΑ; whence the laft is fometimes pronounced in two, and fometimes in three, long fyllables, ΗϜ-ΙΑ and Η-ϜΙ-Α.

The third of thefe verbs exifts only in the termination in ΜΙ, ϜΗΜΙ and ΗϜΗΜΙ or ϜΗΕΜΙ, though it feems antiently to have been in -ΚΩ, ϜΕΚΩ, whence comes the Æolic Aorift ἑηκα, properly ΕϜΕΚΚΑ for ΕϜΕΚΣΑ. According to modern orthography, the fimple afpirate, now fignified by the mark ('), fcarcely ever occurs in the middle of a word, except with the afpirated liquid ῥ, which being necessarily pronounced with a forced as well as conftrained expiration, does not want it, and therefore never has it in any ancient infcription. On the pillars of Herodes Atticus, however, infcribed under the Antonines in imitation of the very antient orthography, we have ΕΝϜΟΔΙΑ for ενδια, and, in the Heraclèan infcriptions ΑΝϜΕ-

---

(1) See Schol. Ven. in Il. Z. 239.

ΩΣΘΑΙ,

ΩΣΟΑΙ, ΠΑΡΗΕΞΕΤΑΙ, &c. for ανεισθαι, παρεξεται, &c. all written according to etymology; which ought therefore to be our guide in this as well as other refpects. Aωρος fhould be ΑΗΩΡΟΣ, αϋπνος, ΑΗΥΠΝΟΣ, &c. &c. Even in the flexions of the verbs, when the Σ was elided from the fecond perfon fingular, the foft vowel afpirate Ͱ was fubftituted in its place, as ΠΟΙΗͰΑΙ for ΠΟΙΗΣΑΙ, now written ποιηαι (1), which may account, in many inftances, for the metrical quantities being fuftained. I have hence ventured to fuppofe, that the verb in queftion fhou'd be written with two afpirates, by which it is not only diftinguifhed from others of fimilar form and different meaning; but a reafon is given why the firft fyllable of the participle ιεμενος is uniformly long, it having been written antiently ͰΙͰΕΜΕΝΟΣ. From this form probably came ιωη, which, in that cafe, muft have been regularly ͰΙͰΟΦΗ. Ιον, or (as in fome editions) ιον, a *miffile dart* or *arrow*, is derived from this verb, and therefore fhould be ͰΙͰΟΝ; as ιον, a *violet*, fhould be ΦΙΟΝ, according to the Latin vIOLA, derived from the fame root.

The fourth verb of this head is varied to ͰΕΔΣΩ and ͰΙΔΣΩ or ͰΙΣΔΩ, the regular flexions of which frequently occur.

The fifth I have fuppofed, from general analogy, to have been written ͰΕͰΩ rather than ͰΕΥΩ; but the prefent orthography may neverthelefs be right in this inftance.

The fixth, I venture to conclude, was written with the F rather than the Ͱ, becaufe the Latin word vESTIS is evidently derived from it, and becaufe the Laconians wrote it with the Β (2); but, as thefe fimple afpirates were fluctuating, and varied with local habit, it is impoffible to decide, without better authority, in what manner Homer wrote it. ῾Εανος, a *robe*, is certainly derived from it, as εανος, *fubtile*, probably is from εαω or ΕΦΑΩ, *to leave* or *permit*. At prefent thefe two words differ only in the quantity of the fecond fyllable; a difference for which there is no apparent reafon; but, if my conjecture is well-founded, the firft ought to be written FΕΑΝΟΣ, and the fecond ΕΦΑΝΟΣ, by which the form becomes as different as the meaning, and a fufficient reafon is given for the A being invariably fhort in the one, and invariably long in the other. Εθος, ηθος,

(1) Etymol. magn. in Voce ενιος. Villoifon, Proleg in Homer. p. 2.
(2) Etymol. magn. & Hefych.

O   &c.

&c. are from this root, and therefore fhould be written, as before obferved, ΓΕΟΟΣ, FHOOΣ, &c. Hence BEΣTON or BETTON fignified, in the Laconian dialect, both a *manner* or *cuftom*, and a *garment*, by a power fimilar to that which the word HABIT has in our own language (1).

XIV.   1. εργω, perf. εοργα, *opero*, FEPΓΩ, perf. FEFOPΓA.

2. ερχω, perf. εεργα or εερχα, *arceo, includo*, � EPΓΩ, perf � EⅠEP-ΓA or ⅠEⅠEPΧA, as in the Heraclean Infcription.

From the firft come FEPΓON, AFEPΓOΣ, &c.; and from the fecond, ⅠEPKOΣ, ⅠEPMA, &c. which are ftill written with the afpirate, though it has been dropt from their root. Dawes perceived that an afpirate or confonant was wanting to each, in order to fupport the metre; but, not attending to the metrical power of the F, nor taking the trouble to trace the different derivations, he prefixed the F to both, and thus confounded two words as different in form as in meaning. The fecond was often written with what Lennep calls the adfcititious E (which he fuppofed to have been arbitrarily prefixed), EⅠEPΓΩ; but this is a new form from the augmented tenfe. It feems alfo to have been written with the old Ionic, or, as the grammarians called it, the Attic I, ⅠEIPΓΩ, for in this dialect they allowed it to have been afpirated (2). They have not, however, inferted the afpirate in απoερσει (Il. Φ. 283), though the natural means by which the fecond vowel was made long, ΑΠΟⅠEPΣEI; for, that fo it ought to be written, and not with the F, as Clarke has conjectured, is, proved by the firft word of the preceeding line:

Ερχθεντ᾽ εν μεγαλω ποταμω, ως παιδα συφορβον
'Ον ρα τ᾽· εναυλος αποερσει χειμωνι περωντα.

XV.   1. ἤ   ἤε   *an? vel*   EF EFE or H, HE.

2. ἦ   *certè*   H or EE.

The firft of thefe words, when in one fyllable, is ufually fuftained before a vowel; whence Dawes concluded that it was written EF. In fome inftances, however, it forms but one fyllable with the negative εκ; whence I am rather inclined to believe that the regular form was always in two fyllables, H E, and that the laft vowel is elided, in the cafe abovementioned, fo as to form H':

(1) Etymol. magn. & Hefych. as reftored by Meurfius in Laconic. lib. III. c. vi.
(2) See Schol. Ven. B. Il. Φ. 282.

XVI.

XVI.   1. θεω or θω   *pono*   ΟΕΩ or ΟΩ.

      2. θεω   *curro*   ΟΕϜΩ.

      3. θεεω or θαεω   *video, miror*   ΟΞϜΕΩ or ΟΑϜΕΩ

From the augmented tenfes of the firft come τιθημι and θηκω or ΟΕΚΩ, which more frequently occur; but θετο, the third perfon fingular of the imperfect or fecond Aorift middle, can only be from the original theme; from which, as Herodotus obferved, is derived the word ΟΕΟΣ, the firft fyllable of which is therefore invariably fhort.

I have ventured to conclude that the fecond was written with the afpirate, not only becaufe it would naturally be diftinguifhed from the firft in a primitive language, remarkable for its perfpicuity, but alfo becaufe the two εs in θεε, the third perfon fingular of the imperfect or fecond Aorift, never coalefce into one fyllable; and the fecond perfon of the future middle is θευσεαι, and the infinitive θευσεσθαι, which, I think, can only be corruptions of ΘΕϜΣΕΑΙ, ΘΕϜΣΕϜΑΙ or ΘΕϜΣΕΣΑΙ, and ΘΕϜΣΕΣΘΑΙ, by the ufual change of the Ϝ into an Υ.

The third has been much difguifed by the introduction of the long vowels, and omiffion of the afpirate; but, neverthelefs, the original form is difcoverable, by regularly tracing the analogy in every flexion; and may in every inftance be reftored, without violence either to the fenfe or metre.

XVII.   1. κεω or κειω   *pono, jaceo*   ΚΕΩ or ΚΕΙΩ.

      2. καω, καιω or κειω   *uro*   ΚΑϜΩ, ΚΕϜΩ, or ΚΗϜΩ.

      3. κεαω or κεαζω   *findo*   ΚΕΑϜΩ or ΚΕΑΔΣΩ.

The forms of the firft appear to be regularly preferved; but the active form occurs only in a neutral fenfe, unlefs it be in Odyff. Ξ. 425, κοψε δ᾽ ανασχομενος σχριζη δρυος ην λιπε κειων, which Clarke, Damm, and others, explain, *that he ſtruck the victim with the ſplinter of oak that he had left off cleaving*; but, befides that κειω no where elfe means to cleave, the tenfe in which it is here employed decidedly precludes that fignification; for, according to Homer's idiom, it muft neceffarily have been the perfect or Aorift, inftead of the prefent. I therefore believe that we fhould apply the latter part of the verfe to the latter part of the action, and underftand *the blow to have been ſtruck with a ſplinter, which he then left, laying it down*. The very learned Chriftian Tobias Damm held that the neutral fenfe, in the antient Greek verbs, was the fame as the active, except that the pro-

                      noun

noun or fubftantive was underftood, which may account for almoft every verb having a neutral as well as an active or paffive fenfe. This is often expreffed by what is called the middle voice, of which more will be faid hereafter. It is poffible, however, that the paffage in queftion may be corrupt, and that, inftead of κειων, we fhould read ΚΕΑΔΩΝ or ΚΕΑΣΑΣ.

The fecond, I believe, fhould be always written with the F, inftead of the I, to diftinguifh it from the firft, whence, in Pindar, it is καυω or ΚΑΓΩ (1). The future, pronounced in the Ionic manner ΚΕΓΣΩ, may, indeed, appear to be thus confounded with the future of ΚΕΓΘΩ, *to hide*, which is now alfo κευσω or ΚΕΓΣΩ, but is regularly ΚΕΓΘΣΩ. The Σ, however, in the flexions of ΚΑΓΩ is elided; whence we have εκγα for ΕΚΑΓΣΑ or ΕΚΕΓΣΑ; and it is poffible that this refinement might have taken place even in the time of Homer, for the Ionian Greeks fhewed their abhorrence of this letter at a very early period. The Θ in ΚΕΓΘΣΩ, ΟΟ-ΣΩ, ΠΕΙΘΣΩ, &c. might have been dropt, for the fame reafons, at the fame early period; for we have fo few monuments of very early ortho-graphy, that it is impoffible to trace accurately the hiftory of thefe re-finements.

XVIII. 1. κλαω   *frango*   ΚΛΑΩ.

2. κλαω, κλαυω, or κλαιω   *lamentor*   ΚΛΑΓΩ or ΚΛΑΙΩ.

The fi ft fyllable of the fecond is always long in the flexions, and that of the firft fhort, which points out the antient difference in the ortho-graphy.

XIX. 1. λις, gen. λιος   *leo*   ΛΙΓΣ, gen. ΛΙΓΟΣ.

2. λις, gen. λιτος   *lævis*   ΛΙΝΣ, gen. ΛΙΝΤΟΣ.

The firft occurs only in the nominative and accufative fingular in Homer, the latter of which is λινα (2) in our prefent copies; whereas it ought to be ΛΙΓΑ according to the rule of flexion here ftated. In a paffage of Callimachus, however, cited in the Venetian Scholia, we have the da-tive plural λιεσσι (3), that is, ΛΙΓΕΣΙ, which proves that the N, in the accufative, is a corruption, introduced to fuftain the fyllable, rendered de-fective by the lofs of the F.

(1) See Nem. X. 65.   (2) Il. Δ. 480.   (3) Ibid.

I have

I have ventured to suppose that the N ought to be added in the second, not only because it is a word of the same signification and etymology as ΛΙΝΟΝ, but because this letter has been dropped, as before observed, out of many words, which in antient Inscriptions are formed with it.

XX. 1. *οιω*   *fero*   ΟΙΩ.
   2. *οιω*   *puto*   ΟΙϜΩ.

The first occurs only in the future, which is therefore usually treated as an irregular flexion of ΦΕΡΩ. In the Heraclean Inscription it is written with the aspirate ͰΟΙΣΟΝΤΙ, for *οισυσι*.

The ɪ in the second, being uniformly long in the Diæresis, must have been followed by the aspirate.

XXI. 1. *ορυω*   *ruo*   ΟΡΟϜΩ:
   2. *ορω*   *concito*   ΟΡΩ.

The first of these verbs is always employed in a neutral sense, and the second always in an active one, except when it occurs with the adscititious augment, as in *ορωρει* and *ορωρε*, which are always neutral, and usually signify the imperfect tense. These singularities are extremely suspicious, and induce me to believe that these forms are corruptions of the regular flexions of the first verb; and that, instead of *ορωρει* and *ορωρε*, we ought to read ΟΡΟϜΕΙ and ΟΡΟϜΕ. When they signify the perfect tenses they were probably written ΟΡΟΡϜΕΙ and ΟΡΟΡϜΕ, the regular augmented forms contracted. From these verbs are derived several words of significations apparently remote from each other, but which have nevertheless a very easy and natural connexion. Ουρος (masculine), the original form of which appears to have been ΟΡϜΟΣ, signifies an *impeller*, or *exciter to action*, and thence a *leader*, *director*, or *guardian*, in general. Hence also a *favourable wind that impels* a ship; and likewise a *slip or channel in the shore, by which a ship is launched or impelled into the water*. Thence it was employed to signify the *ditch or mound that divided the lands of different proprietors*, and, by degrees, a *mounding* or *termination* in general; to distinguish which from its other significations, later writers, and the custom of other dialects, changed the aspirate, and for ΟΡϜΟΣ wrote ͰΟΡΟΣ; but in the Heraclean Inscription it is without any aspirate. Ουρον or ΟΡϜΟΝ signifies *the act of impelling or exciting*; and *υρος*, ΟΡϜΟΣ, or ΟΡΟΣ (neuter), *a mountain*, that is, *a mass of earth, which seemed to have been raised*

6

or

or excited from the reſt. ΟΡΟΣ *is the whey or ſerum of milk, which is pro-*
duced, or ſeparated, from the coagulum by an action ſignified by the verb ΟΡΩ.

From each of theſe many other words are derived by a regular and uniform proceſs; for, as the Greek is an original tongue, the complication
and developement of its elements correſpond exactly with the complication
and developement of the ideas which they repreſent; ſo that the ſtudy of
it leads to an examination of the firſt principles of the mind, and ſoars
above the humble ſcience of common grammar.

XXII.   1. ρυω or ρυεω   *fluo,*   ΡΥΩ or ΡΥΕΩ.

     2. ρυω   *tueor*   ΡΥϜΩ.

     3. ερυω   *traho, detineo*   ϜΕΡΥΩ.

     4. ερυκω   *retraho*   ΕΡΥΚΩ.

The firſt of theſe verbs ſeems to be only a variation of dialect from
ΡΕϜΩ, which was before conſidered.

The three laſt, being ſomewhat ſimilar in their meanings as well as
forms, have been more confounded by the change of the orthography than
any others. To *draw, withdraw,* or *withhold,* may ſignify almoſt the
ſame action; and, when applied to danger, may alſo ſignify *to ſave* or *de-
fend.* The ſecond is, however, uſually diſtinguiſhable ·from the third,
even in the augmented tenſes, by the penultimate ſyllable being long;
for in the third it is naturally ſhort. Whenever, too, the unaugmented
forms of the third are preceeded by a vowel, that vowel is ſuſtained;
which proves that it was written with the aſpirate.

The cuſtom, however, of forming new themes from the augmented
tenſes has created ſuch confuſion in the flexions of theſe verbs, originally
ſimilar in meaning, and rendered ſimilar in form by the loſs of the diſcri-
minating letter, that it will be found extremely difficult to retrieve the
antient orthography, in all inſtances, without the aid of better manuſcripts to aſcertain the true readings.

The derivatives ρυμος, ρυτηρ, and ρυτος, ſeem to be derived from both;
though the firſt ſyllables of thoſe derived from the third being contractions, as in ϜΡΗΤΟΣ, ϜΡΗΤΗΡ, and other words from ϜΕΡΩ; and the
Ϝ being loſt both from theſe and the others, the forms have been utterly
confounded, at the ſame time that the ſenſe of the context has preſerved
the different meanings. Ρυμος ſhould be always written ϜΡΥΜΟΣ, being
derived

derived from FEPΓΩ, as is ρυτηρ in Il. Π. 475, and Odyſſ. Σ. 261, and Φ.
173, where it ſhould of courſe be written FPΥΤΗΡ; but, in Odyſſ. P.
187 and 223,. it is evidently from PΥFΩ, and therefore ſhould be written
PΥFΤΗΡ. Ρυτος,. which only occurs as an epithet to ſtone employed in
building, is uniformly explained by ſcholiaſts and lexicographers to ſignify
adveditious, or *drawn from the quarry*; and, unleſs we had the evidence
of more certain analogy, or antient monuments, to contradict them, the
ſafeſt way is to ſuppoſe that their traditional Information is right, and
conſequently that this word was written FPΥΤΟΣ. Ερυμα, which occurs
only once in Homer, and once in Heſiod, is there uſed to ſignify *defence,*
though the metre ſeems, in both inſtances, to require that it ſhould begin
with the aſpirate—*ην εφορει ερυμα χροος*—and *και τοτε εσσθαι ερυμα χροος*—
χλαιναν μεν μαλαχην, &c. Ariſtophanes and Zenodotus ſaw that this was
corrupt, and therefore propoſed to read *ελυμα,* that is, FEΛΥΜΑ, from
FEΛΥΩ, to *envelope*; but, beſides that no ſuch ſubſtantive occurs any
where elſe, the ſucceeding verb *ερυτο* or ΕΡΥFΤΟ, in the paſſage of Homer, proves that it muſt be derived from PΥFΩ. I would therefore ſubſtitute PΥFΜΑ, now written *ρυμα* in both paſſages—IΗΝ ΕΦΟΡΕΙ PΥFΜΑ
ΧΡΟFΟΣ; and ΚΑΙ ΤΟΤΕ FΕΣΑΣΘΑΙ PΥFΜΑ ΧΡΟFΟΣ - - - - -
ΧΛΑΙΝΑΝ ΜΕΝ ΜΑΛΑΧΗΝ, &c. as *σφαλερον πυργυ ρυμα,* in the Ajax of
Sophocles, and *ρυμα φοινιυ δορος,* in Lycophron. Ερυμα is, however, conſtantly uſed by later writers to ſignify *defence,* they following the text of
Homer as it then was, or, perhaps, adhering to an habitual corruption,
which was ſanctified by uſe, though originating in a literal error; for both
the forms of the Digamma, Ⅎ and F, differing from that of the E only in
a ſmall tranſverſe line, they were often miſtaken for it by the antient tranſcribers, even in engraving the moſt ſolemn public Acts, ſuch as the Heraclèan tablets, which muſt have been much more carefully and delibe-
rately executed than books copied by trading ſcribes and rhapſodiſts. In
the ſame manner, therefore, as in the inſtance before obſerved, ⅬΕΤΟΣ
became ΕΕΤΟΣ, in an age and country where the Ⅎ was regularly in uſe,
PΥFΜΑ became firſt PΥEΜΑ, and then (to avoid a monſtrous and unintel-
ligible word) ΕΡΥΜΑ, in ages and countries where it was wholly diſuſed
and forgotten, and, therefore, more liable to be miſtaken. In another
paſſage of the Ajax of Sophocles, we have, however, *ερυμα,* to ſignify *de-*
fence ;

fence (1); but there, I believe, it was written ρυμα by the poet—προς ερυμα τρωων not being fo regular either in metre or dialect as προς ρῦμα τρωων. In the prefent text of Homer we have alfo ερυσιπτολις; but, as the vowel is always fuftained before it, we may conclude that it was originally ΡΥϜΣΙΠΤΟΛΙΣ.

	XXIII.	1. ρωω	*ruo*	ΡΟϜΩ.
		2. ερωεω	*ceffo*	ΕΡΟϜΕΩ.

Mr. Dawes, by a ftrange inadvertency for a perfon of his learning, would prefix the ϝ to the firft, and for ερρωσαντο write ΕϜΕΡΡΩΣΑΝΤΟ, notwithftanding that the imperfect tenfe occurs frequently in the fame voice, and at the beginning of a line, without any augment, ρωοντο or ΡΟϜΟΝΤΟ. Ερωη, *impetus*, being from the augmented form of this verb, was written ΕΡΟϜΗ, in the fame manner as the fubftantive regularly formed from ΕΡΟϜΕΩ; whence it is one of the very few words in Homer which have two different, and almoft oppofite, meanings.

	XXIV.	1. σοος	*falvus*	ΣΑΟΣ.
		2. σοος	*agitans*	ΣΟϜΟΣ.

The firft of thefe two adjectives is derived from ΣΑΩ, *to fave*, and the fecond from ΣΟϜΩ, *to fhake* or *move violently*; and it appears, from the Venetian Scholia, that fome of the antient Cricks would have difcriminated them as they are here difcriminated. The fecond occurs only in the compound ΛΑϜΟΣΣΟϜΟΣ, *agitator populi*, the epithet applied to the goddefs of difcord, and other warlike and deftructive deities. Neither is the verb from which it is derived ever ufed by Homer, at leaft according to the prefent orthography of his works; but both Herodotus and Sophocles employ it in oblique and difguifed forms. Σᾶσι (2) and συσθω (3) Valkenaer would, indeed, make σῶσι, an abbreviation of σηθυσι, but improperly, for it is the regular Ionic contraction of ΣΟϜΟΥΣΙ and ΣΟϜΟΝΣΙ, as συσθω is the Attic of ΣΟϜΕΣΘΩ. The Lacedæmonians employed the fubftantive συς or ΣΟϜΣ to fgnify any *violent effort* or *impulfe*, according to Plato (4); but it is probable that they themfelves fpelt the verb, in their own dialect, with the Β inftead of the ϝ or Υ, ΣΟΒΩ; whence we have, in Hefychius,

(1) Vf 467.   (2) Σῶσι δια σινδονος.   Herod. L. I. S. 2co.
(3) Σιισθω, βατω.   Sophoc. Ajac. maftig. Vf. 1414.
(4) Cratyl. p. 412.   Ed. Serr.

ΣΟΒΕΙΝ,

ΣΟΒΕΙΝ, διωκειν, τρεχειν, &c. ΣΟΥ, ιε, τρεχε, &c. together with ΣΟΥΣΟ, ΣΟΥΤΑΙ, ΣΟΥΣΘΕΝ, ΣΟΩΜΗΝ, and ΑΠΟΣΟΒΕΙ; all explained to the fame purport, fo as to appear evidently different forms of the fame verb, written according to the different modes of different dialects.

The caufe of the firft adjective's being written with the O inftead of the A was probably the coalefcence of thefe two vowels into the Ω, in the derivatives ΣΩΤΗΡ and ΣΩΤΕΙΡΑ: but this coalefcence is probably of no very remote antiquity, the old words being, according to the regular courfe of analogy, ΣΑΩΤΗΣ and ΣΑΩΤΙΣ, as appears from the Veletrian Infcription (1). The verb feems once to have been written ΣΑΟFΩ, whence the Aorift εσαωσα, or ΕΣΑΟFΣΑ.

SECTION V.

WHEN we confider the fluctuating and uncertain ftate of the Greek pronunciation and orthography, prior to the Macedonian Conqueft, which made the Attic dialect the general criterion of purity and correctnefs, we fhall not wonder that this kind of confufion fhould have crept into the compofitions of an author, almoft coæval, if not (as fome fuppofe) anterior to the general ufe of letters among his countrymen. For, though the poet and the orator are the polifhers, the methodizers, and almoft the modellers, of language, it is to the grammarian and verbal critick that their fine-wrought forms and dazzling colours owe their permanency, as thofe of the painter often do to the chemift and varnifher. Practical eloquence was a fcience regularly taught among the Greeks even be-

---

(1) ΣΩΤΕΙΡΑ occurs as a title of Diana on the brafs coins of Agathocles; but upon more antient ones, of Tarentum, &c. the initials of the fame title are ΣΑ.

fore

fore the Trojan war (1), as being the only means of government where the rights of the *governors* and *governed* were wholly unafcertained; and every chief poffeffed juft as much power as he could perfuade the people to allow him; but the theory of fpeech, or fyftematic grammar, was never regularly treated as a fcience till under the Macedonian kings; when, one dialect being recognifed as the ftandard, men had a given point, from which they could meafure the extent of every deviation, and trace the ramifications of every diftant and obfcure connexion. Unfortunately, however, this dialect was not the parent one; but, on the contrary, that which was moft corrupted, or (as its admirers will fay) moft polifhed, by local and cuftomary peculiarities. Hence the antient grammarians, who confidered this dialect as the criterion of purity, never explored the fources of their own language, but endeavoured to correct the compofitions of their moft antient bard by the practice of thofe who had imitated the very corruptions which obfcured him. Great numbers of antient infcriptions muft then have exifted, which, had they been examined, would have exhibited at leaft the roots of his words in their genuine forms; and from thefe their complete ftructure might have been regularly traced. Few monuments of this kind have come down to us, and thofe few have been too much neglected by Criticks and Grammarians. Neverthelefs, the well-directed labours of Hemfterhuife, Valkenaer, Damm, and Lennep, and, after them, of Villoifon and Lord Monboddo, have difpelled the clouds of grammatical jargon that obfcured the moft important part of the Greek tongue; that is, the flexions of the verbs.

Thofe who wifh to know the progrefs and detail of thefe great difcoveries will confult the printed works of thefe learned perfons, particularly the *Analogia Græca* of Lennep. I fhall here only give the refult of them, in a fhort table, fhowing how the middle voice and the fecond futures and Aorifts have been formed out of different themes of the fame verbs, only fragments of which have continued in ufe. Thefe fragments I fhall place under their proper heads, and with the proper explanations, leaving the fpaces of all the obfolete forms, except the firft, which is the theme itfelf, void.

(1) See Il. I. 443.

6

| | | Indicative | | | Preſent Perf. | Paſt Perf. | Paſt Future. | Preſent Imperf. | Future Imperf. | | Infinitive. | |
Preſent Imperf.	Paſt Imperf.	Future Imperf.	Aoriſt.	Preſent Perf.						Aoriſt.	Preſent Perf.	Future Perf.
ΤΥΠΤΩ	ΕΤΥΠΤΟΝ	———	———				———	ΤΥΠΤΕΙΝ			———	———
ΤΥΠΩ	ΕΤΥΠΟΝ, vulgarly the ſecond Aoriſt. The third perſon plural in ſome dialects, according to Lennep, was in -ΟΣΑΝ, or, from the forms in ΜΙ, in -ΕΣΑΝ; but theſe might have been from the Aoriſt.	ΤΥΠΣΩ	ΕΤΥΠΣΑ	ΤΕΤΥΠ, contracted from ΤΕΤΥΠΕΑ, and adopted for the middle voice.	ΕΤΕΤΥΠΕΙΝ, contracted from ΕΤΕΤΥΠΕΚΕΙΝ, and adopted for the middle voice.	———	ΤΥΠΕΙΝ, vulgarly the ſecond future and ſecond Aoriſt.	ΤΥΠΣΕΙΝ	ΤΥΠΣΑΙ	———	———
ΤΥΠΕΩ	———	ΤΥΠΩ, the Attic future contracted from ΤΥΠΕΣΩ.	———	———	———	———	———	———	———	———	———
ΤΥΦΩ	———	———	———	ΤΕΤΥΦΑ contracted for ΤΕΤΥΦΕΚΑ.	ΕΤΕΤΥΦΕΙΝ, contracted from ΕΤΕΤΥΦΕΚΕΙΝ.	———	———	———	———	———	———
ΤΥΦΗΜΙ											ΤΕΤΥΦΗΝΑΙ	

PASSIVE VOICE.

Preſent Imperf.	Paſt Imperf.	Future Imperf.	Aoriſt.	Preſent Perf.	Paſt Perf.	Paſt Future.	Preſent Imperf.	Future Imperf.	Aoriſt.	Preſent Perf.	Future Perf.
ΤΥΠΤΟΜΑΙ	ΕΤΥΠΤΟΜΗΝ	———	———	———	———	———	ΤΥΠΤΕΣΘΑΙ			ΤΕΤΥΦΘΑΙ,	———
ΤΥΠΩΜΑΙ	ΕΤΥΠΟΜΗΝ, vulgarly the ſecond Aoriſt.	ΤΥΨΟΜΑΙ	ΕΤΥΨΑΜΗΝ, adopted for the middle voice. The ſecond perſon ſingular is contracted from -ΑΣΟ to -ΑΟ -Ω and -Α.	ΤΕΤΥΜΜΑΙ contracted from ΤΕΤΥΠΑΜΑΙ which ſeems originally to have been ΤΕΤΥΠΚΑΜΑΙ.	ΕΤΕΤΥΜΜΗΝ, which has been contracted in the ſame manner.	ΤΕΤΥΨΟΜΑΙ	ΤΥΠΕΣΘΑΙ, vulgarly the ſecond Aoriſt middle.	ΤΥΠΣΕΣΘΑΙ, future middle.	ΤΥΠΣΑΣΘΑΙ, Aoriſt middle.	———	ΤΕΤΥΠΣΕΣΘΑΙ
ΤΥΠΕΟΜΑΙ	———	ΤΥΠΟΥΜΑΙ, the Attic future contracted from ΤΥΠΕΣΟΜΑΙ to ΤΥΠΕΟΜΑΙ, and thence to the preſent form, which is called the ſecond future middle.	———	———	———	———	ΤΥΠΕΙΣΘΑΙ, or ΤΥΠΕΣΘΑΙ, vulgarly the ſecond future middle.	ΤΥΠΗΣΕΣΘΑΙ, vulgarly the ſecond future.	———	———	———
ΤΥΦΘΕΟΜΑΙ	———	ΤΥΦΘΗΣΟΜΑΙ	———	———	———	———	———	ΤΥΦΘΗΣΕΣΘΑΙ	———	———	———
ΤΥΠΗΜΙ, the active form uſed in a paſſive ſenſe.	ΕΤΥΠΗΝ, vulgarly the ſecond Aoriſt.	———	———	———	———	———	ΤΥΠΗΝΑΙ, vulgarly the ſecond Aoriſt.	———	———	ΤΕΤΥΠΕΝΑΙ, adopted for the middle voice.	———
ΤΥΦΘΗΜΙ, the ſame.	ΕΤΥΦΘΗΝ, vulgarly the firſt Aoriſt.	———	———	———	———	———	ΤΥΦΘΗΝΑΙ, vulgarly the firſt Aoriſt.	———	———	———	———

Though

Though I have no doubt but that this hypothefis is true, as far as it fuppofes the fecond futures and Aorifts and the middle voice to be modifications of other tenfes and other voices, yet I cannot fee any neceffity for fuppofing the exiftence of fo many obfolete themes of the fame verb as are here given, fince all the forms now extant may be deduced, by the regular licence of contraction, from two, ΤΥΠΤΩ and ΤΥΦΘΩ (with their refpective terminations in -ΜΙ), which are only variations of dialect, confifting in the infertion or omiffion of the afpirate. The fuppofing a termination in -ΕΩ, in order to produce a future in -ΕΣΩ, is not only unneceffary, but inconfiftent with analogy ; for, as the termination in -Ω formed the *prefent perfect* originally in -ΕΚΑ, it muft, by the fame rule, have formed the future in -ΕΣΩ; which fome contracting by an elifion of the Ε, and others by an elifion of the Σ, it became -ΣΩ and -ΕΩ, corrupted to -Ω͂ and -ΟΥ; fo that ΤΥΠΣΩ, ΤΥΠΕΟ, ΤΥΠΩ͂, and ΤΥΠΟΥ͂ΜΑΙ, are all the fame tenfe, and from the fame theme, which is the common one, ΤΥΠΤΩ, the Τ being elided in the flexions. The regular future from a termination in -ΕΩ muft be in -ΗΣΩ or -ΕΕΣΩ, as the fecond perfons fingular from -ΟΜΑΙ and -ΕΟΜΑΙ were originally -ΕΣΑΙ and -ΗΣΑΙ, changed by the Ionians to -ΕϜΑΙ and -ΗϜΑΙ, and thence contracted to -ΕΑΙ and -ΗΑΙ, and ftill further, by the Attics, to ΗΙ or η.

Lennep fuppofes that the primitive form of the infinitive was the fhorteft, that is, the Doric ΤΥΠΤΕΝ, and that the other common and poetical forms (as they are called) are licentious variations and extenfions of it(1) ; but Lord Monboddo is probably right in taking the longeft form for the original, ΤΥΠΤΕΜΕΝΑΙ, contracted by degrees to ΤΥΠΤΕΝΑΙ, ΤΥΠΤΕΜΕΝ, ΤΥΠΤΕΕΝ, ΤΥΠΤΕΙΝ, and ΤΥΠΤΕΝ(2). In almoft every word of the Greek we meet with contractions and abbreviations, but, I believe, the flexions of no language allow of extenfion or amplification. In our own, we may write SLEEPED or SLEPT, as the metre of a line or rythm of a period may require; but by no licence may we write SLEEPEED.

Though the middle voice confifts of certain forms of tenfes belonging to the other voices, thefe forms were, at a very early period, employed to exprefs a particular meaning. To fignify the *doing of any thing in general*

---

(1) Analog. Græc. p. 157.   (2) Orig. of Languages, Part. II. Lib III. C. XIV.

without

without any particular reference, the active voice was employed; but when it was *done for the use of*, or *with a pointed reference to*, *the doer*, the middle, as in

Το ρα τοτ' εκ χηλοιο λαβων εκαθηρε θεειω

Πρωτον, επειτα δε νιψ' υδατος καλητι ροησι

Νιψατο δ' αυτος χειρας, αφυσσατο δ' αιθοπα οινον.   Il. Π. 228.

and Εξαγαγε προφοως δε, και ηελιι ιδεν αυγας

Ηγαγετο προς δωματ' επει πορε μυρια έδνα.   Ibid. 188 & 190.

In an Athenian law, cited by Æfchines (1), the expreffions of which muft of courfe be precife and accurate, we find that ΜΙΣΟΩΣΑΣ fignified *the perfon who hired out*, ΜΙΣΘΩΣΑΜΕΝΟΣ, *the perfon who hired in, or for himfelf*, and ΜΕΜΙΣΟΩΜΕΝΟΣ, *the perfon who was hired*. This I believe to be the proper ufe of this voice; for, when it is employed *reciprocally* or *neutrally*, the pronoun feems to be underftood; wherefore, it is in fact *actively*.

Though the Greek tenfes are thus fimplified, and reduced to the general principles of rational grammar, which prevail alike in all languages, it is no eafy matter to afcertain their precife meaning, and ftill lefs fo, to exprefs it by the complicated auxiliary verbs, which the ftubborn inflexibility of modern dialects has obliged us to adopt.

Dr. Clarke's note upon it is fpecious and ingenious (2); but he has eluded rather than folved the difficulties, by giving his examples only from neutral and paffive verbs, and thofe too in Latin. His ftatement is,

Time paft
- of an imperfect action
  - abibat, *he was going.*
  - cœnabat, *he was at fupper.*
  - ædificabatur, *it was in building.*
- of a perfect action.
  - abierat, *he was gone.*
  - cœnaverat, *he had fupped.*
  - ædificatum erat, *it was built.*

(1) Κατα Τιμαρχ.   (2) Il. A. 37.

Time

Time prefent	of an imper- fect action	abit, *be is going.*
		cœnat, *be is at fupper.*
		ædificatur, *it is building.*
	of a perfect action	abiit, *be is gone.*
		cœnavit, *be has fupped.*
		ædificatum eft, *it is built.*
Time future	of an imper- fect action	abibit, *be will be going.*
		cœnabit, *he will be at fupper.*
		ædificabitur, *it will be in building.*
	of a perfect action	abierit, *he will be gone.*
		cœnaverit, *he will have fupped.*
		ædificatum erit, *it will be built.*

Lord Monboddo has amply expofed the defects of this fcheme, and given one of his own more complete; but, I fear, not much more fatisfactory. It is as follows (1):

Active.

ΓΡΑΦΩ, *I write.*

ΕΓΡΑΦΟΝ, *I was writing.*

ΓΡΑΠΣΩ, *I fhall or will write.*

ΕΓΡΑΠΣΑ, *I wrote, or did write.*

ΓΕΓΡΑΦΑ, *I have written.*

ΓΕΓΡΑΦΩΣ ΕΣΟΜΑΙ, *I fhall have written.*

ΕΓΕΓΡΑΦΕΙΝ, *I had written.*

Paffive.

ΓΡΑΦΟΜΑΙ, *I am in the act of being written.*

ΕΓΡΑΦΟΜΗΝ, *I was in the act of being written.*

ΓΡΑΠΣΟΜΑΙ, *I fhall be written.*

ΕΓΡΑΦΘΗΝ, *I was written.*

ΓΕΓΡΑΜΜΑΙ, *I have been written.*

ΓΕΓΡΑΠΣΟΜΑΙ, *I fhall have been written.*

ΕΓΕΓΡΑΜΜΗΝ, *I had been written.*

According to this hypothefis, the perfect participle paffive ought to fignify *that which has been done*; but, neverthelefs, ΤΕΤΕΛΕΣΜΕΝΟΝ

(1) See Orig. of Lang. Part II. Book I. Ch. XII.

ΕΣΤΑΙ

EΣTAI does not mean *shall have been finished,* but *shall be finished completely.*
It is difficult to conceive how an action can be *complete,* and yet *present;*
since the very *completion* of it renders it *past;* but, nevertheless, this seems
to have been the sense of the tense which is commonly called the *præter-
perfect,* but which Clarke more properly calls the *present perfect.* The
plusquam perfectum, or *past perfect,* seems, in like manner, to have been
often used to signify the *suddeness* of the action without having reference to
an event *completely past,* as in περι δε σφισιν οσσα δεδηει—τετρηχει δ' αγορη—
βεβηκει and εβεβηκει, in many instances. Lord Monboddo, indeed, supposes
these to be the *present imperfects* of new themes δεδαω, τετρηχω, βεβηκω, &c.
formed from the *present perfect tenses* (1); and it is certain that such new
themes were occasionally used, but, I believe, not so frequently as that
learned writer imagines, for Homer's narrative, when delivered in his own
person, is always in a past tense (2); and it is rather singular that, if he
chose to deviate from his general practice in this respect, he should have
done it only when employing these augmented forms, and thus introduced
a licentious enallage of tenses, which he never allows himself on other oc-
casions, merely to introduce a set of licentious or irregular words. We
may observe too, that δεδηει is certainly a *past perfect* in Il. M. 37, and likewise in Il. K. 187, otherwise it could not accord with the succeeding verb
τετραφατο, as the sense requires it to do. The learned Judge has, indeed,
turned εληλατο and ηρηρειςο, which are equally past perfects, into Aorists;
and, by the same licence of transmutation, he might have made one of
τετραφατο, or, indeed, of any other form; but he should have recollected
that Herodotus, an author whom he professes to have studied so accurately,
employs undoubted past perfects in exactly the same sense as Homer has
these disputed forms—αυτος ανεβεβηκει, και κατ' αυτον αλλοι Περσεων ανεβαινον
—*then he himself suddenly went up, and others of the Persians proceeded after
him* (3). Dr. Clarke has accordingly understood all these forms to be *past
perfects,* though their meaning does not exactly correspond with the use of

(1.) Origin of Languages, Vol. II. p. 157.

(2) I would here be understood to distinguish between *narrative* and *description;* for *description* may properly be in the present tense, when the *narrative* to which it belongs is in
the past.

(3) Lib. I. S. 84.

that tenfe in modern language ; and his opinion certainly does not merit the contempt and afperity with which it has been treated by the learned Judge; for it is juftified in this inftance by the very high authorities of Virgil and Horace, both of whom underftood Homer's expreffions exactly as Clarke has, and thought them beauties worthy of being tranfplanted into their own language. The former has, *fic fata, gradus evaferat altos* (1), exactly correfponding with ὡς ειπων——εϐεϐηκει——and the latter,

> *Ad hoc prementes verterant bis mille equos*
> *Galli canentes Cafarem,*

parallel with

> —— —— —— οσσα δεδηει
> Οτρυνϰσ' ιεναι —— ——

S E C T I O N   VI.

THE learned reader muft have obferved that, in the whole courfe of this enquiry, I have tacitly rejected the evidence of fome very celebrated and important monuments of antiquity, firft publifhed in the Memoirs of the French Academy of Infcriptions and Belles Lettres, and fince cited as authentic by every writer upon this fubject. I mean the infcriptions faid to have been difcovered in the neighbourhood of Lacedæmon, by the Abbé Fourmount, during a journey through Greece, undertaken by order of the late King of France.

M. Fourmont is faid to have been a poring, heavy Antiquary, without tafte or invention, but of immenfe induftry and rigid exactitude in compiling, and fo devoted to antient learning, that he underftood Greek and Hebrew better than his native French (2). Of his proficiency in the two

----

(1) Æn. IV. 685.   (2) Recherches fur les Arts, Vol. II.

latter

latter languages, I am not a competent judge; but of his ſkill in the firſt, I may perhaps be able to give the reader a juſt idea, by a free and candid examination of the inſcriptions which he produced. This examination I feel it incumbent upon me to make, as an apology for my preſumption in differing in opinion with ſo many of the firſt ſcholars of the age, who have quoted theſe inſcriptions as undoubted ſpecimens of the moſt antient writing extant.

When Mr. Fourmont returned from Greece, he gave out that he had made vaſt diſcoveries, having got an antient copy of the laws of Solon, and, by employing two thouſand men to dig in the ruins of Amyclæ, found written monuments of much more remote antiquity than any that had hitherto been produced. Specimens of theſe he publiſhed in the year 1740; but from ſome cauſe or other did not proceed, but left his manuſcripts in the King's Library, from which other ſpecimens have been ſince publiſhed by the Benedictines in their *Traité diplomatique*, and by the Abbé Barthelemi in ſucceeding volumes of the *Memoires* of the Academy. Theſe, however, form but a ſmall part of the collection, the reſt being, as Count Caylus ſays, withheld from the publick on account of the expence neceſſary to make engravings of ſuch a number and variety of characters as are contained in them. A large volume of manuſcripts, copied from Fourmont's originals, under the direction of the Abbé Barthelemi; is, indeed, now ſhown in the Library; but it cannot be to theſe that the Count alludes, for they contain very little variety of character, being chiefly mutilated and incorrect copies of inſcriptions already publiſhed. The originals, however, of theſe are not ſhewn, any more than of the very curious and important ones publiſhed; and as for the laws of Solon, they are now given up, as well as the two thouſand men employed at Amyclæ; it having been diſcovered that the whole Peloponneſus would ſcarcely have afforded ſo many. Fourmont, indeed, did employ all that he could collect, not in diſcovering inſcriptions, but in breaking to pieces thoſe previouſly diſcovered, that future travellers might not detect his errors and frauds (1).

When ſo intelligent and experienced a perſon as Count Caylus talks of the *expence* as the great impediment to publication, we cannot but ſuſpect

---

(1) Of this I was informed by the late Mr. Stuart, who followed Fourmont.

that

that he adduces fo frivolous a reafon merely to cover a more folid one, which he thought proper to fupprefs out of refpect to the Academy; for he muft have known that the expence of engraving or cafting all the d f-ferent variations of character of which the Greek Alphabet is fufceptible, could fcarcely be an object of importance to an affluent individual, and much lefs to an illuftrious public body, or powerful prince. Perhaps the fair and free examination of thofe already publifhed, which I fhall here give, may bring to light the concealed reafon for withholding the reft.

The authority of the Academy, under which they were firft ufhered in-to the world, has hitherto prevented any fuch examination from taking place; otherwise, I am perfuaded that fuch men as the authors of the *Traité diplomatique*, Abbé Winkelmann, Mazochi, M. Auffe de Villoifon, and the prefent Bifhop of Chefter, would never have quoted them as au-thentic; for as to the character of Fourmont, and his want of invention and ingenuity to compofe fuch forgeries, they are but poor palliatives at beft, and will, I think, lofe the little efficacy, which they might otherwise have, when we become acquainted with the exact degree of thefe qualities requifite for fuch compofitions. The author of the *Recherches fur les Arts* has, indeed, adduced feveral other arguments in favour of them, the prin-cipal of which will be hereafter confidered. His reafon for undertaking a formal defence of them, was to anfwer objections which I firft put toge-ther for his ufe, and which I now re-ftate, nearly in the fame form, and fubmit to the judgement of the Learned; only intreating every perfon who fhall again differ with me in opinion, and think my remarks worthy of animadverfion, to make the reply generally to them all, and not, like the learned author abovementioned, oppofe a profufion of argument to thofe parts which appear weak and harmlefs, while the reft are left, unchecked and unnoticed, to prey upon the fpoils of the Academy.

The infcriptions publifhed contain fpecimens of writing from the earlieft period of fabulous tradition down to the fubverfion of the Greek Republicks —from Eurotas, a king fuppofed to have reigned in Laconia feven genera-tions before the Trojan war (1), down to Philip of Macedon. In monu-ments, engraved at periods fo remote from each other, we might expect to

(1) Paufan. Lib. III.

Q   find

find great variations both in the form and use of the letters; but, nevertheless, they are so nearly the same as to appear of one hand-writing, and of one person's composition. We have the terminations of names in the oblique cases the same as in Pausanias; and all the barbarous forms of letters, such as the Ϲ *Sigma* and Ϲ *Epsilon*, employed under the later Roman Emperors. The *Sigma* in the earliest inscriptions is, indeed, taken from the very antient medals of Gortyna, in Crete, upon which we find the word ϚΝΥΤϘΟ1, which Fourmont, like some other Antiquaries of equal sagacity, took for ΓΟΡΤΥΝΣ; whereas it is ΓΟΡΤΥΝΙ, the abbreviation of ΓΟΡΤΥΝΙΩΝ, found upon other medals of the same city; the Iota being of this form, as before observed, on the medals of Lyttus, Posidonia, and in the Veletrian Inscription.

This remarkable conformity has been attributed to the pertinacious adherence of the Lacedæmonians to their antient manners and customs; but it seems to have been forgotten, that these manners and customs were twice totally changed during the period comprehended in these inscriptions; first, by the invasion of the Dorians, and, afterwards, by the Institutions of Lycurgus; and that, in the age of Homer, or, at least, in that of which he writes, which was considerably later than the earliest of these inscriptions, Lacedæmon was the seat of wealth and luxury instead of arms and discipline (1).

The forms of the bucklers also, upon which two of the inscriptions are engraved, are totally unlike the simple round shields of the antient Greeks, or indeed of any other antient people, they being in absurd fanciful shapes, wholly unadapted to the purposes of defence (2). The mode of writing the titles of the magistrates too, in larger letters than those employed in their names, is without example in any genuine monument of antiquity that I have seen (3); and it is observable, that one of the stones is represented as broken in so artist-like and regular a manner, that it could not have been the result of accident (4); for, if so many fractures had been caused by the fall of ruins or the decay of time, the edges would necessarily have been splintered or corroded so as to destroy many of the letters. I shall, however, waive the consideration of these suspicious peculiarities,

(1) Odyss. Δ.
(2) See Pl. V. VIII. & IX.
(3) See Pl. VI. & VII.
(4) See Pl. IV.

as well as the fingular forms of the fhields and letters, becaufe whim and caprice might have operated in antient as well as modern times: but errors in orthography, grammar, and dialect, the blunders of dictionary-makers, tranfcribers, and editors, transferred into monuments attributed to remote antiquity, will, I flatter myfelf, if proved, be deemed of themfelves fufficient evidence of impofture.

The moft antient of thefe monuments is a temple or chapel dedicated to the goddefs ONGA or OGA, which Fourmont pretended to have difcovered, but which no other traveller, has been able to find, notwithftanding the maffive and almoft immoveable ftability with which he fays it was built. As this chapel is fuppofed to have been dedicated in the time of the King Eurotas abovementioned, the father-in-law of Lacedæmon, from whom the city derived its name, it was neceffary to find fome other title for the Lacedæmonians in the dedicatory infcription. Meurfius eafily fupplied this deficiency; for in the text of Hefychius, as it then ftood, he found Ικτευκρατεις Λακωνες, whence he concluded that Ικτευκρατεις, or Ικτεοκρατεις, was an antient name of the people of Laconia (1). Fourmont, therefore, adopted this name with a whimfical alteration, and gave as the votive infcription of his chapel, ΟΓΑΙ ΙΚΤΕΡΚΕΡΑΤΕΕΣ (2). It has fince, however, appeared, that this name is merely the creation of a blundering tranfcriber, who transformed two verbs, the one explanatory of the other, into a fingle noun; fo that, inftead of Ικτευκρατεῖς Λακωνες, we fhould read ικτεῦ' κρατει Λακωνες, as the laft editors have juftly obferved. Thus, by a fucceffion of error and impofture, a fabulous perfonage of antient tradition has been made to anticipate the blunders of a tranfcriber, committed in copying a dictionary-maker of the third century of Chriftianity (3); by which means the French academicians have been enabled, not only to call into being a people that never exifted, but alfo to fix the date of their dominion in the Peloponnefus as readily and accurately as that of the Franks and Normans in their own country (4).

(1) Mifcell. Lacon. Lib. III. C. VIII.   (2) See Pl. III. Fig. 1.

(3) See Fabric. Biblioth. Græc. lib. IV. c. XXXV. Though the original author feems to have flourifhed about that time, his work has been mutilated and interpolated by later hands.

(4) See Mem. de l'Acad. t. XXIII. p. 415.

The

The next infcription is a catalogue or chronicle of the priefteffes of Amyclæ, beginning about the fame time ; Laodamia, the grand-daughter of Eurotas, being the third prieftefs in the lift (1). By a peculiarity of idiom, thefe priefteffes are called ΜΑΤΕΡΕΣ ΚΑΙ ΚΟΥΡΑΙ ΤΟΥ ΑΠΟΛΛΟΝΟΣ ; titles, for which neither M. Barthelemi, nor the author of the *Recherches*, &c. have been able to produce any authority (2), though they feem both to have wandered over the pages of every book extant in the Greek language. The latter has, however, incautioufly fuggefted the correfpondent titles in the modern French convents of nuns, which afford a clear and undoubted illuftration.—LES MERES ET LES FILLES DU BON DIEU were familiar to Fourmont's mind ; and he not only adopted the idea for his antient IKTERKERATEANS, but, by a refinement of inconfiftency and abfurdity, made them exprefs it in all the crudity of its native idiom.

In reading the names we find other peculiarities of idiom not lefs extraordinary, fuch as ΑΡΙΣΕΤΑΝΔΕΡΟ, ΑΡΙΣΕΤΟΜΑΚΟ, ΚΑΛΙΚΕΡΑΤΟ, ΣΕΚΕΠΑΟ, ΣΕΚΟΛΑ, ΣΕΚΙΛΟ, and ΣΕΚΕΝΟΜΑ ; which, I fuppofe, are intended as a fort of Hebræifms, modelled upon the fame plan as IKTEPKEPATEEΣ for IKTEPKPATEEΣ ; thefe names being the genitive cafes, according to M. Fourmont's declenfion, of words, which, in ordinary Greek, we fhould write ΑΡΙΣΤΑΝΔΡΟΣ, ΑΡΙΣΤΟΜΑΧΟΣ, ΚΑΛΛΙΚΡΑΤΗΣ, ΣΚΕΠΑΣ, ΣΚΟΛΑΣ, ΣΚΙΛΛΟΣ, and ΣΚΗΝΟΜΑΣ. This learned gentleman had, it feems, received as incontrovertible truths, the wild opinions, or, as Lennep calls them, the *fplendida deliramenta*, of thofe Criticks, who, foon after the revival of literature, endeavoured to deduce the Greek from the Hebrew, and other oriental roots. He alfo knew from Jofephus (3), that the Lacedæmonians and Jews looked upon themfelves as fprung from a common ftock, and clofely allied by the ties of confanguinity ; whence he naturally concluded that Hebræifms would be more likely to occur in the writings of that people than in thofe of any other

(1) See Pl. III. Fig. 2, l. 7.

(2) See le jeune Anacharfis, vol. I. p. 509, 4to ed.; Recherches fur les Arts de la Grèce, vol. II. p. 251.

(3) Antiq. Jud. Lib. XII. C V. & Lib. XIII. C. IX.; and Meurf. Mifcell. Lacon. Lib. I. C. VII.

Greeks ;

Greeks; and it muſt be owned that, in theſe inſcriptions, he has given them a large ſhare, ſo as utterly to ſubvert the analogy of their own language. Unfortunately, however, the Hebræiſms which he has attributed to theſe fabulous chiefs of the Peloponneſus, who lived (if they lived at all) fifteen centuries before the Chriſtian æra, are the Hebræiſms of the Maſſorethic criticks, who regulated the pronunciation of that language, by adding the vowel points to the text of the Bible, ten centuries after it. The flexions of theſe words are not leſs whimſical and extravagant than their conſtruction. ΣΕΚΕΠΑΟ is terminated according to the old Æolic, or (what is the ſame) the very antient Doric; but ΣΕΚΕΛΑ and ΣΕΚΕΝΟΜΑ are, according to the later Doric, which was either poſterior to Homer, or not known in the country where he compoſed, as no inſtance of it occurs in either of his poems. Theſe names, in the inſcription, are immediately ſubſequent one to the other (1), ſo that the variation could not be intended to mark any revolution, as ſome other changes of orthography are, which will be duly conſidered. ΚΑΛΙΚΕΡΑΤΟ would have remained inexplicable to me had not the author of the *Recherches* expoſed the blunder by participating it. The genitives ΗΕΡΜΟΚΡΑΤΟΣ and ΠΡΟΚΟΝΕΣΙΟ, in the Sigèan Inſcription, he ſays, are alike abbreviations or corruptions of the regular genitive termination in -ΟΥ (2); by which it ſeems that this ingenious author (who has certainly ſhewn great acuteneſs and ſagacity in explaining monuments of art) took his notions of the declenſions from Fourmont's inſcriptions, who has confounded the two claſſes of nouns terminating in -ΗΣ, which are uſually, but improperly, called ſimple and contracted, for both are alike contracted, though the primitive extended forms of the oblique caſes are leſs frequent in the firſt than the ſecond. As imitators generally copy their originals in an inverſe ratio of their merit, that is, by adding as much to their faults as they loſe of their merits, the author of the *Recherches* has added another claſs of nouns, namely, the adjectives in -ΟΣ, to ſwell the confuſion. Fourmont having ſeen that names compoſed of ΚΡΙΤΗΣ formed their common genitives in -ΟΥ, and that this diphthong was repreſented in very antient inſcriptions by the ſingle Ο, concluded that words compoſed of ΚΡΑΤΗΣ

(1) See Pl. IV. l. 13 & 14.   (2) Vol. II. p. 213 & 223.

were

were liable to the fame variation, and therefore wrote ΚΑΛΙΚΕΡΑΤΟ inſtead of ΚΑΛΙΚΡΑΤΕΟΣ, ΚΑΛΙΚΡΑΤΟΥΣ, or ΚΑΛΙΚΡΑΤΟΣ, either of which would have been Greek. This error is ſo groſs, that, were it not perſevered in through the remaining inſcriptions, and illuſtrated by Meſſrs. Barthelemi and D'Hancarville, I ſhould have ſuppoſed it to be an error of the engraver: but we have ΕΥΡΙΚΡΑΤΕΟ, ΑΛΚΑΜΕΝΕΟ, and ΚΛΕΟΜΕΝΕΩ, all upon the ſame principle, for ΕΥΡΥΚΡΑΤΕΟΣ, ΑΛΚΑΜΕ-ΝΕΟΣ, and ΚΛΕΟΜΕΝΕΩΣ.

Nothing expoſes ignorance ſo effectually as an unſucceſsful attempt at ſcientific accuracy. To mark the period of the Dorian invaſion under the Heraclidæ, the terminations of the names of the prieſteſſes are changed, from what Fourmont thought Æolic or Ionic, to Doric. Hence ΑΜΥ-ΜΟΝΕΕ, in the beginning of the inſcription, becomes ΑΜΥΜΟΝΑ after-wards; but the ending of feminine names in two Epſilons inſtead of an Eta is unauthoriſed by any antient monument, and expreſsly contradicted by a paſſage of Plato (1). Neither would this orthography, if juſtified, exhibit the dialect of the antient Laconians, which muſt have been the old Æolic; for Strabo expreſsly tells us, that the fugitives, who quitted the Peloponneſus under the deſcendants of Agamemnon, when invaded by the Dorians, were the founders of the firſt Æolian colonies in Aſia (2).

M. Barthelemi, the editor of this Amyclæan Chronicle, thinks that the beginning of it, comprehending the names of the firſt ten prieſteſſes, has been renewed like the ſecond Sigèan inſcription, but that all the other names, together with the dates of their adminiſtration, were inſerted in order as they ſucceeded to each other; ſo that this chronicle, when entire, muſt have given the dates of all the great events of the fabulous Hiſtory of Greece; for as Laodamia, the daughter of Amyclas, is the third prieſteſs on the liſt, the time of his reign muſt have been correctly aſcertained, and, of courſe, that of his immediate progenitors, Lacedæmon and Eurotas. This would have led to a knowledge of the time of Cadmus's arrival into Greece, of the ſieges of Thebes and Ilios, of the return of the Heraclidæ, and all the other diſtinguiſhed events of poetical tradition, the dates of which none of the great writers of antiquity could fix with any degree of

(1) Ου γαρ Η εχρωμεθα, αλλα Ε το σαλαιον. Cratyl.   (2) Lib. XIII. p. 872.

probability.

probability. This monument, therefore, though exifting (if it exifted at all) in one of the moft celebrated temples, and moft frequented provinces, of Greece, muft have efcaped the notice of all the inquifitive travellers and diligent Antiquaries, who, during feveral fucceffive ages, endeavoured to rectify antient chronology.

I know that arguments fimilar to thefe have been urged againft the authenticity of the Parian or Arundelian Chronicle; a monument, which the furface alone proves to be undoubtedly antient; for no chemical procefs can produce the ftains, corrofions, and calcareous concretions, which mark that marble. It muft be remembered, however, that this Chronicle contains only the private opinion of one of thefe conjectural chronologers, and probably of one not in the higheft repute; wherefore, we need not wonder that it is not cited by any antient author. But the Amyclæan Chronicle, if genuine, muft have afforded undoubted evidence, as far as it went; for though the events which it directly afcertained might have been but few, yet thefe few would have ferved as points of obfervation, from which the bearings and diftances of many others might have been difcovered. In its prefent ftate, the Abbé Barthelemi has afferted that it can be of no fervice to chronology; but M. D'Hancarville has thought differently, and, in a long Commentary upon it, proved that it fixes the reigns of the fabulous kings of Lacedæmon to the period in which Lydiat and Marfham, after the Parian Chronicle, had placed them (1); as, indeed, it naturally would do, it having been fabricated from their writings, and thofe of Cragius and Meurfius.

According to this calculation, Eurotas and Lacedæmon were contemporaries with Cadmus, to whom general tradition has attributed the introduction of letters into Greeee (2). If this tradition be well-founded, Eurotas could have written in no other character than the Phœnician, fuch as we have ftill upon the very antient coins of that people, and their colonies in Africa, Spain, and Sicily. Thefe characters, as is well known, were fixteen in number, written from right to left, and moft of them very different in form from thofe of the Greeks (3). Herodotus, however, obferves, that the Cadmean letters upon a tripod dedicated by Laius, the

(1) Recherches fur les Arts, &c. vol. II.   (2) Ibid. Lib. II. C. II. p. 333.
(3) See Dutens, Differt. fur les Medailles Phœnic. & Paleographie numifmatique.

father

father of OEdipus, which he faw at Thebes, differed but little from the Ionian (1): but whether the letters were changed between the age of Cadmus and that of Laius, or whether the infcription fhewn to the Hiftorian was a forgery, is uncertain. The Ionian letters on the medals and other monuments of his age, now extant, are evidently very different from the Phœnician; and as for thofe upon the temple of Oga, they differ effentially from both, being written from left to right, and having the Omicron triangular like the Delta, and the Rho like the Alpha (2), only turned the other way; which are forms alike unknown to the Phœnician and Ionian alphabets. The other letters, both in this Infcription and the Chronicle, are like the Ionian fantaftically diftorted.

I am willing, however, to abandon this ftrong argument againft the authenticity of thefe monuments, and to admit that letters were known in Greece before the introduction of the Phœnician alphabet by Cadmus; for which my principal reafon is, that the firft piratical fettlers, who brought letters from Greece into Italy, brought an alphabet much lefs perfect, and therefore, probably, more antient, than the Cadmèan. That of the Eugubian Tablet contains only twelve fingle letters, unlefs the Vau is to be reckoned diftinct from the U, with which Gori joins it, as being the afpirated U (3). Thefe are, probably, the original Pelafgian letters, as firft brought into Italy; for, without admitting the conjecture of Gori, that this infcription was engraved two generations before the Trojan war, we may fafely allow it to be more antient than any other written monument extant.

The Pelafgians are faid to have been the firft colonifts who fettled in Italy after the Tyrrhenians (4); and, according to Pliny, brought letters into Latium (5). In this, however, he feems to have been miftaken, for the Latin letters, as well as language, are clearly derived from the Æolian or Arcadian (6), which were nearly the fame as the Cadmèan, and had feveral characters of which the Pelafgian alphabet of the Eugubian Tablet is deftitute. There is, however, a refemblance between the forms of the reft, from which we may infer that they were originally the fame, and

(1) Lib. V. C. LVII.   (2) See Pl. III. Fig. 1.   (3) Proleg. ad Tab. Etrufc.
(4) Dionyf. περιηγ. Vf. 347.   (5) Hift. Nat. Lib. VII. C. LVI.
(6) See Quintil. Lib. I. C. VI. & Corinth. περι διαλεκτων.

only

only varied as they advanced in improvement (1). The Latin are faid to have been introduced by Evander from the Peloponnefus about the time of the Trojan war (2), and were, without doubt, fuch as were in ufe in that country in that age. Their number was then fmall; but the Romans continued to add to them until they produced the alphabet now chiefly prevalent in Europe. The Pelafgian, probably, came into the parts of Italy weft of the Tyber at a much earlier period. The Eugubian Tablet has no B, G, D, or O; the three firft being included in the correfpondent mutes of the fame organs, and the laft in the U, which being employed as a confonant, or rather afpirate, formed the Pelafgian *Vau*, the Roman V, and our W (3). This letter is generally called the Phœnician *Vau*; but, I believe, it is not to be found upon any authentic monument of that people; whereas in the Pelafgian and Etrufcan infcriptions it occurs perpetually.

Whether thefe antient nations received their letters from the Phœnicians at a period anterior to the expedition of Cadmus, or whether both the Phœnicians and Pelafgians received them from the Affyrians (whom Pliny mentions as the inventors of writing (4)), or from fome people ftill more antient, is impoffible now even to conjecture. The Pelafgians appear unqueftionably to have been the firft people of Europe among whom arts and letters were at all cultivated (5); for as to the traditions mentioned by Strabo, of the antient fplendour and civilization of fome nations in Spain, they are unfupported by the teftimony of any exifting monuments, and, therefore, probably fabulous (6). The Athenians derived their origin from the Pelafgians (7), who are faid, by Ephorus, to have founded the Oracle of Dodona (8), the moft antient in Greece; and which, by the account given of it by Homer, feems to have refembled thofe of the Druids (9). They were fpread over all Greece, and part of Afia; and it is probable that moft of the tribes, mentioned by Strabo and Paufanias, as formerly occupying different parts of the Peloponnefus, were only clans of this people; for, according to Ephorus, the whole peninfula was antiently called *Pe-*

(1) See Gori in l. c. (2) Dionyf. Halic. Antiq. Rom. lib. I.
(3) See Fofter on Accent and Quantity, c. IV. (4) Hift. Nat. l. VII. c. LVI.
(5) See Strab. lib. VII. (6) Ibid. lib. III. (7) Herodot. l. VIII. c. XLIV.
(8) Apud Strab. lib. VII. (9) Il. п. 234.

R *lafgia;*

lafgia; and we know that the fame language prevailed and continued through every part of it until the Ionian and Dorian invafions (1). They came into Italy from thence (2); but at what time cannot be afcertained. It was, however, between the arrival of the Tyrrhenians and that of Evander; but when the Tyrrhenians arrived is quite uncertain, for Dionyfius of Halicarnaffus very prudently reje&s the ftory of Tyrrhenus, the grandfon of Hercules (3), whom we may fafely rank among thofe imaginary heroes, who were called into being to account for the name of a country; and, I believe, if we add Eurotas, Lacedæmon, and Amyclas, to the fame lift, we fhall do perfe&ly right, notwithftanding the pretended coæval infcriptions which bear their names. At all events, the expedition of the Pelafgians could not have been anterior to the period in which thefe princes are fuppofed to have reigned; for the Grecian fea was then, and for a long time after, poffeffed by the Phœnician and Carian pirates, who, having fettlements on moft of the adjoining iflands, muft have reftrained the inhabitants of the Continent from making any confiderable naval expeditions (4).

Minos, King of Crete, was the firft of the Greeks who acquired a naval power, and opened the fea for his countrymen, by expelling the Phœnicians and Carians from the iflands. They then became pirates in their turn, and extended their predatory expeditions all along the coafts of Afia and Italy (5). Minos, according to Homer, was two generations before the Trojan war, his grandfon Idomeneus having been a leader in it; but, as he was then advanced in age, we may, in calculating, allow Minos to have been three generations before the war, which will ftill place him four generations later than the fabulous king Eurotas.

If the Pelafgians could not have come from the Peloponnefus into Tufcany before the fuppofed time of Eurotas, it naturally follows, that the alphabet which they brought with them could not be more antient and imperfe& than that then in ufe there. But how does this accord with the votive infcription attributed to him, where we find the Γ in the common Ionian form (which is that of the Pelafgian Π), and the O diftorted into the form of the Δ (6), whilft neither of thefe letters exift in the Eugubian

(1) Strab. lib. VIII.   (2) Dĭonyf. περιηγ. 348.   (3) Antiq. Rom. lib. I.
(4) Thucyd. lib. I.   (5) Ibid.   (6) See Pl. III. Fig. I.

6   infcription?

Infcription ? The reft are Ionian characters varioufly diftorted, and written from left to right; whereas both the Phœnicians and Pelafgians wrote from right to left.

Thefe infcriptions, therefore, appear to be falfe, whichever hypothefis we adopt, that of the Cadmèan being the primitive alphabet of Greece, or that of the Pelafgian having preceeded it.

The next monument that offers itfelf to our conſideration is one of the votive fhields abovementioned, upon which is infcribed the pedigree of Teleclus, King of Sparta, who is faid to have reigned early in the eighth century before the Chriftian æra (1). This pedigree is taken exactly from Meurfius (2), except a trifling variation in the fpelling, fuch as a K for a X in the name ΑΡΧΕΛΑΟΣ. Where the author found fuch a genitive cafe as ΛΑΒΟΤΑΣ is difficult to guefs, unlefs he copied fome error of the prefs, as I am inclined to fufpect. The word ΒΑΓΟΣ for ΑΓΟΣ, *a leader*, he might have got from Cragius or Meurfius, who took it from an erroneous or interpolated paffage of Hefychius, who firft explains it to be κλασμα αρτης, μαζης, *a fragment of a loaf or cake*, which is right; for αγω or αγ-νυμι, *to break*, was, as before obferved, written with the F, which the Laconians changed to a B. He afterwards adds και βασιλευς και ϛρατιωπης, *and a king and a common foldier*, which is certainly erroneous, and probably interpolated; for αγω, *to lead*, appears always to have been begun with a vowel, and many of the explanations in Hefychius are of later date than the original work, and of no authority. Fourmont, however, was not fkilled in criticifm, and therefore took every thing for granted which he found in the Dictionary, that common oracle of dunces.

The next infcriptions, according to the order of their pretended dates, are two tables, containing lifts of the kings, fenators, and magiftrates, of Sparta, during the celebrated Meffenian war, which employed the arms of that Republick during a confiderable part of the eighth century before the Chriftian æra (3). To commemorate the events of this war, M. Fourmont and his commentators think thefe infcriptions were engraved; and indeed we know of no other purpofes for which they could have been engraved. There is, however, no mention of the war, or any thing elfe in them, but merely

(1) See Pl. V.   (2) Laconic. in Græc. Thef. Antiq.
(3) See Pl. VI. & VII

                   the

the titles and names of magistrates, the former all taken from Cragius and Meursius. As an excuse for this peculiarity, he cites the known taciturnity and concisenefs of the Lacedæmonians; not recollecting that this concisenefs confisted in expressing a great deal of meaning in a very few words, and not in employing many words to exprefs no meaning, which is the cafe with thefe infcriptions; for, had there been no other memorials of the war, no one could have guefsed that they had related to it; or, indeed, that it had ever exifted. Many of the magiftrates could not have had any fhare in it, as their offices were merely civil; neither is it probable that the faftidious modefty of the Lacedæmonians would have recorded the names of thofe who had; fince they did not condefcend to mention a fingle individual, not even Leonidas himfelf, in the infcription which recorded their noble facrifice at Thermopolæ.

In the titles of magiftrates infcribed, we find all the miftakes of Cragius and Meurfius exactly followed, fome of which are confiderable. The former, in fpeaking of the Ἁρμοϛαι, or *regulators*, had afferted, that they were called Ἁρμοϛηρες by Hefychius (1), whence we find ΑΡΜΟΣΤΕΡΕΣ in the infcription: but the words of Hefychius are, Ἁρμοϛης. ὁ πεμπομενος επιμελητης εις ὑπηκοον πολιν. και λιθοι δυο προς τω αυτω της φλιας τιθεμενοι Ἁρμοϛηρες λεγονται. The latter part of this paffage is evidently corrupt, and in its prefent ftate conveys no meaning; but if, inftead of αυτω, we read ὐδω, as has been propofed, the fenfe will be, *two ftones adapted to the foundation of the door-cafe are called* Ἁρμοϛηρες. The provincial governors of the Lacedæmonians are always called Ἁρμοϛαι; but it does not appear that there were ever any regular domeftic magiftrates of this kind; though there might have been fuch occafionally elected to controul private manners. Thefe, however, were probably called Ἁρμοσυνοι, a title of the fame import; which, Hefychius fays, belonged to certain magiftrates of Sparta, chofen to regulate the conduct of the women. Fourmont, however, who fearched no farther than Cragius, has put thefe down as another clafs of regular magiftrates; and, what is more extraordinary, put them down in a record intended to commemorate a war. In fome inftances he does not appear to have read more of his compilers than the heads of their chapters;

(1) De Rep. Lacon. lib. II. c. XIII.

T   otherwife

otherwife he would not have given us fuch a magiftrate as the BOΥΑΓΟΡ, who, according to all accounts, was only the head-boy of each clafs or company of the youths who were educated by the State. There were of courfe feveral of them at the fame time; and as the ϖαιδονομος, or public tutor (whofe office Fourmont meant to fignify, but miftook the title), could not attend perfonally to all, he made thefe leading youths his depu-ties. That an antient Lacedæmonian fhould have committed fuch a blun-der as this, is as improbable as that an Etonian fhould miftake PROPOSTOR for PPOVOST.

Another extraordinary magiftrate in thefe infcriptions is the ANIOKA-PATHP; the ἡνιοχαρατης, or *public riding-mafter*, of Hefychius. The word is evidently corrupt, and fhould be either ἡνιοκρατης or ἡνιοχαρτης, probably the latter from ἡνιον, εχω, and αρω, as has been conjectured. The Dorians would naturally have begun it with the A; but that A would, in the time of Theopompus and Polydorus, have been preceeded by the afpirate Ϝ or H in this title, as well as thofe of the ἁρμοϛαι and ἁρμοσυνοι. The Digamma would probably have been alfo employed, fo that the regular word would have been ϜΑΝΙΟΧϜΑΡΤΗΣ. The Lacedæmonians did, indeed, as before obferved, employ the P for the Σ; but they probably did it regularly, and not capricioufly, as it appears in the infcriptions, and as Fourmont found it in the compilations of Cragius and Meurfius, gleaned from different au-thors, of different ages, and different dialects. ΒΑΓΟΣ ought to have been written ΑΓΟΡ or ΒΟΥΑΓΟΡ, ΒΟΥΒΑΓΟΣ; ΑΓΕΣΙΛΑΟΣ, ΒΑΓΕΣΙΛΑΟΣ; &c. but Fourmont has written the names as he found them in the books which he confulted, without confidering this inconfiftency. Even the name of the fame perfon is written in the ordinary manner, ΘΕΟΠΟΜ-ΠΟΣ, in the one infcription, and half Laconized to ΣΙΟΠΟΜΠΟΣ in the other. The name ΛΕΟ is even Latinized; for, I believe, in every dialect of the Greek it muft have been ΛΕΩΝ or ΛΕΟΝ.

The I for the Υ was employed in fome inftances by the Lacedæmonians, as Fourmont had probably heard; whence we have fuch words in the in-fcriptions as ΝΟΜΟΦΙΛΑΚΕΣ and ΕΥΡΙΚΡΑΤΕΟ, which I fhould have fufpected to be errors of the engraver or copyift, had not the termination of the latter made even a groffer blunder perfectly confiftent with the learning and fagacity of the author. This termination is evidently a fyftematic, and

not

not an accidental, error, as it is perfevered in through many words, and formally illuftrated and defended by Meffrs. Barthelemi and D'Hancarville; the firft of whom very gravely tells us that it is Doric; and the latter, to corroborate his affertion, cites the word ἙΡΜΕΩ from Theocritus, of whofe Doricifms he had of courfe heard. That he was any otherwife acquainted with them I cannot but doubt, fince the poem, which he has cited to illuftrate the peculiarities of that dialect, has not a fingle inftance of it, being wholly compofed in the common poetic language formed upon that of Homer and Hefiod. Even if it had, the word adduced would not be relevant, it being of a different clafs or declenfion, fuch as, in the Æolic and Doric dialects, has the nominative in -A and -AΣ, and the genitive in -AFO, -AO, and -A; and in the Ionic and Attic, the nominative in -HΣ, and the genitive in -EO, -EΩ, and -OΥ; whereas the words alluded to in the infcriptions have the nominative in -HΣ through all the dialects, and the genitive in -EOΣ, -OΣ, or -OΥΣ, according as local cuftom had contracted or corrupted it; but to omit the Σ would be to fubvert all analogy of fpeech (1).

The form of thefe infcriptions is not lefs extraordinary than the fubftance of them, they being both figned by the public fecretary, and authenticated by the public feal (2), upon which is engraved the name ΛΑΚΕΔΑΙΜΟΝ. That the public fcribe or fecretary fhould fign a public record or decree for putting up an infcription is very natural; but that he fhould think it neceffary to put his fignature to the ftone itfelf, feems wholly inconfiftent with the manners of the Lacedæmonians, or, indeed, of any other people poffeffed of common-fenfe: but, even if they had been guilty of fuch an abfurdity, they would not have done it in the form here employed; for the officers of the public affemblies in the States of Greece did nor authorife their fignatures, by adding the mere title of an office to the name of him who bore it, but by ufing a verb which expreffed, not only the office, but the actual exertion of it at the time of figning the record on which it appeared. Thus, in the infcription of Minerva Polias, we have ΝΙΚΟΦΑΝΕΣ ΜΑΡΑΘΟΝΙΟΣ ΠΡΟΤΟΣ ΕΓΡΑΜΑΤΕΥΣΕΝ, and, in the burlefque imitation of the proceedings of a public affembly, acted

(1) Τῆς δὲ πεμπτης ἰδιον, το την γενικην των ἐνικων εις -ΟΣ ἐχειν. Theod. Gaz. lib. II.
(2) See Pl. XI. and VII.

by

by the women in one of Ariftophanes's comedies, the herald proclaims the decree of a council, in which ΤΙΜΟΚΛΕΙ' ΕΠΕΣΤΑΤΕΙ, ΛΥΣΙΛΛ' ΕΓΡΑΜΜΑΤΕΥΕΝ, ΕΙΠΕ ΣΩΣΤΡΑΤΗ. *Timoclea prefied, Lufilla acted as fecretary, and Softrata made the motion, which had been voted* (1).

The putting the public feal to a ftone, in order to authenticate it, feems ftill more abfurd than the having it fubfcribed by the public fecretary; but neverthelefs, M. Fourmont affures us, that he found every day at Lacedæmon infcriptions with the names of the kings and magiftrates, and the feal affixed to them. The author of the *Recherches*, indeed, obferving that no other traveller or Antiquary had been fo fortunate as to find a fingle inftance of it in any other part of the world, fuddenly tranfmutes the feal to a buckler, notwithftanding the diffimilarity of its form to thofe publifhed by Fourmont, and the impoffibility of affigning any reafon for its being introduced. It is rather wonderful that he did not turn it into a cart-wheel, to which it has fome refemblance, and which, being the emblem of Fortune, might, by a little of his ingenuity, have been explained to fignify the various fortunes of the war; which thefe infcriptions are fuppofed to commemorate becaufe they fay nothing of it. Fourmont, without doubt, would have made them fpeak very plainly of it, had not the fame caufe deterred him which prevented the appearance of the laws of Solon, namely, the confcioufnefs of his own weaknefs, which, however capable he might think it of forging titles and proper names (and fuch are all the infcriptions publifhed), fhrunk from the encounter of grammatical accuracy, to which any thing like compofition would have expofed him.

The next monument to be confidered is another of the votive fhields abovementioned, which is infcribed with the name of Anaxidamus, the fon of Zeuxidamus, who reigned at Sparta towards the clofe of the eighth century before the Chriftian æra (2). Underneath, upon the bafe, is his

(1) Thefmophor. Vf. 372. The reader may obferve in thefe two quotations the nice employment of the tenfes. The verb in the infcription, being merely to *commemorate*, is in the Aorift; but in the decree, it being to *authenticate*, it is in the paft imperfect. The *action*, when *commemorated*, was *completely paft*; but when *employed to authenticate, ftill exifting*, though *paft* with reference to the *promulgation* of the *act authenticated*.

(2) See Pl. VIII.

pedigree; which, differing entirely from that given by Meurſius from Pauſanias, has afforded matter of much triumph to the defender of theſe inſcriptions. The difference, however, proceeds merely from a blunder of Fourmont, who, caſting his eye careleſsly over the prolix pages of Meurſius, and obſerving the name of Anaxidamus, the ſon of Zeuxidamus, to follow thoſe of Eurycrates and Anaxander in the catalogue of the Agidæ, and not attending to the words *ex altera familiâ*, confounded the two royal houſes that reigned together, and transformed the partners of Archidamus into anceſtors. Hence the pedigree is, *Archidamus, the ſon of Zeuxidamus, the ſon of Anaxander, the ſon Eurycrates*; whereas, according to all antient authors who have ſpoken of theſe princes, Zeuxidamus and Anaxidamus were the ſon and grandſon of Theopompus, who were of the houſe of the Proclidæ; and Eurycrates and Anaxander, their contemporaries, the ſon and grandſon of Polydorus, who was of the Agidæ (1).

The peculiarities in the word ΕΥΡΙΚΡΑΤΕΟ have been already noticed, and, I believe, are wholly unjuſtified by antient authority. That of the Δ for the Z in ΔΕΥΚΣΙΔΑΜΟ is, however, authoriſed by the Zanclèan medals, from which Fourmont undoubtedly took it. He did not, however, recollect that the Zanclèans were an Ionian colony, whoſe dialect favoured the eliſion of the Σ; whereas the Dorians would certainly, in that age, have prefixed it to the Δ, as they always did to expreſs the Z of the other Greeks. The Ξ too in this name muſt have been compoſed of the Γ and Σ, and of the Κ and Σ, as it is derived from ΖΕΥΓΣΩ, the regular future of the verb ΖΕΥΓΩ, otherwiſe written ΖΕΥΓΝΥΜΙ.

The foxes and ſerpent, repreſented on this ſhield, allude to a ſilly fiction, probably the invention of later times, concerning a public ſacrifice, at which theſe animals appeared miraculouſly upon the reſpective altars of the Meſſenians and Lacedæmonians, to prognoſticate the event of the war in which they were engaged (2).

The laſt of theſe inſcriptions is alſo upon a votive buckler and its baſe, which contain the name of the city Lacedæmon, and of its king Archidamus, the ſon of the great Ageſilaus (3). This prince was killed near Tarentum in the hundred and ſixth Olympiad (4), about three hundred and

---

(1) See Meurſ. Reg. Lacon. c. XI. and XVII.   (2) See Apoll. lib. II. ſ. V.
(3) See Pl. IX.   (4) Pauſan. lib. III. p. 230.

fifty-five years before the Chriſtian æra; ſo that he flouriſhed when arts and letters were in the higheſt ſtate of perfection: yet the form, both of the ſhield and the letters, is as rude and barbarous as any of the others. The only eſſential peculiarity, however, conſiſts in the OO for the Ω in the word ΛΑΚΕΛΑΙΜΟΟΝ, which, I believe, cannot be juſtified either by authority or etymology in words of this claſs.

I ſhall now truſt to the candour of the reader to decide whether or not I have judged right in rejecting the authority of theſe inſcriptions. When I look them over, I am inclined to think that I have ſaid more than enough to detect them; but when I conſider the pertinacious obſtinacy with which forgeries, equally bungling, have been defended againſt perſons of ſo much greater learning and ability (1), and the daring confidence with which others, long ſince detected and exploded, have lately been adduced as authentic compoſitions of remote antiquity, to ſupport the wild paradoxes of viſionary theoriſts(2), I am apprehenſive that I have ſaid too little.

It has been my endeavour to avoid any inſulting reflexions upon the conduct of thoſe learned perſons who have quoted theſe inſcriptions as authentic ſources of important information; for, though it is the duty of every impartial inveſtigator of truth to expoſe fraud and detect error whereever he can find it, yet if he can accompliſh his end without wounding the feelings of any man, or the reputation of any writer, his merit will be the greater. Fraud, indeed, deſerves no favour, being little leſs criminal when gratifying vanity than when gratifying avarice (3); but of this I am inclined to acquit every one, in the preſent inſtance, except the original author, Fourmont, whoſe want of genius and ability will, I flatter myſelf, never be again urged as a proof of his ſincerity; for that which excites our

(1) See the controverſies concerning Phalaris, &c.

(2) See *Divine Legation of Moſes demonſtrated*, and *new Syſtem of antient Mythology*; particularly the latter, vol. II. p. 229, and vol. III. p. 77, of the firſt edition. The former does indeed tell us, that his Letter of Alexander has been ſuſpected, and offers the beſt arguments that he could find in its defence: but the latter boldly quotes the bungling and long-exploded forgeries of the ſecond century of the Chriſtian æra as the certain and unſuſpected compoſitions of remote antiquity; though he, as well as every other ſcholar, muſt have known that they were fraudulent, and could only hope to avoid detection by the obſcurity into which they are deſervedly fallen.

(3) This conſideration will excuſe the preceeding reference.

S   admiration

admiration at his forgeries, is not the ability employed in compofing them, but the impudence exerted in publifhing them; and this is a quality which generally prevails in an inverfe ratio with the others.

That the authors of the *Jeune Anacharfis*, and the *Recherches fur les Arts*, fhould, by being the dupes of the impofture, become partakers in it, is extremely to be regretted, as both thefe learned writers have rendered confiderable fervices to polite literature, and are, I believe, both alike incapable of any intentional guilt of this kind.

The former is a perfon of a very elegant mind, and has produced the only work extant upon the fubject of antiquities that can boaft of any acquaintance with the Graces. The fcholar and philofopher may indeed be diffatisfied with many parts of his work; but the mifcellaneous reader will be every where amufed with variety, and foothed with urbanity, without having his underftanding too much fatigued with deep refearches, or ftrained by long and complicated deductions. He will find himfelf led gradually over the wide and variegated furface of Grecian literature; but as his guide never analyfed the foil, nor examined the productions, he can only fhow him general forms, and teach him unconnected facts; the firft of which intereft but little, unlefs we know their mutual bearings and particular relations to each other; and the fecond not at all, unlefs we know the fprings which gave rife to them, and the ends to which they are directed.

The author of the *Recherches* dived deep into the matter, which he profeffedly undertook to difcufs; and, had he confined his enquiries to that, he would have done honour to himfelf and fervice to the publick; for many of his explanations of the monuments of antient art fhow a degree of acutenefs and fagacity almoft unparalleled. But when he invades the province of grammarians, and endeavours to explain antient words, he almoft makes us doubt whether or not he continued to poffefs the fame faculties, fo totally is he changed by changing his fubject.

SECTION

S E C T I O N VII.

THE Decree of the Lacedæmonians against Timotheus, as it is pre-
served in Glareanus's edition of Boethius *de Musicâ* (lib. I. c. I.), is,
with marginal variations, as follows:

Ἐπεὶ δὲ Τιμόθεορ ὁ Μιλέσιορ παραγιμενορ ἐν τὰν¹ ἀμέτέραν πόλιν, τὰν παλαιαν μολπὴν ἀτιμασας. χ τὰν δια πᾶν² ἐπ]ὰ χορδᾶν
κιθαρίζει, ἀποςρεφόμενορ πολυφωνίαν εἰσάγων³, λυμαίνεται τὰρ
ακοὰρ τῶν νέων διά τε τὰρ πολυχορδᾶρ, χ τάρ καινο]άταρ τύτων⁴
μέλεορ ἄγεννε, χ ποικίλαν ἀντὶ ἀπλόαν, χ τεταγμέναν ἀμφιαῦῖεν
μολπὴν ἐπὶ χρώμαϊορ συνείςαμεν⁵ τύτυ μέλεορ διὰςασιν. Αντι γὰρ
Εναρμονίω ποιὰν ἀνῂςρεφον ἀμοιϐᾶν. Παρακαλαθεὶς δὲ ἐν τόν ἀγῶνα
τὰρ Ελευσινίαρ Δαμαΐορορ⁶ ἄιςχορ⁷ διεφημίζαϊο τὰν τῷ μυθῷ κίδνησιν.
Τὰν γὰρ Σεμέλα ὀδύναν ὐκ ἐνδέκατορ Νέορ διδαχὴν ἐδίδαξε. Εἶτα
περὶ τύτων τὸν βασιλέαν⁸ χ τὸν ῥῇϊορορ⁹ μεμψαϊαι Τιμόθεον. Επα-
ναϊίθεϊαι δὲ χ τὰν ἔνδεκα χόρδαν ἐκτανώρ τὰρ¹⁰ περιαςᾶρ¹¹, ἐπειλει-
πόμενορ τὰν ἐπἰάχορδον ἄςορ. Τὸ γάρ πόλιορ βαρορ¹² ἄπιον τε-
τάρϐηϊαι ες τὰν Σπαϊὰν¹³ ἐπιφὲρειν: Τιθῶν¹⁴ μὴ καλῶν νῆτῶν, μή-
ποϊε ταρᾶτῂϊαι κλέορ ἀγόρων¹⁵.

¹Ἐλθὼν ²τὰν
³ῥιπῶν ⁴τῦτο
⁵συνιςάμεϑορ
⁶Δαμαῖος
⁷ἀπρεπει
⁸τοῦς βασιλέαρ
⁹τῶν ῥητόρων
¹⁰γαρ
¹¹περιταρ
¹²μίαν βαρὺς
¹³Σπαρτῶν
¹⁴τίμὲν
¹⁵ἀγόνϑων

Gronovius first endeavoured seriously to restore it, and, in the Preface to
the fifth volume of his Collection or Greek Antiquities, published it as
follows:

Επειδὴ Τιμόθευρ ὁ Μιλήσιορ παργίμενορ ἐτ τὰν ἀμεϊέραν πόλιν τὰν παλαιὰν μῶαν
ἀτιμάσας δὴ, χ τὰν δια τᾶν ἐπζὰ χορδᾶν κιθάριζιν ἀποςρεφόμενορ, πολύφωνον εἰσά-
γων λυμαίνεϊαι τὰρ ἀκοὰρ τῶρ νέωρ, διάτε τὰρ πολυχορδίαρ χ τὰρ καινίταϊορ τῶ μέλεορ ἀγεννῆ χ ποικίλαν ἀντὶ ἀπλόαρ χ τεταμέναρ ἀμφιέννυϊαι τὰν μῶαν ἐπὶ χρώμα-
τορ συνιστάμενορ τὰν τῶ μέλεορ διασκείαν ἀντὶ τὰρ ἐναρμονίω ποτ τὰν ἀπόςροφον
ἀμοιϐάν· παρακληθεὶς δὲ χ ἐτ τον ἀγῶνα τὰρ Ελευσινίαρ Δάματρορ ἀπρεπῆ λιεσ-

πίυσα,ο ταν τῶ μύθω διασκείαν, ταρ ταρ Σεμέλαρ ὠδῖιαρ ουκ ἐν δίκω ταρ νέωρ δί-
δακκε· διδοκται φᾶν περὶ τύτων ταρ βασιλέαρ, χ̣ ταρ ἐφόρορ μέμψατ]αι Τιμό-
θεος, ἐτ..αγκᾶται δὲ χ̣ ταν ἐνδεκαχορδίαν ἐκταμεῖν ταρ περιτ]ὰρ ὑπολιπόμενον ταρ
ἐπτα· ὅπερ ἕκασ]ορ·τὸ ταρ πόλιορ βάρορ ἱρῶν ἱύλάϚηται ἐτ ταν Σπάρταν ἐπιφέρεν
τε τῶν μὴ καλῶν ἐθᾶν, μή ποτε ταράτ]ηται κλέορ ἀγώνων.

In the year 1777 a more correct copy was published from some Manuscripts at Oxford, accompanied with variations found in other Manuscripts
belonging to that University; and a critical and explanatory Commentary
by the learned and respectable Prelate who published it. This copy, with
the variations, was as follows:

Επειδη[1] ο Τιμοθεορ ο ·Μιλησιορ ϖαργημενορ[2] ετ]αν[3]
αμετεραν ϖολιν ταν ϖαλαιαν[4] μοαν[5] ατιμασδε και ταν
δια ταν επ]αχορδαν κιθαριξιν[6] αποςρεφομενορ ϖολιφωνιαν[7] εισα]ον λιμαινεται[9]·ταρ·ακοαρ τὸν νεον[10] δια τε
ταρ ϖολιχορδιαρ[11] και ταρ κανοταταρ[12] το[13]·μελεορ
αγεννε[14] και ϖοικιταν[15] ἀντι·ἁπλοαρ και·τεταμεναρ
αμφιεννιται[16] ·ταν μοαν επι·χρωματορ[17] ·σινεισταμενορ
ταν το μελεορ διασκεῖν[18] αντι ταρ εναρμονιο ϖοιταν[19]·
αντιστροφον[20] αμοιϚαν. ϖαρακλεθειρ[21] ·δε και ετον
αγονα[22] ταρ ·Ελειϟινιαρ Δαμάτρορ απρεπε[23] διεσκει-
σατο·ταν το·μιτω διασκειαν ταν ταρ Σεμελαρ οδιναρ
κκ ειδικα·ϟορ νεορ διδακκε. Δεδοχθαι[24] φα[25] ϖερι[26]
·τυτοιν·τορ βασιλεαρ και·τορ εφορορ ·μεμψατ]αι[27] Τι-
μοθεεν επανακαται[28] δε κκι ταν ε.δεκα χορδαν εκτα-
μον ταρ ϖε::]αρ υπολιπομενο[29] ταρ επ]α οπορ[30]
εκαστορ το ταρ ϖολιορ Ϛαρορ ϛρεν ευλαϚεται[31] ετ]αν
Σϖαρταν επιφε:..ν[32] τι·τον[33] μὲ[34] καλον νετον μεϖο]ε[35]
ταϟαϟεται[36] κλεϟρ αγοντϟν[37]·

[1] Επι...αν Codd. al. Oxon.
[2] ϖαρατιμιϟορ Cod. Bal. [3] ιν ταν
Codd. al. [4] ϖαλιϟν Codd. al.
[5] μωαρ Codd. al. [6] κιϟαριϟιν Cod.
Bal. κυθαριϟιν Seld. [7] ϖολιφωνιαν
Cod. Magd. [8] εισαγων Magd. ει-
ϟατον al. [9] λυμαινεται Seld. [10] νεων
Magd. [11] ϖολυχορδιαρ Seld. [12] κι-
νοτατορ Magd. [13] τω Magd. [14] α-
τιϟνι al. [15] ϖοικλϟαν Magd. [16] αμ-
φιηννται Seld. αμφιηννυτοι Bodl.
[17] χρωματο; Seld. χρωματορ Bodl. &
·Magd. [18] διασκιιαν·Magd. [19] ϖο-
·ητιαν Bal. ϖοϟαν Magd. ϖο...αϟ
Bodl. [20] αιτισθροϖον Bodl. αιτιϟο-
φον Bal. αϟοϟροφον Seld. [21] ϖαρα-
κλιτιιρ Seld. ϖαρακαιθιιρ Magd.
[22] ατονα. Magd. [23] Seld. & Bal.
ατϟιϟι cæter. [24] Magd. διδοκται.
cæter. [25] φαρ Bodl. [26] ὑϖερ al.
[27] Seld. μιμψαται cæter. [28] ιϟα-
ϟακαϟαι Bal. &c. CCC. [29] ὑϖολι-
ϖωμηνω CCC. ϟλιϖοιϟν al. [30] ϟϟορ
Bodl. & Seld. [31] ϟλαϚιθϟι Bodl.
ελαϚειται Seld. [32] Seld. ϟνϟιϟιν al.
[36] Seld. ταϟαϟιϟϟι Bodl. ταϟαϟϟαι

[33] Bodl. ταϟ Magd. [34] μη Magd. & cæter. [35] Bal. μη ϖοτϟ al.
Bal. [37] αϟϟϟται al. ατϟϟϟν al.

To this the learned Editor, in order to give his reader a more complete
and accurate idea of it, subjoined the following reformed copy, restored to
what he thought its original orthography:

ΕΠΕΙΔΕ

ΕΠΕΙΔΕ ΤΙΜΟΣΙΟΡ ΗΟ ΜΙΛΑΣΙΟΡ ΠΑΡΑΓΙΝΟΜΕΝΟΡ ΕΝ ΤΑΝ ΗΑ-
ΜΕΤΕΡΑΝ ΠΟΛΙΝ ΤΑΝ ΠΑΛΕΑΝ ΜΟΑΝ ΑΤΙΜΑΔΔΕΙ ΚΑΙ ΤΑΝ ΔΙΑ
ΤΑΝ ΗΕΠΤΑΧΟΡΔΑΝ ΚΙΣΑΡΙΤΙΝ ΑΠΟΣΤΡΕΦΟΜΕΝΟΡ ΠΟΛΥΦΟΝΙΑΝ
ΕΙΣΑΓΩΝ ΛΥΜΑΙΝΕΤΑΙ ΤΑΡ ΑΚΟΑΡ ΤΟΝ ΝΕΟΝ, ΔΙΑ ΤΕ ΤΑΡ ΠΟ-
ΛΥΧΟΡΔΙΑΡ ΚΑΙ ΤΑΡ ΚΕΝΟΤΑΤΟΡ ΤΟ ΜΕΛΕΟΡ ΑΓΕΝΝΕ, ΚΑΙ ΠΟ-
ΙΚΙΛΑΝ ΑΝΤΙ ΗΑΠΛΟΑΡ ΚΑΙ ΤΕΤΑΜΕΝΑΡ ΑΜΠΕΝΝΥΤΑΙ ΤΑΝ
ΜΟΑΝ ΕΠΙ ΧΡΟΜΑΤΟΡ ΣΥΝΙΣΤΑΜΕΝΟΡ ΤΑΝ ΤΟ ΜΕΛΕΟΡ ΔΙΑΙΡΕ-
ΣΙΝ ΑΝΤΙ ΤΑΡ ΕΝΑΡΜΟΝΙΑΡ ΠΟΙΟΝ ΑΝΤΙΣΤΡΟΦΟΝ ΑΜΟΙΒΑΝ.
ΠΑΡΑΚΛΑΘΕΙΡ ΔΕ ΚΑΙ ΕΝ ΤΟΝ ΑΓΟΝΑ ΤΑΡ ΕΛΕΥΣΙΝΙΑΡ ΔΑΜΑ-
ΤΡΟΣ ΑΠΡΕΠΕ ΔΙΕΣΚΕΥΑΣΑΤΟ ΤΑΝ ΤΟ ΜΥΣΟ ΔΙΑΣΚΕΥΑΝ ΤΑΝ
ΤΑΡ ΣΕΜΕΛΑΡ ΟΔΙΝΑ ΟΥΚ ΕΝΔΙΚΑ ΤΟΡ ΝΕΟΡ ΕΔΙΔΑΚΣΕ ΔΕΔΟΧ-
ΘΑΙ .. ΠΕΡΙ ΤΟΥΤΟΙΝ ΤΟΡ ΒΑΣΙΛΕΑΡ ΚΑΙ ΤΟΡ ΕΦΟΡΟΡ ΜΕΜΨΑΣ-
ΘΑΙ ΤΙΜΟΣΙΟΝ ΕΠΑΝΑΓΚΑΣΑΙ ΔΕ ΚΑΙ ΤΑΝ ΗΕΝΔΕΚΑ ΧΟΡΔΑΝ ΕΚ-
ΤΑΜΕΝ ΤΑΡ ΠΕΡΙΤΤΑΡ ΥΠΟΛΕΙΠΟΜΕΝΩΝ ΤΑΡ ΗΕΠΤΑ ΗΟΠΟΡ ΗΕ-
ΚΑΣΤΟΡ ΤΟ ΤΑΡ ΠΟΛΙΟΡ ΒΑΡΟΡ ΗΟΡΟΝ ΕΥΛΑΒΕΤΑΙ ΕΝ ΤΑΝ
ΣΠΑΡΤΑΝ ΕΠΙΦΕΡΕΝ ΤΙ ΤΟΝ ΜΕ ΚΑΛΟΝ ΕΣΟΝ ΜΕΠΟΤΕ ΤΑΡΑΤ-
ΤΕΤΑΙ ΚΛΕΟΡ ΑΓΟΝΟΝ.

This, however, only ferves to prove that the learned Prelate did not exactly know the value of his own publication ; for moft of his emendations
are either unneceffary, or tend to the fame end as thofe of the old tranfcribers, that is, to eject every curious provincial peculiarity, not readily
underftood, and to fill its place with a word from the more known dialects. Like other editors, both antient and modern, he found it more eafy
to alter than explain.

The change of the Θ to the Σ is unneceffary ; for, though the Laçedæ-
monians pronounced thefe two dental afpirates in the fame manner, it does
not appear, from any genuine monuments of their writing, that they confounded them in orthography, or expreffed them by one fign, any more
than we do the τ and sh in the words FACTION and FASHION.

The fame may be faid of the change of the Ι for the Υ in all the inftances where this laft vowel is ufually employed ; for Euftathius tells us,
that it was the practice, in the later Doric and Æolic, to put the Ι for the Υ(1);

(1) Ὁι δε νεωτεροι τρεψαντες κατα το δυφρος διφρος, μυσο; μισος, μουσα μοισα, τυπﺍﺎﺎﺎﺎﺍﺍﺎﺎﺎﺎﺎﺍﺍﺍﺍﺍﺍﺍﺍﺍﺍﺍﺍﺍﺍﺍﺍﺍﺍﺍﺍﺍﺍﺍﺍ τυπλοισα,
και ὁσα τοιαυτα δωρικα και αιολικα. p. 1913. l. 32.

                                                                    and

and the uniformity of it in this copy of the Decree fhews that it was intentional.

The inferting the common afpirate too, and not the Digamma, is improper; for both thefe letters were dropt from the alphabet nearly at the fame time, and neither of them occur in infcriptions of fo late a date as this Decree, unlefs indeed it be upon fome coins of Elis, Heraclèa, and Tarentum, the age of which cannot be afcertained, and the columns of Herodes Atticus, written in imitation of the antient orthography (1). It was alfo cuftomary in the antient dialects to drop the afpirate from the confonant, as has been fhewn in the inftances of the Zanclean and Theban medals; whence I have no doubt but that ΜΙΤΟΣ, which occurs (in the genitive cafe) in the manufcripts of the Decree, for ΜΥΟΟΣ, is the true word, and not ΜΥΣΟΣ, which the Editor would fubftitute, though it has a different and incompatible meaning.

The change of the τ to the Λ in ΠΟΙΚΙΤΑΝ is right, and alfo that of the A to the O in the laft fyllable of ΚΑΝΟΤΑΤΑΡ; but the fubftituting an E for the A in the firft is wrong. Gronovius's reading ΚΑΙΝΟΤΑΤΟΡ is probably right.

ΑΤΙΜΑΣΔΕ feems to be the proper form, and not ΑΤΙΜΑΣΔΕΙ, the fenfe requiring a paft imperfect rather than a prefent tenfe, and the omiffion of the augment being common to Homer, Hefiod, and Herodotus.

Κιθαριξιν, or ΚΙΘΑΡΙΚΣΙΝ, is alfo more confiftent with the roughnefs of this dialect, and more conformable to the antient terminations of the verbs in -ΚΩ (whence the future -ξω or -ΚΣΩ) than ΚΙΣΑΡΓΤΙΝ, given by the Editor, or ΚΙΤΑΡΙΤΙΝ, which one manufcript has, and which is lefs objectionable.

ΔΙΑΙΡΕΣΙΝ for ΔΙΑΣΚΕΙΝ, or ΔΙΑΣΚΕΙΑΝ, is too violent an alteration, if any alteration were neceffary, which none is; for the latter word is juftified by the authority of a Manufcript, and accords perfectly with the context. Even the firft may poffibly be right; for, though I have not met with fuch a form as ΔΙΑΣΚΕΙΣ or ΔΙΑΣΚΕΦΙΣ, the termination of thefe abftract fubftantives in -ΙΣ is as confiftent with the idiom and analogy of the language as in A.

(1) To thefe, perhaps, may be added the Heraclèan tables, which have both afpirates; but the age of them is uncertain.

ΠΟΙΤΑΝ

ΠΟΙΤΑΝ the Editor has turned to ΠΟΙΟΝ or *ποιων*. The old Bafil edition of Boethius has ΠΟΙΑΝ, which may be the Doric contracted form of ΠΟΙΑΩΝ, the fame as ΠΟΙΕΩΝ, and therefore right. I prefer, however, the reading of the manufcripts ΠΟΙΤΑΝ, confidered as the accufative feminine of the participle aorift, contracted, after the Doric manner, from ΠΟΙΣΑΣΑΝ to ΠΟΙΣΑΝ; and, by the change of the Σ to the Τ, ΠΟΙΤΑΝ. A paft tenfe is more fuitable to this place than a prefent; and it may refer to the preceeding fubftantive ΔΙΑΣΚΕΙΝ, or ΔΙΑΣΚΕΙΑΝ.

The change of ΠΑΡΑΚΛΕΟΕΙΣ to ΠΑΡΑΚΛΑΟΕΙΡ may be right, as far as fubftituting the Α for the Ε; but terminating words of this clafs in Ρ is unjuftified by authority, and inconfiftent with analogy, and certainly not admiffible in any dialect.

The fyllable ΦΑ or ΦΑΡ, which the Editor rejects as ufelefs and inexplicable, relates either to the fenate who enacted, or the fenator who moved, the Decree; probably the latter; for the decrees, or *ψηγισματα*, of the Greek Republicks, were recorded in the form of minutes, and had the mover's name adjoined to each, even after they were voted, as, Ἱπποκρατης *ειπε Πλαταιης ειναι*, &c. (1).

ΔΙΔΑΚΚΕ in the manufcripts is right, as before obferved; the Editor's alteration to ΕΔΙΔΑΚΣΕ being the fame as a change of *θηκε* or *δωκε*, in Homer and Hefiod, would be to ΕΟΗΚΣΕ and ΕΔΩΚΣΕ.

ΜΕΜΨΑΣΟΑΙ and ΕΠΑΝΑΓΚΑΣΑΙ, given by the Editor, are likewife wrong, the forms ΜΕΜΨΑΤΤΑΙ and ΕΠΑΝΑΚΑΤΑΙ in the manufcripts being more confiftent with the dialect, which transformed the Σ into a Τ, as well as dropt the afpirate. If any alteration is neceffary in the laft word, it muft be merely the infertion of the Ν—ΕΠΑΝΑΝΚΑΤΑΙ—according to the mode of fpelling obferved in moft antient infcriptions. I believe, however, that no alteration is neceffary; for, though this verb does not occur elfewhere, in the fame form, we have other words of the fame extraction and fignification, as *ακος*, *care*, and *ανακως*, *carefully*; which, as Euftathius obferves, are from the fame root as *αναξ* and *ανασσω*, words which do not imply, in Homer, the office and power of a king in the

(1) Demofth. in Neær.

prefent

prefent fenfe, but merely a *curator*, or *fuperintendant* (1). The future in -ξω or -ΚΕΩ proves that the verb ανασσω was, at fome period, or in fome dialects, terminated in -ΚΩ, and, by the variations common in the Greek tongue, in -ΚΕΩ and -ΚΑΩ; fo that ΕΠΑΝΑΚΑΤΑΙ was probably the regular Aorift infinitive, in the Laconian dialect, of the verb which fignified *that exertion of authority* by which the kings and ephori were to compel Timotheus to quit the city.

NETON in the manufcripts is only wrong in the firft letter, which fhould be a B, BETON, or (as in the Etymologicum magnum) BETTON, the regular Laconian form of FEΘON (2). Probably it is fo in the manufcripts, for the barbarous N and B of the lower ages are eafily miftaken for each other. ΕΣΟΝ, fubftituted by the Editor, is taken from a note upon Hefychius, who gives BEΣON as Laconian for EΘΟΣ, and ΠΑΣΟΝ for ΠΑΘΟΣ, by which he feems to exprefs rather the vicious pronunciation, than the eftablifhed orthography, of that people,

ΤΑΡΑΡΕΤΑΙ in the manufcripts is right, and not ΤΑΡΑΤΤΕΤΑΙ, given by the Editor, it being the Laconian form of the fecond Aorift fubjunctive middle, and not the prefent of the fubjunctive paffive. In common Greek it would be ταρχσηται, or ταρατηται, from ταρασσω, or ταραττω. This accords with the preceeding verb ΕΥΛΑΒΕΤΑΙ, or ευλαβηται. Though thefe forms are called fecond Aorifts, they have almoft always a future fignification in the early writers, as in ως αν μη καταδηλος γενηται, Herodot. lib. I. c. 3. Ὁρκιοισι γαρ μεγαλοισι κατειχοντο, δεκα ετεα χρησεσθαι νομοισι τες αν σφισι Σολων θηται. Ibid. c. 29.

(1) Ανακ]ας εκαλεν τας βασιλεις οι παλαιοι διατο ανακως, ηγεν επιμελως; εχειν των ὑποτεταγμενων. Euftath. p. 21. 15. See alfo 1425. 56. Ανακως δε εχειν των πορθμεων (Περιανδρον). Herodot. lib. I. c. XXIII.

(2) ΒΕΣΤΟΝ το ιματιον ὑπο Λακωνων. οι δε ΒΕΤΤΟΝ. Διογενες. I have before obferved the double power of this word, fimilar to that of HABIT in our own language.

INDEX

ERRATA.

P. 1.

5	n. 2	for 5 r. 6.
9	4	come r. came.
16	20	Pafidonia r. Pofidonia.
19	n. 1	6 r. 5.
25	6	Bæotians r. Bœotians.
32	18	*a complete* r. *an incomplete.*
35	15	ΚΑΡ'ΗΥ r. ΚΑΡ'ΗU.
48	10	dele *fo.*
58	10	for καληοιμην r. καλεοιμην.
85	2	no r. nor.
	19	*it* r. *the feventh.*
92	10	ιλιδον r. ιλαδον.
99	26	σχριζη r. σχιζη.
103	12	εσοθαι r. εσσασθαι.
104	27	and r. or.
127	3	prefied r. prefided.
128	12	were r. was.

F I N I S.

Fig. 1.

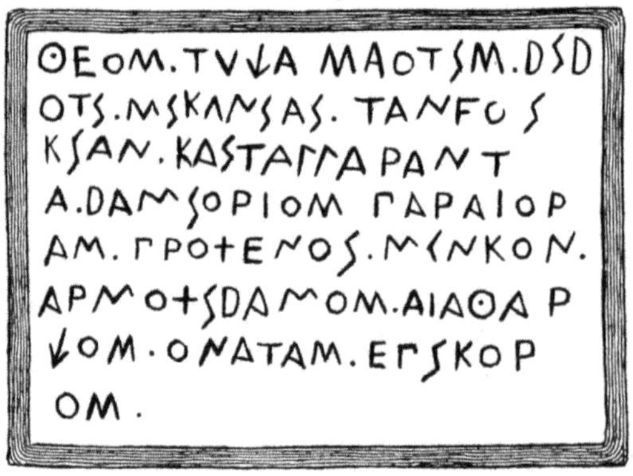

ΘΕΟΜ.ΤΥΛΑΜΑΟΤΣΜ.DSD
OTS.ΜSΚΛΝSΑS.ΤΑΝΡΟS
ΚSΑΝ.ΚΑSΤΑΓΓΑΡΑΝΤ
Α.DΑΜSΟΡΙΟΜΓΑΡΑΙΟΡ
ΑΜ.ΓΡΟΤΕΝΟS.ΜΙΝΚΟΝ.
ΑΡΜΟΤSDΑΜΟΜ.ΑΙΛΘΑΡ
ΛΟΜ.ΟΝΑΤΑΜ.ΕΓSΚΟΡ
ΟΜ.

Fig. 2.

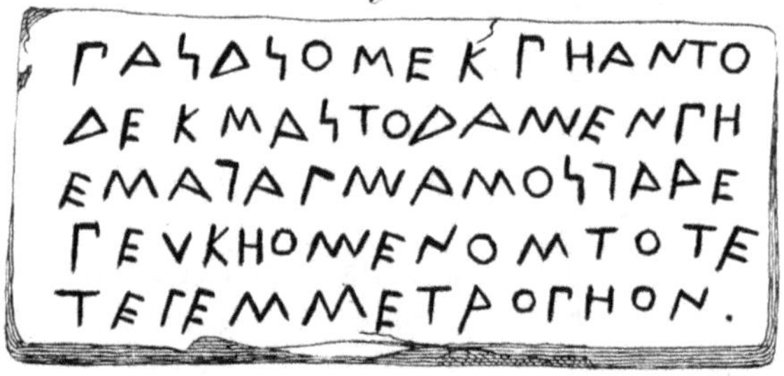

ΓΑΛΑΛΟΜΕΚΓΗΑΝΤΟ
ΔΕ ΚΜΑΛΤΟDΑΜΕΝΓΗ
ΕΜΑΤΑΓΝΑΜΟΛΤΑΡΕ
ΓΕΥΚΗΟΝΕΝΟΜΤΟΤΕ
ΤΕΓΕΜΜΕΤΡΟΓΗΟΝ.

Fig. 3.

ΟΛΛΥΤΟΜΦΟΕΜΧΑΝΔΡΙΑSΚΛΙΤΟSΦΕΓΑS

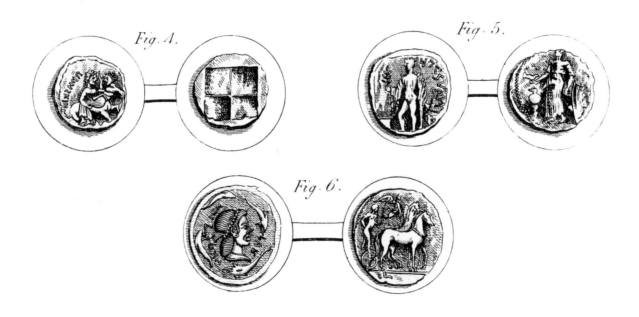

Fig. 4.   Fig. 5.

Fig. 6.

ΘΑΝΟΔΙΚΟ
ΕΜΙΤΟΝΜΟ
ΡΑΤΕΟΣΤΟ
ΗΜΟΚΟΜΗ
ΣΙΟΚΡΗΤΗΡ
ΚΟΤΥΙΑΚΑΙΕΔΑ
ΡΗΤΗΡΙΟΝ:Κ
ΑΙΗΟΜΟΜΟΗΙΑ
ΡΥΤΑΝΗΙΟΝ
ΕΔΟΚΕΝ:ΣΙΚΕ
ΕΥΣΙΝ

ΦΑΝΟΔΙΚΟ:ΕΙΜΙ:ΤΟΗ
ΕΡΜΟΚΡΑΤΟΣ:ΤΟΠΡΟΚΟ
ΝΕΣΙΟ:ΚΑΛΟ:ΚΡΑΤΕΡΑ
ΜΦΙΣΤΑΤΟΝ:ΚΑΙΗΕΘ
ΟΝ:ΕΣΠΡΥΤΑΝΕΙΟΝ:Ε
ΔΟΚΑ:Μ:ΜΝΗΣΙΚΑ
ΑΠΙΤΑΔΕΠΟΙΕΣΕ
ΟΜΕΛΕΣΔΑΙΜΕΝ:ΜΕΟ
ΣΙΛΕΙΕΣ:ΚΑΙΜΕΠΟ
ΙΣΕΝ:ΗΑΙΣΟΛΟΣΙΗ:ΜΕΣΙΣ
ΗΑΔΕΛΦΟΙ

ΔΛΡΙ

ΙΚΕΤΕΡΚΕΡΑΤΕΕϞ.

Fig. 1.

ΟϿϿΟ7Δ ΥΟΤ ΙΔΔΥΟϿ ΙΔϿ ϞϿΒϿΤΑΜ	1
2 ΝΟϞΚΑΙ ΕΤ . . . . ΜΑΤΕΡΟΝ	
3 ΔΕΔΚΑΛΙϞΔΕΡΑΤΟΥ ΜΑΤΕΕΡ Δ	
ΔΕΕΟ7Δ ΟϞΥΔΟΥ ϞΟΥΔΑ Δ7ΟΔϿϿΔ	4
ΔΜΜΟΝΕΕ ΔΙΔΔΚΕΟϞ ΜΑΤΕΕΡ	5
6 ΔΙΙΙ ΛΝΔΟΟ ΔΔϞΙΟΥ ΚΟΥΔΑ	
ϿΛΟΔΜΕΕΔ ΔΜΝΚΕΔ ΔϿϿΜΑΥΟΔϿ	7
8 ΙϟΕΟϞ ΜΑΤΕΕΡ ΙΙΙΙ ΛΝΔΟΟ .. ϞΙΟΥ	
Δ ΔΥΟϿ	9
ΙΙΥΥΥ ΔϿϿΤΑΜ . . . . ΑϞΥΔ ΑϞ . . . . Δ	10
11 ΙΔϞΙϞ ΙΔϞΟΥ ΚΑΙ Γ .. ΟΕΕ ΔΕΔϞΤΟΥ	
ϞΟΥΔΙ	12
ϿΛΟΔΜΕΕΔ ΔΔΛΔΟΥ ΔϿϿΜΑΥΟΔϿ	13
14 ΕΡ ΔΙΙ ΚΑΛΙϞΤΟ ΟΕΟΓΟΜΓΟΥ ΚΟΥΔΑ	
7 ΔϿϿΤΑΜ ΥΟΜΑΔϿΧΔΑ ΔϿ	15
16 ΚϟΙΟ ΑΡΙΟΝΟϞ ΚΟΥΔΑ	
ΔΟΔ ΔϿϿΤΑΜΥΟΤϟΔΔΔΔ ϿϿΟΔϟΙΔϟ	17
18 ΔΕΔΚΔΛΛΙϞ ΟΕΟΚΛΕΟϞ ΚΟΥΡΑ	
ΔϿϿΤΑΜ ϟΟΝΟΙΔϿΤϟΔ ΔϟϟΔΝΟΜΔΔ	19
20 ΥΥΥΥΓΙΙΙΙ ΑΝΑΤΟ ΑΡΙϞΤΟΒΟΥΛΟΥ ΚΟΥΡΑ	
ΙΙ7ΥΥΥΥ ΔϿϿΤΑΜ ΥΟϟΟΥ ΥϟΟΤΤ .. ΝΟΟΧ	21
22 ΓΡΟΚΡΙϞ ΓΟΛΥΜΕϞΤΟΡΟϞ ΚΟΥΔΑ	
ΙΙΥΥΥΥ ΔϿϿΤΑΜ ΥΟΧΔΜϿΔΟΝ ΑΙϟΑ	23
24 ΓΟϟΥΔΟΡΑ	

```
 1  ··ᗡƎᗡᗺMᗺ⅃   ᗡT  ᗝIᏐᗝMƎ  ⊡ M
 2  TEEP EϜᗗ⅃ᒥᗝK4·····Tᗝ  Kᗗ⅃IᏐᗝKᗡ
 3  MᗡTEEᗡ MTᗗᏐI  ᗡT ᗝ IᗝᗝTM  ᗝƎƎTᗝM
 4  MᗡTEEᗡ K KᗡᗝᗝᗡᗡEᗝIᏐ Tᗝ KᗡᗝᗝᗝEᗝᗝ
 5  ᗡᗝƎᗝ ᗡT ᗝMᗝMᗝMᗝ ᗝK ᗝƎƎTᗝM
 6  4Eᗝ MᗡTEEᗡ MEᗝMᗝMᗝ MᗝTᗝ
 7  MᗝᗝᗝMᏐᗝᗝ  ᗝ  M ᗝƎƎTᗝ  ᗡᏐIᒧ
 8  Tᗝ ᗝᗝIᏐETᗝMᗝEᗝᗝTᗝ ᗝᗝIᏐETᗝ MᗝKᗡM
 9  ᗝTEEᗝ ⅃ᗝ M ᗝᗝᗝᗝᗝM ᗝᗝ  ᗝƎƎTᗝ
10  MᗝTEEᗡ KEᗝ ᒥᗝIᗝ Tᗝ KᗝᒪIKEᗝᗝTᗝ
11  ᗝᗝᗝMIᗝᗝᗝ ᗝT ᗝMᗝMᗝMᗝ ᗝM ᗝᗝᗝᗝ
12  Kᗝᗝᗝ ⅃ᗝMᗝMᗝMᗝ Tᗝ 4EKEᒥᗝᗝ MᗝTEEᗝK
13  4ᗝ⅃ᗝMI4 Tᗝ 4EKEᒥᗝᗝMᗝTEEᗝᗝ ᗝT 4I Mᗝᗝᗝ4
14  4EKᗝᒪᗝ Tᗝ 4EKIᒪᗝ MᗝTEEᗝ Mᗡ⅃
15  4EKEMᗝMᗝ Tᗝ ᗝ⅃KIᗝᗝ ᗡT ᗝMᗝMᗝMƎᗝ4
16  ᒥE4ᗝᒥI4 ᗡT ᗝᒥKIᗝᗝMᗝ MᗝTEEᗝ ᗝ
17  ᗝᗝ ᗝƎƎTᗝM ᗝᗝƎMᗝ ƎᗝOT ᗝMƎMᗝᗝƎᗝ
18  ᒥᗝᒪᗝK4ᗝ Tᗝ ᒥI4ᗝMᗝᗝᗝ MᗝTEEᗝ Kᗝ
19  ⅃ᗝ⅃Vᗺᗝ4Iᗝ Tᗝᗝ MᗝᗝᗝMᗝTᒧIᗝᗝ VᗝT ᗝI ᗝᗺV⅃ᗝᒧ
20  ᗝ ᗝ K MEᒪᗝMIᒥᒥᗝ Tᗝᗝ M MᗝᏐᗝMᗝ4
21  Kᗝᗝᗝ ᗝ 4ᗝ⅃ᗝMI4 Tᗝᗝ ᗝᗝI4TᗝMᗝKᗝᗝ ᗝ ᗝᗝᗝᗝ
22  Kᗝᗝᗝ KMEᒪᗝMIᒥᒥᗝTᗝᗝ MELᗝMIᒥᒥᗝᗝ KᗝᗝᗝK
23  ᗺᗝ ᗝᗝᗝᗝ VᗝᗝᗝM ᗝᏐIᒧ VᗝT ᗝᗝƎᗝᗝM
24  MEᒪᗝMIᒥᒥᗝ Tᗝᗝ ᒥI4ᗝMᗝᗝᗝᗝ Kᗝᗝᗝ ⊞
25  MEEᗝᏐIKIᗝƎᗝƎM YᗝᗝᒥᒥIMᗝᗝƎM YᗝT ᗝT4ᗝKIᒧƎᗝƎᗝM
26  ᗝᒥᗝIᗝ Tᗝᗝ ⅃ᗝᒧᒥ4TᗝᗝTᗝᗝ Kᗝᗝᗝ Kᗝ
```

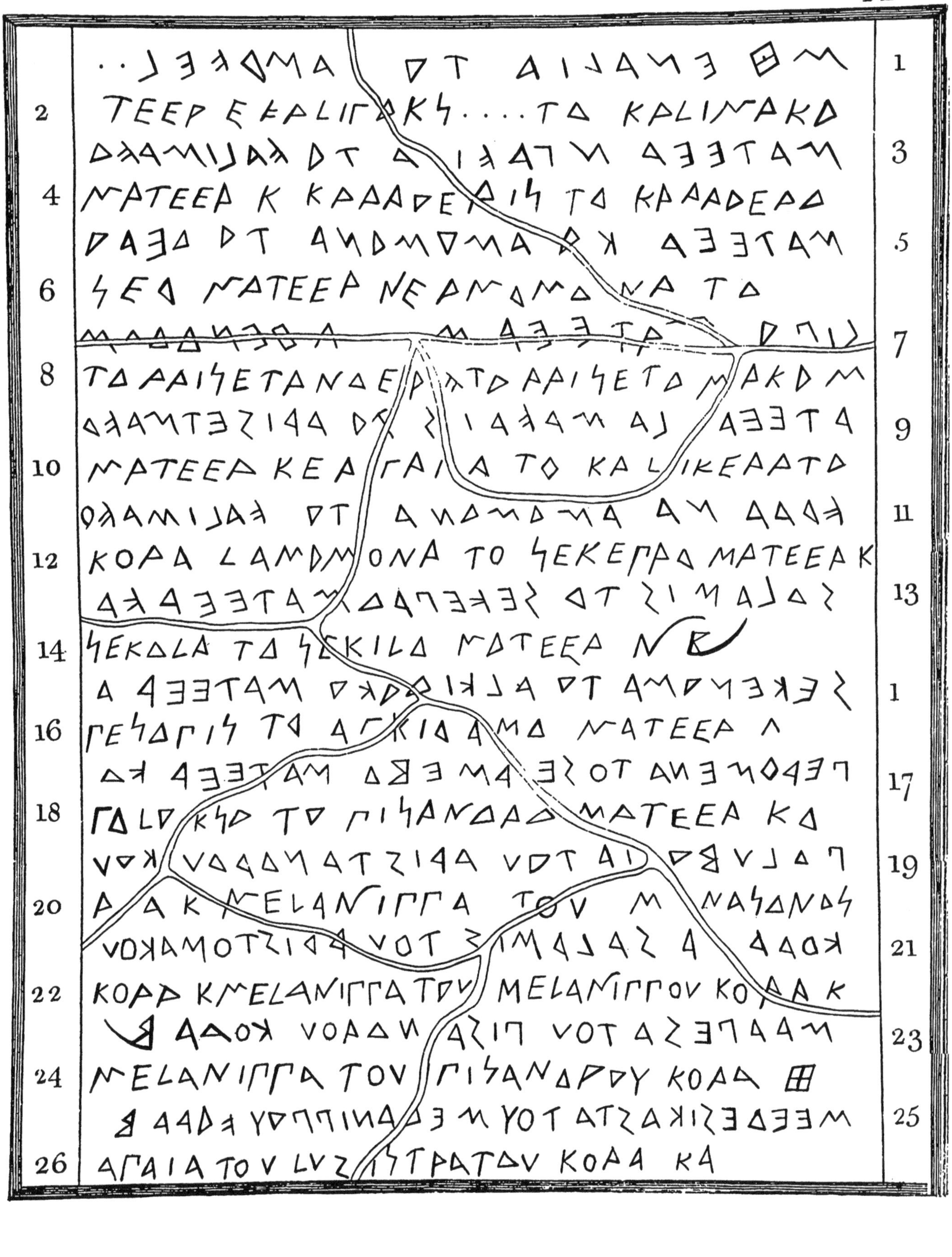

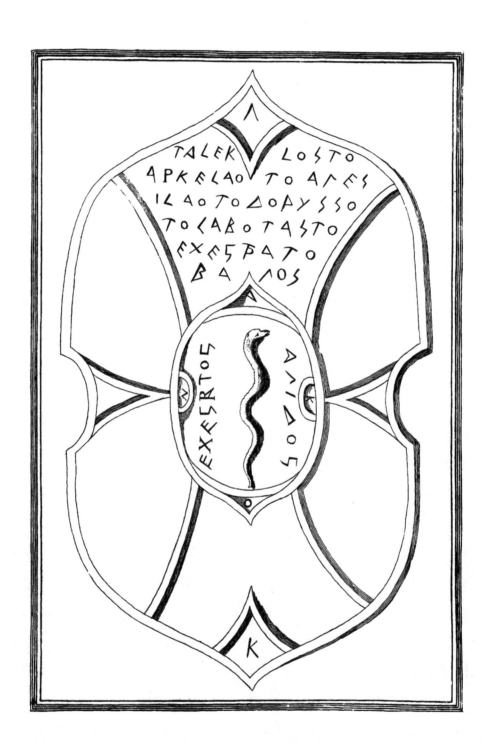

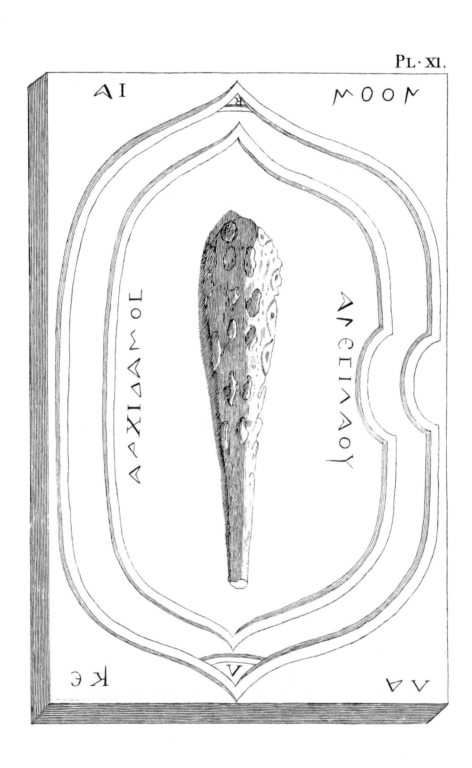

For EU product safety concerns, contact us at Calle de José Abascal, 56–1°,
28003 Madrid, Spain or eugpsr@cambridge.org.

www.ingramcontent.com/pod-product-compliance
Ingram Content Group UK Ltd.
Pitfield, Milton Keynes, MK11 3LW, UK
UKHW051028150625
459647UK00023B/2859